THE WORLD TURNED INSIDE OUT

Henry Corbin and Islamic Mysticism

by

Tom Cheetham

SPRING JOURNAL BOOKS
WOODSTOCK, CONNECTICUT

© 2003 by Thomas Cheetham.
All rights reserved.
First Spring Journal Books printing 2003.

Published by
Spring Journal, Inc.;
299 East Quassett Road;
Woodstock, Connecticut 06281

Printed in North America.
Text printed on acidfree paper..

General editor JFL.
Book edited and indexed by Nancy Cater.

The cover image is of the Archangel Gabriel
by Martin Schongauer (German, c.1450-1491).
The image is used by permission from
the National Gallery of Art, Washington, D.C.

Library in Congress Cataloging in Publication Data
Pending

Printed in Canada

This book is dedicated to the memory of

F. Edward Cranz
1914-1998
Rosemary Park Professor of History, Emeritus

and

Lester J. Reiss
1933-1999
Lucretia L. Allyn Professor of Philosophy

two great teachers at Connecticut College.

Acknowledgements

Reading and certainly writing about Henry Corbin is a humbling experience in part because it requires at least modest familiarity with so many different disciplines. I want to extend special thanks to Charles Adams, retired Head of the Department of Islamic Studies at McGill University, for reading over the manuscript and making some helpful comments. I am of course responsible for any errors of fact or interpretation. I am also indebted to a small number of students with whom I have had the pleasure of discussing Corbin's work and related issues over the last several years, both at Wilson College and at the College of the Atlantic. Gisela Behrens of the C. G. Jung Center of Philadelphia provided generous hospitality and the opportunity to present parts of this work to interested audiences. Bob Doan of Unity College helped with some of the idiosyncrasies of French. Without the help of many long-suffering librarians at Wilson College, Unity College, and the Bangor Public Library, this book would have been impossible to write. Special thanks go to Luwanda Youngblood and Claire Smart. Not least, I am grateful to Jay Livernois for encouraging me to write this book in the first place.

Portions of Chapters 1 and 5 have appeared in earlier versions in *Spring Journal* Volumes 64 and 67.

Contents

Introduction

> Hegel said that philosophy consists in turning the world inside out. Let us say rather that this world is here and now inside out. The *ta'wil* and the prophetic philosophy consist in putting it right side out once more.[1]

Henry Corbin's work deserves to be far more widely known in the English-speaking world. Although much remains untranslated, many of his most important books are available in English. But his writings require familiarity with a greater diversity of subjects than can be reasonably expected from all but the most widely read scholars. He was at once a Neoplatonic philosopher, a theologian with interests in Immanuel Swedenborg and Johann Georg Hamann, Jacob Boehme, and Martin Heidegger, and an Orientalist specializing in Islamic mysticism. He was a scholar of the first rank, a formidable linguist and a prolific translator, editor, and commentator. But he was more than a scholar. He was an exponent of a kind of mystical theology that has seen its fortunes eclipsed by the rise of materialism and rationalism, and his work has significance far beyond that of most academic specialists.

One obstacle for the reader is the fact that the "Oriental" philosophy in which he came to find his home is little known. Corbin's heart lay in Iranian Shi'ism, for many people an obscure branch of a poorly understood religion. The mention of Iran or of Shi'ite Islam conjures up for too many only visions of violence and intolerance. Yet the message that he brings from Iran and from Islam is potentially of such psychological and cultural importance as to make the effort of familiarizing ourselves with his work and the traditions from which it springs more than worthwhile.

Corbin is known to some as a major source, along with C. G. Jung, for the intellectual foundations of archetypal psychology. Its focus has often been on two major aspects of his work: the rediscovery of the reality of the *mundus imaginalis* and the effort to loosen the grip of dogmatic monotheism on Western consciousness by disclosing the polytheistic faces of Divinity.[2] More recently Harold Bloom has brought Corbin's books to

---

1. Henry Corbin, *Spiritual Body and Celestial Earth: From Mazdean Iran to Shi'ite Iran*, xiii.

2. See James Hillman, *Archetypal Psychology: A Brief Account*; Thomas Moore, *The Care of the Soul*; Benjamin Sells, *Working with Images*.

the attention of a different audience.[3] But his work is immense and complex and should be approached on its own terms. Within archetypal psychology a good deal of attention has been paid to the lines of affinity leading back from Jung to alchemy and to the rediscovery of classical mythologies in the Renaissance of Europe. Yet Corbin leads in other directions. While Corbin drew comparisons in nearly all of his works with aspects of the Western Christian tradition, the territory that he opened up in Islamic thought remains for most people unknown.

Beyond difficulties resulting from his erudition, Corbin's writings are often hard to penetrate in spite of a prose style that is elegant and precise. One reason for this is that in Corbin's work, as Marshall Hodgson has said of the *Qur'an*, "almost every element which goes to make up its message is somehow present in every passage."[4] Corbin's first major essays to be translated into English were already the product of his maturity, and one can find in them most of the themes that were to dominate his thinking for the rest of his life. He amplified, modified, and added to this complex structure of ideas with each work that he produced during a long and prolific career. Each of his works repays detailed study for the light that it throws on all the others.

There is as yet no book in English that provides more than a brief introduction to Corbin's life and work.[5] This book is an attempt to provide a context in which his writings can be situated, highlight some of the ideas and issues that are important to an understanding of his work as a whole, and to provide references for anyone interested in pursuing the topics further. I have quoted extensively from his writings and have tried through-

---

3. Harold Bloom, *Omens of Millennium: The Gnosis of Angels, Dreams and Resurrection*. Bloom has also contributed a preface to the new edition of Corbin's *Creative Imagination in the Sufism of Ibn 'Arabi*, which has been retitled *Alone with the Alone*.

4. Hodgson, quoted in Norman O. Brown's "The Apocalypse of Islam."

5. Daryush Shayegan's outstanding comprehensive book-length study, *Henry Corbin: La topographie spirituelle de l'islam iranien*, has not been translated. The best summary available in English is Christopher Bamford's "Esotericism Today: The Example of Henry Corbin," which appears as the introduction to Corbin's *The Voyage and the Messenger*. Hermann Landolt has recently written, "Henry Corbin, 1903-1978: Between Philosophy and Orientalism," a useful essay on Corbin and his understanding of the relation between Orientalism and philosophical phenomenology.

out to let him speak for himself. It is by the selection and arrangement of the topics and, admittedly, by their sometimes artificial separation that I hope to provide an overview. I have tried to write the kind of short introduction that I would have found helpful in my first encounter with his thought. This is in no way intended as an exhaustive study. That would require a far larger book and a different author. My hope is that by providing some guideposts this book will make his writings accessible to a wider audience. There is no substitute for a close reading of Corbin's own writings. If I can stimulate readers to turn to Corbin's work, I will have achieved my purpose.

In surveying such an enormous opus, it would be presumptuous to pretend to completeness or to objectivity. I should say something of my biases and limitations. I am not an Orientalist. My initial contact with Corbin's writings came about because of interests in archetypal psychology and ecological philosophy. Corbin's work and those aspects of the Abrahamic tradition which it represents offer an approach to the psyche and the natural world that provides a stark and illuminating contrast with that of the Western tradition. It raises and answers, for those who are able to follow it, such fundamental questions about the place of humans in nature that it would be foolish and arrogant to ignore it. Corbin's ecumenical treatment of the religions of the Book suggests ways of understanding ourselves and how we have become who we are that are unobtainable almost anywhere else. Anyone concerned with the psychological, social, and ecological problems of contemporary life will find Corbin's work valuable, whether in the end they are able to adopt his perspective or not.

A Brief Biography of Henry Corbin

Even a quick sketch of Corbin's life reveals a capacity for philosophical research and diverse interests that are breathtaking.[1] He was born in Paris on the 14th of April 1903 to Henri Arthur Corbin and Eugenie Fournier. His mother died six days later. His health was fragile in his early years, and he was frequently forced to interrupt his studies. He showed a strong affinity for music and studied organ and theory. Corbin attended the monastery school at St. Maur, later the Seminary School of Issy, and received a certificate in Scholastic philosophy from the Catholic Institute of Paris in 1922. In 1925 he took his *"licence de philosophie"* under the great Thomist Étienne Gilson at the *École Practique des Hautes Études* in Paris, with a thesis entitled "Latin Avicennism in the Middle Ages." Corbin was entranced by Gilson's scholarship and his ability to bring medieval texts to life. Gilson was then beginning his own study of the role of Islamic philosophy in the development of Scholastic thought in the West. Corbin admired him immensely and took the master interpreter as his model. He writes, "This was my first contact with Islamic philosophy. I discovered there a complicity between cosmology and angelology…and this angelological concern has not, I believe, left me during my entire life."[2]

During the same period he attended Emile Bréhier's lectures on the relation between Plotinus and the *Upanishads*: "…how could a young philosopher avid for metaphysical adventure resist this appeal: to study deeply the influences or traces of Indian philosophy in the work of the founder of Neoplatonism?"[3] A "notorious period of mental asceticism" followed on his decision to undertake the simultaneous study of Arabic and Sanskrit. He had already mastered both Latin and Greek.

---

1. Corbin's own account is in "Repères biographiques" and "Post-scriptum à un entretien philosophique" found in *Henry Corbin*, ed. Christian Jambet. Daryush Shayegan in *Henry Corbin: La topographie spirituelle de l'islam iranien* and Seyyed Hossein Nasr in *Henry Corbin: The Life and Works of the Occidental Exile in Quest of the Orient of Light*, both of whom worked closely with Corbin for many years, also discuss the biographical details of his life.

2. Corbin, *Henry Corbin*, ed. Jambet, 39. My translation. I have used published translations wherever possible. All other translations are my own.

3. Corbin, *Henry Corbin*, ed. Jambet, 39.

In 1928 Corbin encountered Louis Massignon, the Director of
Islamic Studies at the *École des Hautes Études*. The contrast
with Gilson's methodical and rigorous style was "incredible."

> It used to happen that a lesson would commence with
> one of the flashing intuitions of which the great mystic
> Massignon was unsparing. And then a parenthesis would
> open, and then another, then another.... Finally the lis-
> tener found himself stunned and bewildered, arguing
> with the master about British politics in Palestine....[4]

Corbin's proclivity for the mystical element in oriental studies was confirmed by contact with Massignon.

> There was no escaping his influence. His soul of fire, his
> bold penetration into the arcana of mystical life in Islam,
> where no one had before penetrated in this way, the no-
> bility of his indignations at the cowardice in the world,
> all of this inevitably made its imprint on the spirit of his
> young listeners.[5]

It was Massignon who first turned Corbin's attention to the
writings of Shihab al-Din Yahya al-Suhrawardi, the Iranian
theosopher of the Oriental Light, whose writings were to affect
the course of his life.

> Thus it was that one day, it was, I think, in the year 1927-
> 28, I spoke to him of the reasons that had led me as a
> philosopher to the study of Arabic, questions that posed
> themselves to me concerning the connections between
> philosophy and mysticism, and that I knew, through a
> scanty resume in German, of a certain Suhrawardi... Then
> Massignon had an inspiration from Heaven. He had
> brought back from a trip to Iran a lithographed edition of
> the major work of Suhrawardi, *Hikmat al'Ishraq*,
> "The Oriental Theosophy." With commentaries, it formed
> a large volume of more than 500 pages. "Take it," he said

4. *Ibid.*, 40.
5. *Ibid.*

x

to me, "I think there is in this book something for you." This something was the company of the young Shaykh al-Ishraq, who has not left me my whole life. I had always been a Platonist (in the broad sense of the term); I believe that one is born a Platonist as one is born an atheist, a materialist etc. Unfathomable mystery of pre-existential choices. The young Platonist that I was then could only take fire at contact with the one who was the "Imam of the Platonists of Persia...." Through my meeting with Suhrawardi, my spiritual destiny for the passage through this world was sealed. Platonism, expressed in terms of the Zoroastrian angelology of ancient Persia, illuminated the path that I was seeking.[6]

There were no longer any doubts about the direction the main lines of his research would take, and he began the study of Turkish, Persian, and Arabic.

As if this was not already enough for several lifetimes, Corbin's interests extended nearly as far in other directions. He never considered himself primarily an Orientalist or a philologist or a scholar of Scholasticism or of modern Western philosophy. He was a philosopher pursuing a quest. At the age of seventy he wrote,

> To be a philosopher is to take to the road, never settling down
> in some place of satisfaction with a theory of the world,
> not even a place of reformation, nor of some illusory

---

6. Corbin, *Henry Corbin*, 40-41. Recently John Walbridge and Hossein Ziai have challenged the interpretation of Suhrawardi that Corbin shares with S. H. Nasr and others. They are critical of Corbin's gnostic approach and emphasize the philosophical aspects of Suhrawardi's teachings in their translation of Suhrawardi's *Hikmat al'Ishraq* called *The Philosophy of Illumination*. They write: "Corbin's interpretation is expressed not just in his studies of Suhrawardi but also in his translations and even his critical editions of Suhrawardi's works. The use of renderings like 'theosophy' and 'oriental' indicate the fundamentally mythological focus of Corbin's interests and interpretations. His translation of *The Philosophy of Illumination* omits the logic, and his editions of the three 'Peripatetic'...works omit the logic and physics of each work and contain only the sections on metaphysics. Such methods inevitably downplay the strictly philosophical aspects of Suhrawardi's thought." See Walbridge and Ziai's Introduction to Suhrawardi's *The Philosophy of Illumination: a new critical edition of the text of Hikmat al-ishr̄aq*, xix, and references therein.

> transformation of the conditions of this world. It aims for self-transformation, for the inner metamorphosis which is implied by the notion of a new, or spiritual rebirth.... The adventure of the mystical philosopher is essentially seen as a voyage which progresses towards the Light....[7]

His own quest was not confined to the study of Islamic thought. During the 1920's and the early 1930's, he simultaneously pursued studies that in and of themselves would have clearly marked him as a brilliant and eclectic Protestant theologian. He became deeply engaged wih the German theological tradition, what he would later call the "lineage of hermeneutics:" Jacob Boehme, Martin Luther, Johann Georg Hamann, Friedrich Schliermacher, Wilhelm Dilthey, Martin Heidegger, and Karl Barth. In 1931 he was a co-founder, along with two Protestant pastors, of a short-lived periodical called *Hic et Nunc*, a journal for theological renewal inspired by the early writings of Barth. He lectured and delivered papers on Luther, Kierkegaard, and Hamann, at the same time publishing translations of Suhrawardi in 1933, 1935, and 1939. He was also the first to translate the early works of Barth into French.

The writings of both Luther and Hamann profoundly affected Corbin's understanding of Islamic mysticism. The primary importance of Luther was to provide insight into the contrast between the Revealed and the Hidden God and into the meaning of *significatio passiva:* the presence in us of those characteristics by means of which we know God. Hamann provided the foundations of a "mystical hermeneutics" which was central to Corbin's philosophical development. But it was his reading of Heidegger's *Being and Time* in 1930 that was to be the defining moment in his struggle to grasp the meaning of hermeneutics as the science of interpretation. The two met for the first time in Freiburg in 1931. Corbin traveled there again in 1936 to submit the first French translation of any of Heidegger's works, which was to appear in 1939 as *Qu'est ce que la metaphysique?*

He tended the oriental collection at the Bibliotheque Nationale in Paris beginning in 1928. In 1933 he married the woman who was to be his

---

7. Corbin, *The Voyage and the Messenger: Iran and Philosophy*, 140.

lifelong companion, Stella Leenhardt. In 1939 they traveled to Istanbul for what was intended as a six-month stay to collect manuscripts for a critical edition of Suhrawardi. Corbin served as the only member of the French Institute of Archaeology there until the end of the war. When his replacement arrived in September of 1945, the Corbins left Istanbul for Teheran and arrived on the 14th of September in the country "the color of heaven." In November, Corbin was instrumental in launching a project to create a Department of Iranology in the new Institute Française. They returned finally to Paris in July 1946.

In 1949 he first attended the Eranos Conferences in Ascona, Switzerland, where he was an important figure until his death. In 1954 he succeeded Massignon in the Chair of Islam and the Religions of Arabia. The three major works upon which his reputation rests in the English-speaking world were first published in French in the 1950's: *Avicenna and the Visionary Recital, Creative Imagination in the Sufism of Ibn 'Arabi,* and *Spiritual Body and Celestial Earth.* The work which is generally regarded as his *magnum opus*, as yet untranslated, is the four volume *En islam iranienne: aspects spirituels et philosophiques*, which appeared between 1971 and 1973. From the 1950s on he spent the autumn in Teheran, winter in Paris, and spring in Ascona. In 1974 he and a group of colleagues, including Gilbert Durand and Antoine Faivre, founded the University of St. John of Jerusalem: The International Center for Comparative Spiritual Research.[8]

His life was spent teaching, writing, lecturing, and editing critical editions of Persian and Arabic manuscripts. His published work includes over two hundred critical editions, translations, books, and articles.[9] He presented his last paper in June 1978, "Eyes of Flesh, Eyes of Fire: The Science of Gnosis." He died on October 7th of that year and thus was spared the anguish of witnessing the chaos into which Iran was plunged.

---

8. This organization operated until 1988 and published fourteen volumes of *Proceedings* (Paris: Berg International). Corbin's contributions are in the first five *Proceedings*. It has since been succeeded by *Cahiers du groupe d'études spirituelles comparées*, Gilbert Durand, President (*Proceedings* published by Arché: Paris).

9. A complete bibliography of works published in his lifetime can be found in *Henry Corbin*, ed Jambet.

CHAPTER ONE

Against the Times: Primordial Space, Primordial Time

The Act of Presence

If there is a single first step on the road to the cosmos that Corbin invites us to enter, it may be the simple, passionate refusal to accept the understanding of ourselves and the world that dominates modern secular consciousness. The foundations for this worldview are historical and materialist throughout. All of our means of understanding converge upon a single unified vision of reality. History, sociology, psychology, biology, physics, and engineering—all of the "human" and all of the "natural" sciences—are versions of the same reductive program. All are based on laws of historical causality in a world composed wholly of matter in space.

In a world so conceived, nothing can be more real than anything else. In a world so conceived, consciousness is reducible to and explicable in terms of physical, biological, social, and historical forces. Such a world is radically incompatible with the existence of persons. This is nihilism. As long as we feel alienated and exiled in such a world, there is hope. But the very real danger is that we will abandon ourselves to this world in our hopelessness, abandon ourselves to those impersonal forces which drive us blindly to our ends, and in doing so, we will disappear: There will no longer *be* persons.[1]

All of this Corbin refuses in its entirety. His claim is that in order to understand how it came about and in order to escape from it, we must understand it as a spiritual, philosophical, and metaphysical problem. This does not mean that it is an abstract and merely philosophical undertaking; the only philosophy that interests him is one that is effective. That we conceive of

---

1. Henry Corbin, *Le paradoxe du monothèisme*, 240.

metaphysics and of philosophy as merely intellectual is symptomatic of our problem. An understanding of ourselves and our situation which is true and therefore effective in guiding the soul towards its truth, requires metaphysical comprehension at the most personal and immediate level.

A focus on the reality of the human person in reaction to the scientific rationalism of the Enlightenment, the abstraction of Hegelian Idealism, and later against fascist and totalitarian ideologies, took many forms in late nineteenth and early twentieth century European theology and philosophy. But of most importance for understanding Corbin is the phenomenological philosophy of Edmund Husserl and his student Martin Heidegger.

The significance of Heidegger's monumental *Being and Time* for Corbin is not so much that it caused a revolution in his outlook, but rather that it provided a crystallization of themes and issues which were already gathering in his thinking through his study of both Western philosophy and Islamic thought. Like Corbin, Heidegger had been deeply engaged in the study of medieval philosophy and theology and wrote his first major academic treatise on Duns Scotus. As Corbin points out, this provides a significant link between Heidegger's intellectual background and his own, in particular since the Medieval concept of *grammatica speculativa* which is fundamental to Luther's thought had a profound impact on Corbin, as we shall see.[2] But without question Heidegger's work was, in Corbin's own words, of "decisive" importance.[3]

2. *Henry Corbin*, ed. Christian Jambet, 25.

3. See, *ibid*, 28ff. The relationship between them is complex and interesting. Corbin himself discussed in some detail the influences of Heidegger's early work. See "De Heidegger à Sohravardi, entretiens avec Phillipe Nemo," "Post-scriptum à un entretiens philosophique," and "Transcendental et existential" in *Henry Corbin*, ed. Jambet. Roberts Avens has written perceptively concerning Heidegger's relation to Corbin and to James Hillman. See, Avens, *The New Gnosis* and "Things and Angels, Death and Immortality in Heidegger and in Islamic Gnosis." See also Avens, *Imagination is Reality: Western Nirvana in Jung, Hillman, Barfield and Cassirer*, "Theosophy of Mulla Sadra," "Henry Corbin and Suhrawardi's Angelology," "Corbin's Interpretation of Imamology and Sufism," and "The Subtle Realm: Corbin, Sufism and Swedenborg" which emphasize Heidegger's later, more Gnostic writings. Corbin explicitly avoided such an analysis in his conversations with Nemo, claiming that an analysis of the later Heidegger and his potential affinities with mystical theologies of any sort would require and repay the work of several lifetimes. Daryush Shayegan in *Henry Corbin: La topographie spirituelle de l'Islam iranien* also devotes considerable space to a discussion of Heidegger's relations to Corbin.

As is the case with Corbin, Heidegger's life work involves a fundamental critique of Western thought and of the course of Western history.[4] That this rather sweeping plan was intended from the start is evident even at the beginning of *Being and Time*: Section 6 is somewhat immodestly entitled "On the Task of Destroying the History of Ontology." His hope is to provide a radical critique by getting at the roots of what it means for us to "be" at all. *Being and Time* is ostensibly about the question of the meaning of being. Of the utmost importance is Heidegger's choice of standpoint for his task:

> Looking at something, understanding and conceiving it, choosing, access to it—all of these ways of behaving are constitutive for our inquiry, and therefore are modes of Being for those particular entities which we, the inquirers, are ourselves. Thus to work out the question of Being adequately, we must make an entity—the inquirer— transparent in his own Being. The very asking of this question is an entity's mode of *Being*; and as such gets its essential character from what is inquired about— namely, Being. This entity which each of us is himself and which includes inquiring as one of the possibilities of its Being, we shall denote by the term "*Dasein*."[5]

"*Dasein*" is Heidegger's way of naming that about us that has, in some sense, "ontological priority over every other entity,"[6] that about us which allows anything to appear at all. This *Dasein* that we are has a complex ontological and phenomenological structure which had not been noticed explicitly before and which Heidegger intends to uncover. In order to begin the revelation of these structures of being, he distinguishes those aspects that pertain to the fundamental structure of *Dasein* from those which are characteristic only of our

---

4. One of the best short introductions to Heidegger's work as a whole and to the intellectual climate in Europe in 1927, when *Being and Time* was first published, is George Steiner's *Martin Heidegger*.

5. Heidegger, *Being and Time*, 26-27.

6. *Ibid.*, 62.

everyday existence in the world. The former, deeper level he calls ontological and existential; the latter, more superficial level he calls ontic and *existentiell*. This distinction is basic. It is on the deeper, more obscure level that the ontological priority of *Dasein* resides.

Dasein is, literally translated, "being-there." It provides the condition for the possibility of anything being present at all. This is the crucial intuition that will make Heidegger's work so important for Corbin. He stresses that the *da* of *Dasein* is the "act of Presence."[7] The analysis thus begins with Presence as the fundamental given. Not with a knowing subject, or with energy, or with matter; not with any kind of "thing" at all. This kind of presence, for Heidegger, is ontologically prior to the appearance of a subject or an *ego*, prior to anything as restricted as human consciousness. In this way he attempts to stand outside all the vexing metaphysical dualisms: *phenomena/ noumena*, subject/object, idealist/materialist. This analysis is an attempt to provide a way of understanding ourselves and the world which is at once rigorously philosophical and metaphysical but not in any way abstract. This analytic of *Dasein* is to be rooted in the multitude of ways in which we are in the world and is situated outside positivist or indeed of any of the traditional categories of philosophical thought.[8] This is a revolutionary ontology within the tradition of

---

7. Corbin, *Henry Corbin*, ed. Jambet, 32. We might ponder here a comparison between Heidegger's attempt to provide a trans-human centrality to something like "consciousness" and Jung's African revelation on the Athi plains in November, 1925. The relationship between Jung's psychology and the phenomenology of Husserl, Heidegger, Merleau-Ponty, and their followers is interesting and important and throws light on Corbin's appropriation of themes from both groups. See Roger Brooke, *Jung and Phenomenology*.

8. Whether he succeeds in accomplishing his purpose has been the subject of a cascade of academic production since 1927. Avens cites Hans Jonas, a scholar of Gnosticism and a former student of Heidegger's. Jonas observes that Heidegger objects to calling man a "rational animal" since it places humans too low. Jonas says, "in reality, the lowering to Heidegger consists in placing man in *any* scale, that is, in a context of *nature* as such." Cited in Avens, "Things and Angels," 17. Heidegger and Corbin differ fundamentally on the question of where *Dasein* is situated ontologically, as we will see. For Corbin and the mystical theosophers, there is no autonomous natural order except that posited when we deceive ourselves into immobilizing nature by conceiving it as simply objective. See below, especially Chapter 6.

Western metaphysics, one which is, in Heidegger's terminology, "concrete," and which takes as fundamental a close examination of the ways in which we exist in the world.

The analysis of *Dasein* is, in other words, phenomenological: it begins with a descriptive analysis of how phenomena appear. This is explicitly not an attempt to reduce or explain one thing or appearance by another. The aim is the disclosure, the uncovering, of that which shows itself in the appearances. Corbin's understanding of the methods and goals of phenomenology is deeply influenced by his understanding of Heidegger, but at the same time, he was to find resonances in this method with aspects of Islamic thought which were to allow him to go far beyond Heidegger's analysis.

Everyone who reads *Being and Time* is confronted with the difficult task of making sense of the numerous neologisms. The text is subtle and complex. The notoriously tortuous writing is not difficult because it is abstract. It is difficult because Heidegger is attempting to create a vocabulary that can break through the traditional categories of Western thought into a language which can reveal the most primordial and concrete images but at the same time hidden from our everyday consciousness. Corbin's response to the challenge is revealing: his copy of *Being and Time* was marked throughout by glosses in Arabic.[9]

Corbin's genius is in part as a comparative phenomenologist, and part of his work is to make real, to "valorize," as he likes to say, the worlds of other times and other cultures. He will move in worlds where the basic conditions of experience are radically different from those of the modern West and, increasingly of course, from the entire Westernized world. And it is partly by means of Heidegger's understanding of the primordial priority of *Dasein* that he found the means and the philosophical justification for doing so. As a philosopher placed between two cultures, Corbin is in a nearly unique position to stand on the boundaries of the worlds and feel the full force of the encounter. He will need to orient himself, to find that Center that he is seeking, and

---

9. Corbin, *Henry Corbin*, ed. Jambet, 26.

that very need will help him towards it. The orientation required must contain within itself the answer to the question of "relativism" which Corbin calls "spiritual universes." Heidegger's primordial ontology helps to provide that standpoint.

A phenomenology of primordial presence goes right to the root of our experience of both space and time and, of course therefore, of the very stuff of the world. If space and time are founded upon something deeper, on a mode of presence which in some way determines their characteristics and which is not separable from how they appear, then it is to that mode of presence that we must turn our attention if we are truly to understand ourselves and our world, and here is the place to focus if we wish to free ourselves from it. It is upon the mode of being of this *Dasein*, this being centered on the act of presence itself, that all else depends. The analysis of space and time must not begin by regarding them as given, but rather by investigating the mode of presence by means of which they themselves are revealed.

To begin with, we must realize that we are not in space in the way in which we have come to believe that we are; it is truer to say rather that we spatialize a world:

> Orientation is a primary phenomenon of our presence in the world. A human presence has the property of spatializing a world around it, and this phenomenon implies a certain relationship of man with the world, *his* world, this relationship being determined by the very mode of his presence in the world. The four cardinal points, east and west, north and south, are not *things* encountered by this presence, but directions which express its *sense*, man's acclimatization to the world, his familiarity with it. To have this sense is to orient oneself in the world.[10]

The ways in which we experience space depend, not upon a presumed objective, uniform extension given prior to our existence and into which we fit, but rather upon the status of the presence that we adopt, usually unconsciously, and which determines our relationship to those

---

10. Corbin, *The Man of Light in Iranian Sufism*, 1.

categories of experience we call spatial. This practice of phenomenology marks a profound departure from the positivism of science
and the uniform and public objectivity of Newtonian absolute space.

This is difficult enough for a modern consciousness to accept,
but with Corbin's Heideggerian analysis of time, an even more radical break with the tradition of modernism occurs. As presence provides
the possibility of spatial orientation, so there is a primordial structure
that provides the possibility of the "time" of history. For Heidegger,
one of the fundamental characteristics of *Dasein* is "historicality."[11]
Historicality is an ontological structure of *Dasein*, and it is this that
provides the possibility of the occurrence of anything like "history."
That is, in terms that Corbin will come to use, the manifest history of
human events is only possible because there is a deeper, hidden structure of *Dasein*, which makes possible the characteristics of temporality
in a more fundamental sense. Again however, the deep structure is
covered over by the everyday, the commonplace: the ontological is
hidden by the ontic. As with our perceptions of space, so our experience of manifold modes of temporality can be forgotten, covered over,
by the modes of being emphasized and established by our culture and
by the everyday, superficial modes of presence which we adopt or
rather fall into most of the time.

Heidegger's treatment of temporality was pivotal for Corbin:

> I must say that the course of my work had its origin in the
> incomparable analysis that we owe to Heidegger, showing
> the ontological roots of historical science, and giving
> evidence that there is a historicity more original, more
> primordial than that which we call Universal History, the
> History of external events, the *Weltgeschichte*, History in
> the ordinary sense of the term... There is the same relation-
> ship between historicality and historicity as between the
> existential and the *existentiell*. This was a decisive moment.[12]

11. Heidegger, *Being and Time*, 41.
12. Corbin, *Henry Corbin*, ed. Jambet, 28. In the MacQuarrie and Robinson translation, the German *geschichtlich* is rendered "historicality" in English, and Corbin translates it
as *historialité*. Likewise French *historicité* is English "historicity" from the German *historizität*.

But the decisive realization is not merely that this more ontologically primordial level exists, but that because the history of external events is somehow subordinate to and takes place within this more basic structure of Presence, we are not entirely at its mercy. The phenomenology of Presence means that we do not confront a world of

> *things* that are separate from the soul in the manner of objects...that form "currents" in the manner of a river, [for then] the dilemma can arise: either to throw oneself into the current or to struggle against it.[13]

Corbin wants neither to be submerged in the inexorable current of the time of material things nor to fight it. Neither option will suffice because either way we are at the mercy of independent objects in quantitative space. We must realize that it is not things or history which have us, which give us life or death, it is we who have them.

The Great Refusal

The phenomenology of Presence thus understood provides the grounding for Corbin's greatest refusal:

> This historicality appears in effect as motivating and legitimating the refusal to let ourselves be inserted into the historicity of History, into the web of historical causality, and which we are calling an uprooting[14] of the historicity of History. For if there is a "meaning of History" it is not at all in the historicity of historical events; it is in this historicality, in the secret, esoteric, existential roots of History and the historical.[15]

Corbin does not claim that to step out of history or out of the Faustian space of modern science is easy or simple; quite the contrary, it requires "spiritual combat" of the highest order. But the intimation that it can be done at all is the necessary and crucial realization in our almost wholly

---

13. Corbin, *Avicenna and the Visionary Recital*, 10.
14. French *arracher*: to tear out, to tear away, to pull out, to uproot.
15. Corbin, *Henry Corbin*, ed. Jambet, 28.

materialist and secular world. If we see that it can be done, then we realize we are not irremediably bound by the deepest, most far reaching presuppositions of our time. But notice what is required: an aptitude for the "the secret, esoteric, existential roots of History." Without the ability to penetrate to the hidden levels of temporality, we remain at the mercy of the inexorable flux of linear time.

The image of the current of history has deep resonances for Corbin. The way to step out of it is by means of gnosis: transformative knowledge that changes the mode of presence of the knower and which is synonomous with esotericism. More than once he has quoted the Sixth Imam of the Shi'ites: "We, the Imams, we are the Sages who instruct; our Shi'ites are those initiated by us; as for the rest, they are as the foam rolled along by the torrent."[16] Throughout the entire range of Corbin's work, the emphasis is everywhere upon the secret hidden realities of soul and the conviction that it is here that one must turn to escape the secular, the superficial, the material, the public, and the merely literal. It is only by means of the subtle realities of soul that objectivity can be found. Without doubt Corbin saw in Heidegger's program an intent comparable in part to that of the Shi'ite gnostics whose struggle is to protect and guard the realities of the hidden Divine Trust that is the true reality of Creation. The spiritual combat of Shi'ism is against all the literalizing, secularizing tendencies of any age.[17] While Heidegger's own strategy includes breaking away from dogmatic theology, it is clearly directed against narrow materialism or any commonplace, everyday interpretation of the world and human life. His disdain for the opinions of *das Mann* is, it seems clear, not merely an ontological attitude, but a moral one as well, and so his program seems in this sense not so far from that of Corbin, though he lacked the capacity to move into the worlds in which Corbin was to live. And from the point of view of Islamic esotericism, ontology and ethics are inseparable.

Gnosis requires a commitment of the whole person in order that the change extend to the roots and alter the mode of presence. To

---

16. Corbin, *En islam iranienne: aspects spirituels et philosophiques*, v. 1, 117.
17. See, *ibid.*, Vol. 1, Ch. III.

tear ourselves away from historical time, we require far more than an abstract intellectual recognition of the possibility. For Corbin, phenomenology itself implies a movement of the whole being, since the phenomena in question include all the emotions and sympathies of the human person. We require a movement of the whole soul, a deep desire, a resolve, and the "courage of love."[18] But Corbin's conception of phenomenology is in many ways most un-Heideggerian.[19] For Heidegger too, phenomenology is a passionate enterprise involving the authentic self. But characteristically for Heidegger, this involves Resolve: we must be Resolute in our Being-towards-Death, since our inevitable mortality defines our deepest reality. But Corbin says there is no necessity whatever to remain Present in Heidegger's *Weltanschauung*. What to Heidegger seemed our rock-bottom mode of being, that is, "Being-towards-Death," is really not ontologically foundational, but is itself historically conditioned, and we need not adopt it. We can use the key he has given us to free ourselves from his world as well.

The modern world has fallen prey to a deadly agnosticism that can only end in nihilism and has nearly lost the capacity to achieve those modes of being which are oriented towards the eternal, towards that which is "on the other side of death."[20] There are modes of Presence and the World they entail, the World they make possible, which have become lost to modern historical consciousness, and that World has become for us a lost continent because the modes of Presence it requires are oriented towards the Eternal. This is the World that Corbin wants to make accessible once more, and it is in the Islamic imagination and in that of pre-Islamic Iran as well that he found it.

The move to Islam is a move out of linear, historical time. Nwyia says: "Schooled in the *Koran*, Muslim consciousness is spontaneously anhistorical, that is to say, mythic...the historical event evaporates

---

18. Corbin, *En islam iranienne*, v. 1, 38.

19. In "Henry Corbin, 1903-1978: Between Philosophy and Orientalism," Hermann Landolt, following Jambet, sees Corbin's view of phenomenology as closer in spirit to Husserl's than to Heidegger's.

20. Corbin, *Henry Corbin*, ed. Jambet, 32-33.

and all that is left is a vague memory submerged in a story which has become mythic."[21] Norman O. Brown comments,

> The *Koran* backs off from that linear organization of time, revelation, and history which became the backbone of orthodox Christianity, and remains the backbone of Western culture after the death of God.... Islam is committed by the *Koran* to project a meta-historical plane on which the eternal meaning of historical events is disclosed.... History *sub specie aeternitatis*.[22]

Thus there is a great deal at stake when we attempt to step out of the current of the history of material causality. What we are stepping into is mythic time, mythic space, a mythic reality, where the historicist priority of time over space is reversed. The step out of secular, linear temporality requires relation to Eternity. Corbin is engaged in reawakening our archaic potential for archetypal, transhistorical experience. His royal road lies through soul and leads into the transhistorical consciousness of mystical Islam.[23]

Corbin is concerned throughout his work to counter the forces of nihilistic materialism which he saw destroying the fabric of the traditional cultures of Islam. But his efforts apply to all such cultures threatened by the spread of modern consciousness and its social and economic results. In a world that is rapidly losing bio-diversity and cultural diversity, Corbin's work can be seen as an attempt to safeguard human spiritual diversity against the ravages of narrow-minded dogmatisms, whether spiritual or scientific. Within that most monotheistic of Abrahamic religions, Corbin, student of Louis Massignon, reveals

---

21. Cited in Norman O. Brown, "The Apocalypse of Islam," 87. Brown prefers "folkloric" to "mythic." I use "mythic" here to refer to modes of consciousness which are not "rationalist, materialist and historicist" and which reflect the archaic consciousness of traditional, pre-modern cultures.

22. *Ibid.*, 86-88.

23. This kind of analysis of mythic versus historical time is central to the work of Corbin's friend and colleague at Eranos, Mircea Eliade. See for example Eliade's *The Myth of the Eternal Return.* Especially pertinent is the last chapter, "The Terror of History," which expresses many of the same feelings about the dilemma of modern humanity that drove Corbin's search.

a primordial relation to the world and to divinity. Brown writes,

> The Islamic imagination, Massignon has written, should be
> seen as the product of a desperate regression, back to the
> primitive, the eternal pagan substrate of all religion.
> …Islam stays with the dream life of the masses…discarded
> by the Enlightenment as superstition…[24]

That Corbin could find in Heidegger's ontology a path towards
Islam understood in this way is perfectly consonant with Heidegger's
own "pagan" tendencies. In his later work, Heidegger's analysis of
Presence and its relation to time and space can be clearly seen as a
move towards mythic, and perhaps mystic, consciousness. He further
develops his early intuition and describes a sense in which both the
past and the future are somehow contained and implied within an expanded
sense of Presence. David Abram writes that in his mature thought,

> *past* and *future* are…articulated as hidden powers that
> approach us, offering and opening the present while never-
> theless remaining withdrawn, concealed from the very
> present that they make possible…
> …[H]e writes of the past and the future as *absences*
> that by their very absence concern us, and so make them-
> selves felt within the present.[25]

Yet, even in *Being and Time* which so deeply affected Corbin,
the horizons of time are contained in the act of Presence itself. The
primordial phenomenon of the future is that it "comes towards us."[26] The
past and the future are both somehow contained in the present.

---

24. Brown, "The Apocalypse of Islam," 92.
25. Abram, *Spell of the Sensuous*, 211-12. Abram's lucid analysis of Heidegger
occurs in the context of his own attempt to shake us loose from the material, historical
consciousness of the technological West and make possible a return to something more
archaic, more grounded, and more real. Abram's focus is on the imagination of tribal
and traditional cultures, which never achieved the status of great civilizations as Islam
certainly did, and therefore on the more obviously pagan consciousness.
26. Heidegger, *Being and Time*, 372.

The implications of Heidegger's analysis for our experience of both time and space are made explicit by Abram when he says that the primordial experience of the future can be found in the Present as the *"beyond-the-horizon"* and that of the past in the *"under-the-ground."*[27] That a similar experience of the world is in the primordial revelation of Islam is suggested by this comment of Corbin's about Islamic thought as a whole:

> Forms are thought of as being in space rather than in time. Our thinkers perceive the world not as "evolving" in a horizontal and rectilinear direction, but as ascending: the past is not behind us but "beneath our feet."[28]

This archetypal emphasis on space rather than time and on the eternal significance of the present moment runs throughout Islamic consciousness. The space of a mosque

> is as if reabsorbed into the ubiquity of the present moment; it does not beckon the eye in a specific direction; it suggests no tension or antinomy between the here below and the beyond, or between earth and heaven; it possesses all its fullness in every place.[29]

So Corbin's uprooting of the soul from the current of historical causality is a freeing from its entrapment in a secular world in which it is swept along to an inevitable demise, and it is a freeing to a world of archetype and myth. It is therefore in a double sense that Corbin says we are freed to "give a future to the past:" the past as the merely no-longer-present of other cultures, other histories, and the Past as the Eternally Present.

---

27. Abram, *Spell of the Sensuous*, 212-13.

28. Corbin, *History of Islamic Philosophy*, 5. This attitude towards time and mere temporal change underlying Islamic thought explains the vehemence of the attack on "evolutionism" in such a sophisticated and powerful thinker as Seyyed Hossein Nasr and in most of the proponents of Traditionalism. See, for instance, Nasr, *Knowledge and the Sacred*, especially Ch. 7. From within the worldview of modern biology, his critique is absurd. On the Traditionalists see Chapter 5 below.

29. Titus Burckhardt, from *Art of Islam: Language and Meaning*, cited in Brown, "The Apocalypse of Islam," 86.

The past and the future,

> are not attributes of exterior things; they are attributes
> of the soul itself. It is we who are living or dead, and who are
> responsible for the life and death of these things.[30]

We determine the status of "the past," and we determine the nature
of the world in which we find ourselves:

> Yet nothing fluctuates more than the notion of "past"; it
> depends actually on a decision, or a pre-decision, which
> can always be *surpassed* by another decision which re-
> stores a future to that past.[31]

What gives a future, a "life," to the past, for instance, to a
history of being other than that of the modern West, is the soul
opening that possibility to itself. It is up to us whether we succeed or
fail in making a future for the past:

> The decision of the future falls to the soul, depends upon
> how the soul understands *itself*, upon its refusal or accep-
> tance of a new birth.[32]

But this does not mean that we can necessarily take some past
system as a whole and adopt it from the outside as our own. For
instance, Corbin says of Avicenna,

> It may prove that the *letter* of his cosmological system is closed
> to the immediate consciousness of our time. But the personal
> experience entrusted to his recitals reveals a *situation* with which
> ours perhaps has something in common. In this case, his whole
> system becomes the "cipher" of such a situation. To "decipher" it
> is not to accumulate a vain erudition of things, but to open our
> own possibilities to ourselves.[33]

---

30. Corbin, *En islam iranienne*, v. 1, 37.
31. Corbin, *Man of Light in Iranian Sufism*, 13.
32. Corbin, *Avicenna*, 10.
33. *Ibid.*

So a history of philosophy or a comparative study of philosophical or religious systems is for Corbin always based upon a phenomenological method that assumes the potential effectiveness of the systems under scrutiny for the soul in the present. Any other kind of history is vain erudition. Corbin's philological, historical, and comparative research is always the work of a man devoted to *philosophia*, a seeker. And he himself emphasized the unity of his quest:

> What I searched for in Heidegger, what I understood thanks to Heidegger, is the same thing that I searched for and found in Irano-Islamic metaphysics.... But with this last, everything was situated from then on at a different level....[34]

Heidegger's search for an alternative to modern materialistic nihilism remained entirely within the Western philosophical tradition. His attempt to escape the post-Cartesian world led him in the end to the origins of Western thought in the Pre-Socratics, searching the texts for the roots of a failed metaphysics, in order to uncover what he called the "history of Being" and "destroy the history of ontology" and so recover the phenomena of a lost world. Corbin's path led east to Iran, "a world where the 'history of being' is something entirely other than that imposed by the transition from Greek to Latin,"[35] and to an alternate history, but one having roots, like ours, in both the primordial monotheism of Abraham and in the philosophy of ancient Greece. It is there that he found the world for which he was looking and which he called the *mundus imaginalis*:

> For a long period I have been searching, like a young philosopher, for the key to this world as a real world, which is neither the sensible world, nor the world of abstract concepts. It was in Iran itself that I had to find it, in the two ages of the spiritual world of Iran.[36]

And it is to the history of these two ages that we now turn.

---

34. Corbin, *Henry Corbin*, ed. Jambet, 24.
35. Corbin, *Voyage and the Messenger*, 215.
36. Corbin, *Spiritual Body and Celestial Earth*, viii.

CHAPTER TWO

An Oriental Theosophy

Massignon's transmission of the great work of Suhrawardi into Corbin's hands was a defining event in his life. The Shaykh al-Ishraq, Master of Oriental Light, was born in Suhraward, in Northwest Iran in 1155 and died martyred by Saladin and his religious inquisitors in the city of Aleppo, in what is now Syria, in 1191.[1] Suhrawardi saw himself as the resurrector of the wisdom of ancient Persia within the context of the Islamic Revelation. Iran was to occupy an especially important place in Corbin's personal spiritual iconography. Central to much of his work is the idea that the spiritual history of humanity will be truncated until we come to understand the possibilities that the specifically Iranian experience opens up to us. In the course of his early studies, the young theologian from the Christian West pursued both Arabic and Sanskrit: Islam, on the one hand, and Indian philosophy and Hinduism on the other. But with the discovery of Suhrawardi, the die was cast:

> Persia was situated at the center, a median and mediating world, because Persia, ancient Iran, is not only a nation or an empire, it is a spiritual universe, a focus of the history of religions.[2]

---

1. The term *ishraq* is a verbal noun meaning the illumination of the rising sun. The term applied to Suhrawardi's followers, *Ishraqiyun*, is translated either Illuminationists or Orientals, referring to their focus on the Light of the Orient, but not in a geographical sense.

2. Corbin, *Henry Corbin*, ed. Jambet, 41.

He understood Iran as a mediating world both geographically and metaphysically. It symbolized for him the *mundus imaginalis* and the freedom of the soul that this announces. The history of Iranian Islam is closely tied to the fate of Shi'ism. In the 16th century Shi'ism became the official state religion of Iran. It is largely in Shi'ite terms that Corbin understood prophetic religion, or perhaps it is better to say that it is in Shi'ism that he found best expressed the inner core of prophetic religion.

In order to make our way around in Corbin's world, it is essential to be familiar with at least the roughest outlines of Iranian and Islamic history. Here we can only briefly review those facets of that long and complex story which are the most indispensable for a grasp of Corbin's work. As he himself said, this is a lost continent for most Westerners.[3]

Persia and Mazdaism

The first of the two ages of Iranian spirituality to which Corbin refers is the pre-Islamic era, which can be dated from the origins of a specifically Iranian complex of beliefs and practices in the middle of the second millennium B.C.E. and that extended through four dynasties: the Achaemenid, Seleucid, Parthian (or Arsacid), and Sassanian.[4] The second

3. It lies far beyond the scope of this book to survey the esoteric traditions of Christianity and Judaism that are pertinent to Corbin's projects. The interested reader should see Antoine Faivre, *Access to Western Esotericism*; Seyyed Hossein Nasr, *Knowledge and the Sacred* and *Religion and the Order of Nature*; Philip Sherrard, *The Eclipse of Man and Nature* and *Human Image—World Image*; and Arthur Versluis, *Theosophia: Hidden Dimensions of Christianity* for treatments of the Christian tradition. For Judaism see Gershom Scholem, *Origins of the Kabbahlah* and Moshe Idel, *Kabbalah: New Perspectives*.

4. Sources for this section include Norman Cohn, *Cosmos, Chaos and the World to Come: The Ancient Roots of Apocalyptic Faith*; Corbin, *Creative Imagination in the Sufism of Ibn 'Arabi, A History of Islamic Philosophy*, and *Spiritual Body and Celestial Earth: From Mazdean Iran to Shi'ite Iran*; Mircea Eliade, *A History of Religious Ideas, Vol. 1: From the Stone Age to the Eleusinian Mysteries, Vol. 2: From Gautama Buddha to the Triumph of Christianity*, and *Vol. 3: From Muhammad to the Age of Reforms*; Marshall S. Hodgson, *The Venture of Islam: Conscience and History in a World Civilization* (3 vols); Clive Irving, *Crossroads of Civilization: 3000 Years of Persian History*; Sandra Mackey, *The Iranians: Persia, Islam and the Soul of a Nation*; Rustum Masani, *Zoroastrianism: The Religion of the Good Life*; S. Murata & W. Chittick, *The Vision of Islam*; Ninian Smart, *The Religious Experience of Mankind*; and Jean Verenne, "Pre-Islamic Iran" *Mythologies*, Vol. 2, edited by Yves Bonnefoy.

age is the Islamic, beginning with the collapse of the Sassanid empire in 637 C.E. and extending to the present day.

Ancient Persia was a vast domain, which by 1800 B.C.E. extended from the Zagros Mountains to Transoxiana. The Iranian religion was closely related to that of the Vedas with a panoply of gods and spirits. Central to this system of beliefs was the significance of fire and light. Zarathustra, or as he was known to the Greeks, Zoroaster, was a priest of the religion and saw himself as a reformer of this complex faith which he believed to have degenerated. He was born in northern or eastern Persia and lived between 1500 and 1200 B.C.E.[5] His prophetic calling began with the appearance of the angel Vohu Manah, who escorted him on a visionary voyage to the supreme deity, Ahura Mazda (Wise Lord; Ohrmazd in Pahlavi). Subsequent revelations confirmed his prophetic mission. His chief concerns were to institute an eschatological monotheism based on the primacy of Ahura Mazda over all other deities, establish a cosmology in which the Divine Light engages in a struggle with Darkness, and to purge what he saw as excesses in the religion, such as blood sacrifice and ritual use of intoxicants.

The sacred text of Zoroastrianism, or Mazdaism, is the *Avesta*. The earliest parts are traditionally attributed to Zarathustra. The latest texts were perhaps written down in the fourth century B.C.E., but the text was altered at times, even after the Islamic conquest. There is little doubt that portions of the earliest pre-monotheistic texts have been lost due in part to the "purification" instituted by the prophet. The final canonical form was given to it during the Sassanian Empire (226-635 C.E.).

The content and subsequent development of Zarathustra's message was to be crucial for the monotheistic religions of the Near East: Judaism, Christianity, and Islam.[6] In contrast to the prevailing static view of Time and Creation shared by Egyptians, Sumerians, Canaanites, all the Aryan peoples, both Indian and Iranian, and the pre-exilic Israelites, Zarathustra proposed a cosmology based upon the experience of purpose and

---

5. These early dates have only recently been established with confidence. See Cohn, *Cosmos, Chaos and the World to Come*.

6. *Ibid.* Cohn argues this view of the role played by Mazdean eschatological concepts.

directionality in the world. In this cosmology Creation is the stage for a divine drama, the struggle between Light and Darkness, which will one day come to an end with the final battle in which the savior Shaoshyant will complete the victory of Light. Each human soul is free to choose its own part in this drama, and its ultimate fate, in Heaven or in Hell, will depend on this choice. In a reworking of an ancient Indo-Iranian theme, after death each soul is said to meet its celestial Self in the form of a young woman on the road to the Beyond which passes over the Çinvat Bridge. This "bridge of sorting" appears wide to the Just and as narrow as a razor to the Evil who plummet into hell. If the origin of this eschatological worldview lies with Mazdaism, as Cohn argues, then it was the Zoroastrians and not the Israelites[7] who served as the original midwives for the birth of history.

While, strictly speaking, Mazdaism is neither polytheist nor dualist, it was never a rigid and abstract monism, and over time the ancient mythic and polytheistic past reasserted itself. Even during the time of the prophet, Ohrmazd is surrounded by a group of divine beings, the *Amesha Spentas*, who personify such attributes as Justice and Devotion. He is also father to several other beings, including a pair of twins, one of whom freely chose evil over good and became the destroying Spirit, Ahriman. The Evil One is thus not evil by nature, but by choice. This initiates the Cosmic Drama. The defining characteristic of Mazdaism is the centrality of this cosmic struggle, and this vision of the moral structure of Creation sounds the primary note of a theme that was to resonate through the centuries in the great religions of the Middle East. In the words of a modern day Zoroastrian:

> Not by mere negation of evil, not by retreat before it,
> but by facing it boldly and fighting it with all one's might
> may man hope to fulfill his lofty destiny to redeem the
> world from evil and establish the kingdom of righteous-
> ness on this earth. He was but animal yesterday. He is

---

7. As argued by Eliade, for instance.

man today. His destiny is to be angel, if not all at once, in the not distant hereafter, as the result of the gradual process of self-perfection.[8]

In Mazdean cosmology Ohrmazd created the world for the very purpose of annihilating evil, and so cosmology and eschatology are indistinguishable. Limited or finite, eschatological Time is created in order for the struggle to take place. This inaugurates the conception of a linear, purposive time, rather than the primordial time of cyclical mythologies. Time is linear in so far as the events which occur in it take their meaning from the sequence of their occurrence. Ohrmazd is originally finite since he is delimited by his opposite, Ahriman. In the initial event of this drama, Ahriman attacks. But Ohrmazd had foreseen this and had produced a concrete but spiritual Creation, the world of the *menok*, which in order to counter the attack, is made corporeal, or *getik*, so that Ohrmazd can become infinite in space as well as time. This world is created as the battleground of Good and Evil. But before transferring Creation to the *getik* state, Ohrmazd asked the innumerable heavenly spirits, the Fravartis, if they would take on corporeal existence in order to help in combating Ahriman's forces. They agree to this. Thus the origin of their name, which means "those who have chosen." "This testifies to the attachment for incarnate life, for work, and in the last analysis, for matter—an attachment that is a specific characteristic of Zarathustra's message."[9]

This is to be contrasted in the strongest terms with the pessimism and radical dualism that were characteristic of Manicheanism and the various movements generally called Gnostic, which sprang up in the centuries preceding and following the birth of Christ. Material creation is good; it is only Ahriman that corrupts it. The material world is not the realm of Darkness—it is made of the same substance as the soul. Each person has a subtle body, which exists in the *menok* world, as a resurrection body of light. It is only after Ahriman enters and pollutes the *getik* world that it becomes

---

8. Masani, *Zoroastrianism*, 7-8.
9. Eliade, *A History of Religious Ideas, Vol. 2*, 316.

a world of mixture. By virtue of their freedom, humans can collaborate in the work of redemption of the material world.

> For in the eyes of Mazdaism, the material Creation—that is, matter and life—*is good in itself* and worthy to be purified and restored. Indeed the doctrine of the resurrection of bodies proclaims the inestimable value of the Creation. This is the most rigorous and the most daring religious valorization of matter that we know of before the Western chemist-philosophers of the seventeenth century.[10]

This is not to say that there is an indiscriminant celebration of matter. The polluted matter of Ahriman must be eliminated from the mixture, and therefore there is an emphasis on ritual purity. The ordered world must be kept apart from the disordered. Any contact of the impure creation with the good creation must be avoided in order to prevent the former from undermining the latter: ". . . dirt, rust, mould, blight and also . . . anything that issues from the human body," are all impure, as are certain kinds of creatures that it is the Zoroastrian's duty to destroy. Ants, beetles, scorpions, lizards, snakes, and wolves are among the instruments of Ahriman.[11]

Therefore, through both active ritual and moral struggle against the forces of Ahriman, the Zoroastrian was "directly and constantly involved" in the processes helping to sustain the order of the world. "All members of the community took part, through the ordinary tasks of everyday life, in sustaining and strengthening the ordered world...." Thus the rules of the religion served both to democratize its members and to set them off from others of different faiths.[12] Humans were understood to be active participants in the course of this new sense of history. Not as in the modern conception, merely technicians moving matter around in space, hoping perhaps for utopian better days to come, but cosmically important moral agents whose very being has an impact on

---

10. Eliade, *A History of Religious Ideas, Vol. 2*, 320.
11. Cohn, *Cosmos, Chaos and the World to Come*, 89.
12. *Ibid.*

the outcome of the struggle. The modern philosophical sense of ontology, which Heidegger hoped to undermine, pales to embarrassing insignificance in comparison. In trying to grasp what eschatology and history meant for these people and what it means today for the esoteric and ahistorical Muslims, history must be understood against the background of the mythic sensibility that gave birth to it.

The nature and role of esoteric or ecstatic rites in Mazdaism is not clear, but that such rites existed is certain. Zarathustra seems to have opposed at least the uncontrolled use of trance-inducing intoxicants. The illuminative knowledge that was to be obtained by rites and rituals is thought to have been a visionary illumination and *gnosis* of initiation in which botanical intoxicants played a small part. This illumination itself, which transfigures the soul, ensures salvation, and at the final Resurrection at the end of limited time, the world itself derives from Ohrmazd who is the source of the divine light, Xvarnah. This transforming light appears as the result of the unmixing of the Ahrimanian pollution with the original pure Creation. It is in the Light of Xvarnah that Suhrawardi will find the Orient of Pure Light of the ancient Iranian sages that he found raised to another level in the *Quran*:

> God is the light of the heavens and the earth. The sem-
> blance of His light is that of a niche in which is a lamp,
> the flame within a glass, the glass a glittering star as it
> were, lit with the oil of a blessed tree, the olive, neither
> of the East nor of the West, whose oil appears to light
> up even though fire touches it not,—light upon light
> (*Quran* 24:35).[13]

Over time Mazdean orthodoxy progressively hardened the dualism between the powers of Ohrmazd and Ahriman. This was opposed by Zervanite theology, which seems to have developed under the Arsacids, although how widespread this movement became is not known. In Zervanism, both Ohrmazd and Ahriman are sons of

---

13. Translation by Ahmed Ali, *al-Quran* (Princeton: Princeton UP, 1984). All translations of the *Quran* used in this book are from this edition.

Zervan, a figure who can be dated as far back as the Achaemenid period. Zervan is referred to as both Time and Space so that "speculations on time-space as the common source of the two principles of Good and Evil...were familiar to the Iranians."[14]

The structure of limited, finite time is made clear by three figures: Gayomart, Zarathustra, and Saoshyant. Gayomart is the androgynous primordial Macanthropos, sprung from the coupling of Ohrmazd and Spandarmat, the Angel of the Earth. The planets proceed from his body, and from his semen springs rhubarb, from which comes the first human pair. He is killed by Ahriman, but transmits the Revelation to the first humans. He is the equal of both Zarathustra and Saoshyant as an exemplar of the Just and Perfect Human. Zarathustra himself stands midway in time between the Primal Human and the Savior. The figure of Saoshyant, the Final Savior who will appear at the end of time, is a crucial element in the Mazdean schema that will have a long history in the religions of Abraham.

During the reigns of the Achaemenids Cyrus (d. 530 B.C.E.) and Darius (d. 486 B.C.E.), the Persian Empire grew by conquest until it stretched from beyond the Nile in the west to the Indus in the east, and a distinct Persian culture was established. Zoroastrian fire temples were prominent landmarks in public places, and the magi,[15] the official priest class of the kings, became the "guardians of the flame." Although Darius had decreed that the *Avesta* was to be recorded in gold and silver on twelve thousand ox hides, there is some dispute among scholars as to whether Mazdaism should be regarded as the official religion of state. There is reason to think that even the Achaemenean kings regarded themselves as Ohrmazd's representatives on earth.

---

14. Eliade, *A History of Religious Ideas, Vol. 2*, 309.

15. The origin of this term comes from the *Magioi*, the Greek name for the tribe that provided the priest class for the ancient nomadic Medes, who conquered the Assyrians in 612 B.C.E.

The end of the Achaemenid Empire began with the defeat of Xerxes by the Greeks at Salamis in 481 B.C.E. In 332 B.C.E., Alexander of Macedon crossed the Zagros mountains, entered the magnificent capitol at Persepolis, and destroyed it.

> In less than a hundred years—from Cyrus's rise to the death of Xerxes—the Persians had produced a religion that replaced idols and blood rites with a god and a moral system; a government reigning over a diversity of nations living in peace; a philosophy concerned with ethics, tolerance, and justice; and finally an art that celebrated an extraordinarily high level of civilization.[16]

With the collapse of Alexander's empire, his cavalry commander Seleucis seized Persia, and the Seleucids maintained control for one hundred and sixty years. In the end they were ousted by the nomadic Parthians from the steppes of the north. The first Parthian chief, Arsaces, established a dynasty that lasted from 163 B.C.E. to 224 C.E. and, although tumultuous and unstable, managed to keep the Romans at bay. The history of Persian culture from the Alexandrian period on is marked by the effects of its contact with Hellenic civilization. Alexander's great empire had the effect of bringing together a multitude of diverse elements from a variety of traditions. This grand melting pot included the monotheism of Judaism, and later, of the early Christian sects, Greek philosophy and religion, and the traditions of the East.

Under the Arsacids, the effects of the spread of Hellenistic mystery religions, particularly the cult of Mithra, begin to be felt. Mithra occurs in the *Avesta* as a figure subsidiary to Ohrmazd, yet is himself one of the great gods. He is a solar god associated with light, a god of war, and a universal provider. With these attributes it is easy to see how he came to be connected under the Arsacids with the concept of a messianic King-Savior. The deification of the King is a characteristic feature of the Hellenistic and post-Hellenistic

---

16. Sandra Mackey, *The Iranians*, 31.

dynasties, and the connection of the Magian priests involved in the sacrificial cults of Mithra with the ruling families connects the cosmic eschatological mythology with the political structures of the time. The cult of Mithra seems to have begun in Mesopotamia and Asia Minor but was to spread throughout the Hellenistic world.

Another thread woven into the fabric of Hellenistic culture is the group of beliefs collectively referred to as Hermeticism. The texts that have come down to us as evidence of this system were composed between the third century B.C.E. and the third century C.E. They are held to have been revealed by Hermes Trismegistus (the Thrice Great). The content of the Hermetic religion combines astrology, magic, alchemy, and other occult sciences in a Judeo-Egyptian-Iranian matrix suffused with Platonic and later, neo-Platonic elements. The magical cosmology central to Hermeticism is based on the perception of a cosmic system of sympathies and correspondences, most importantly, between the human microcosm and the macrocosm of the world of nature. The influences of this cosmology in the West can be seen in the heretical and magical undercurrents in theology and philosophy down through Marsilio Ficino and the Renaissance Platonists—Paracelsus, Robert Fludd, and Isaac Newton. Characteristic of Hermeticism is the doctrine of the esoteric transmission of secrets. Eliade writes:

> We must not lose sight of the fact that the revelations contained in the great treatises of the *Corpus Hermeticum* constitutes a supreme Gnosis, that is, the esoteric knowledge that insures salvation; the mere fact of having understood and assimilated it is equivalent to an "initiation." This new type of individual and wholly spiritual "initiation," made possible by attentively reading and meditating on an esoteric text, developed during the Imperial period and especially after the triumph of Christianity.[17]

---

17. Eliade, *A History of Religious Ideas*, *Vol. 2*, 300.

As we shall see, the Hermetic corpus, like the works of Aristotle and Plato, was preserved to return to the Latin West by the civilization of Islam.

In the year 208, in Fars, the original seat of the Achaemenids, Ardeshir succeeded to the throne of a tribal monarchy surrounded by the chaos of a Arsacid Empire collapsed into internecine warfare. His success in establishing his authority over the rival monarchs began the rule of the Sassanians[18] which lasted until 637 when, nearly destroyed by the Byzantines, the weakened Persian army was finally defeated by the Arabs at Qadisiyyah on the Euphrates. The Sassanian period marks a burgeoning of Persian art and culture but also a rigidification of Mazdaism and the strengthening of the power of the absolute monarchy and of the priesthood. Ardeshir realized that emphasizing the divine right of kingship, a tradition inherited from the Achaemenids, would help cement his authority. He made Mazdaism the official religion of the state, and the Magi, who had maintained the old religion for hundreds of years independently of the kingship, were now officially in the service of the rulers. "In a grand manipulation of symbols, the sacred flame of the temple...became the flame of the king as well as Ahura Mazda."[19] By the end of the Sassanian dynasty, the Magi had become largely tools of the power of the state, and the religion had lost touch almost entirely with the original teachings of the prophet. Persian culture, however, remained stable. Mackey writes,

> The themes of ethics and behavior bred by religion, kingship and justice, art and customs, tolerance for diversity and an eagerness for assimilation lived on as they had lived on after the Achaemenians... That the uniquely Persian culture and identity survived and prospered must be credited to the Sassanians... However, in the end, it was the Iranians themselves who defended a unique form of nationalism which came from an emotional commitment to culture. When

---

18. The name comes from Ardeshir's grandfather.
19. Mackey, *The Iranians*, 34.

> Iran fell to the Arabs in the seventh century, Persian culture
> stayed intact to fertilize Islam and define it for Iran.[20]

The early years of the Sassanian dynasty are marked by the rise of the religion of Mani, who was born near Ctesiphon around 216. By 242 his influence had spread to the point that the emperor Shapur I recognized the religion and allowed him permission to preach throughout the empire. Mani conceived his mission to be to establish a universal religion of salvation from the suffering inherent in this world, based on the "Knowledge that saves:" gnosis. Thus it represents perhaps the most popular and widespread of that group of beliefs referred to collectively as Gnosticism.[21] There is much controversy and confusion in the vast and complex literature concerning Gnosticism. It is important in reading Corbin to distinguish Gnosticism *sensu stricto* from gnosis as Corbin uses the term. The former is based upon a radical dualism of Evil and Good, a denigration of the material world, and a pessimistic view of the human condition. The latter refers to the esoteric, inner spiritual essence of any religion. It is this meaning of the term which is pertinent to Corbin's work. There can thus be a Christian gnosis, a Jewish gnosis, an Islamic gnosis, without necessarily implying any particular cosmology. Roberts Avens summarizes:

> Historically, gnosis constitutes the esoteric element in
> the official or exoteric religious traditions of the world.
> As such it must be distinguished from gnosticism which
> flourished before, during, and after the rise of Christian-
> ity. The predominant view of gnosticism is that of a
> radically dualistic religious movement positing the ex-
> istence of two equal and contrary forces in the universe: a
> good God and an evil Demiurge. The good God did not
> produce the world, and he doesn't rule over it: he is
> transmundane, acosmic, unknowable. The Demiurge is

---

20. Mackey, *The Iranians*, 38-39.

21. For some clarification see Michael Adams Williams, *Rethinking "Gnosti-cism:" An Argument For Dismantling a Dubious Category.*

> an inferior God responsible for the creation of the world
> and all the calamities issuing from this act. Gnosticism
> sees man as a misplaced spark (*pneuma*) of the divine
> light, engulfed in darkness through no fault of his own.
> He must struggle to free himself from the mortal encasement
> and soar back to the empyrean realm from which he came.[22]

This contrasts strongly with Mazdean cosmology and adds an additional element of heterogeneity to the cultural palette that Islam was to confront.

It was during the Sassanian dynasty that much of the work of cultural assimilation of traditions from the West and the East was accomplished. This was to lay the groundwork for the cultural climate which existed in Persia at the time of the Islamic triumph and which guided the course that Islamic theology was to take there. The range of intellectual developments in Sassanian Persia can be indicated by events at opposite ends of the Empire. First, in the south and west, the translation of Greek texts was to have a profound influence on the course of Islamic thought. Second, in the

22. Avens, *The New Gnosis*, 132. Since Harold Bloom has written the preface to the new edition of Corbin's *Creative Imagination in the Sufism of Ibn 'Arabi*, it should be noted that Bloom's treatment of Gnosticism in his own work, *Omens of Millennium: The Gnosis of Angels, Dreams and Resurrection* is influenced to a large extent by Hans Jonas, although it is ostensibly based in large measure on Corbin and tends in the end to emphasize a pessimist view of Creation, which is not that of Corbin himself. I will risk the suggestion that perhaps Bloom's view of Gnosticism and of Corbin can be correlated with his claim that Shakespeare represents the pinnacle of Western literature. George Groddeck has proposed that with Shakespeare we find the culmination of a literature that brings us "news of the human," one which has ultimately proved narrowing since it is focused upon the ego that is now essentially bankrupt, complete, and dying. The other strain in Western literature, represented for Groddeck by some of Goethe's works, brings us "news of the universe" and is based upon an awareness of divine instinctuality, of *Gott-natur*. A champion of the former literature would perhaps be more at home in a world-denying Gnosticism than in the gnosticism of theophany that Corbin represents. For a discussion of Groddeck, see Bly, (ed.) *News of the Universe: Poems of Twofold Consciousness*, 280-85. For further treatment of the positive evaluation of Creation in the esoteric gnostic tradition, see Versluis, *Theosophia*; Sherrard, *The Eclipse of Man and Nature*; and Nasr, *Religion and the Order of Nature*, especially Chapters 6, 7, and 8.

north and east, the Graeco-Oriental tradition of what Oswald Spengler termed a "magical culture" was preserved and developed and was to enter eventually into the Islamic culture of Persia.

Of enormous importance to the history of philosophy and theology in Islamic Iran is the complex relationship among Mazdean eschatology, Greek philosophical speculation, and the Islamic Revelation. The influence of the Greek tradition on Islamic thought is largely mediated by translations of Greek texts, first into Syriac and then later, into Arabic. One of the chief centers for the translation of these texts was the School of the Persians at Edessa (modern Urfa in southeastern Turkey). The Byzantine emperor closed the school in 489 because of heretical tendencies there, and many of the scholars relocated to Nisibis in what is now northern Iraq. There they founded a school of theology and philosophy. Another school, likewise comprised largely of Syrian scholars, was in Jundi-Shapur (near Dezful in the western part of modern Iran). Many of these translators and scholars were Nestorian or Monophysite Christians whose views on the nature of the Incarnation of Christ were to be rejected by the official Church at the Council of Chalcedon in 451. The continued existence of these and other heretical formulations concerning the relation of spirit and body in the lands east of the Mediterranean is a crucial element in the history of theology in Islam. Also of significance for the interpretation of Greek philosophy is the fact that many of these writers did not distinguish clearly between the ancient Greek philosophers and the early monks and Fathers of the Church. This conflation of Greek philosophy and Abrahamic Revelation made quite natural what we shall see is one of the fundamental ideas of Islamic gnosis: that the Angel of Intellect and the Angel of Revelation are the same.

In the northeastern part of the Sassanian Empire (what is now eastern Iran and parts of central Asia), the cultural milieu was a rich combination of traditions retaining the diversity brought about by Alexander's establishment of trade and contact between the East and West. In Balkh, for instance, everything that this "'mother of cities' had absorbed over the centuries from the various cultures—Greek, Buddhist, Zoroastrian, Manichean, Nestorian, Christian—lived on in it."[23] Here, as in other cities lining the trade routes of the Alexandrian Empire, the traditional sciences of mathematics and astronomy, astrology and alchemy, medicine and mineralogy were alive and flourishing as they could not do under the increasingly anti-magical influence of the Roman Church. And so a great deal of the intellectual and cultural diversity which was driven out by the Christian culture of the West moved into, or remained alive and available for transformation, in the lands that were soon to become Islamic.

The Age of Islam

A brief sketch of the religion of Islam is bound to be unbalanced and runs the risk of being misleading, but may nonetheless be useful for those who have little or no prior knowledge. Any serious student of Corbin will need to have some familiarity with this rich and complex tradition.[24] At the same time it must be clearly kept in mind that Corbin does not represent Islam, and his attitude and approach to things Islamic is colored by his affinity for Shi'ism and by his personal philosophical project.[25] With these caveats in mind,

23. Corbin, *A History of Islamic Philosophy*, 20.

24. One of the best general introductions is *The Vision of Islam* by Murata and Chittick. The best short historical survey is Karen Armstrong's *Islam*. Among the many excellent works that are helpful in providing an overview of Islam and Islamic culture are the following: Sheila Blair and Jonathan Bloom, *The Art and Architecture of Islam: 1250-1800*; Norman O. Brown, "The Prophetic Tradition" and "The Apocalypse of Islam;" Henry Corbin, *A History of Islamic Philosophy*; Mircea Eliade, *A History of Religious Ideas, Vol. 3*; Richard Ettinghausen and Oleg Grabar, *The Art and Architecture of Islam: 650-1250*; Marshall S. Hodgson, *The Venture of Islam*; S. Murata, *The Tao of Islam*; S. H. Nasr, "Henry Corbin" (Ch. 17 in *Traditional Islam in the Modern World*), *Knowledge and the Sacred*, and "Shi'ism and Sufism;" M. Sells, *Early Islamic Mysticism* and *Approaching the Qu'ran*; and Annemarie Schimmel, *Mystical Dimensions of Islam*. On Shi'ism in particular, see S. H. Nasr, et al., *Shi'ism: Doctrines, Thought and Spirituality* and *Expectation of the Millennium: Shi'ism in History*.

25. See Charles J. Adams, "The Hermeneutics of Henry Corbin" and W. Chittick, *The Sufi Path of Knowledge.*

we turn to an outline of those aspects of Islamic religion and history which are perhaps most essential for an initial approach to Corbin's work.

Arabia in the seventh century was a cultural backwater that had remained isolated throughout the history of the Fertile Crescent civilizations because of its remoteness and harsh climate. Many of the semitic Arabs lived a largely nomadic existence, but trade routes from Yemen to the Mediterranean and Persia had allowed the establishment of a handful of small cities and the development of a prosperous merchant class. The influence of Judeo-Christian beliefs on the prevailing religion seems to have been minimal. The religious center was Mecca, where the temple of the *Ka'aba* (literally, "the Cube") was located. The ritual circumambulation of the *Ka'aba* and the Black Stone of celestial origin that it contains was a part of the annual pilgrimage to Arafat. The Lord of the *Ka'aba* was Allah, which means simply "God," but this figure had been eclipsed in importance by the three feminine deities who were his daughters.

The Prophet Muhammad was born to a family of merchants in Mecca in about 570 C.E. At the age of forty, after a series of ecstatic experiences during spiritual retreats into the hills and caves surrounding the city, he received in his sleep the first of the often overpowering revelations which were to come to him periodically until the end of his life. The angel Gabriel appeared to him and commanded him four times to "Read!" (or "Recite!"). Recovering from his shock, Muhammad finally asked, "What shall I read?" Gabriel said: "Read in the name of your Lord who created, created man from an embryo; Read! for your Lord is most beneficent, who taught by the Pen, taught man what he did not know"(96:1-5). Thus began the Revelation of one of the most influential sacred books in history. It was produced by or through a single man in the course of one lifetime. Mohammad was illiterate as were most of his countrymen, and the individual revelations which make up the *Quran* were not gathered into a canonical form until after his death. It was memorized by the faithful in its entirety, as it is still by many today, as is not at all unusual in an oral culture.

Muhammad was at first both frightened by the intensity of the experience and doubtful of its validity. He confided in his wife, Khadija, who supported him during the crisis brought on by these powerful experiences. The continued eruption of the revelations in the end convinced him of their truth, and in 612 he began his public prophetic mission. According to tradition, in the year 617 or 619, partly in answer to the doubts of unbelievers, the Prophet was taken up into Heaven in a Celestial Ascent called the *Mi'raj*. This event, mentioned briefly and allusively in the *Quran* (17:1), was to become the archetypal mystical experience in Islam.

The Prophet's life from then on was one of political, spiritual, and social action of a high order. Unlike the figure of Christ, Muhammad was immersed in the life of the world. He is regarded by Muslims (those who have submitted to God's will) as the exemplary human: supreme mystic, loving husband and father, fierce warrior, just statesman, revered teacher. But he was human. He was the Messenger, not the Message. The Message, the Revelation, the Divine Word, is the Book. The status accorded to Muhammad as the most holy man has puzzled Christians who are accustomed to the quiet otherworldliness of most traditional accounts of Christ. But from the beginning, Islam has been a religion rooted in this world. For Islam everything belongs to Allah; there can be no giving to Caesar what is Caesar's and to God what is God's.

There is a very real sense in which Islam is a most ecumenical religion and has from the beginning contained within its teachings a broadminded attitude to religious diversity, though of course in practice this has often conflicted with reality. Islam sees itself as the culminating Revelation and Muhammad as the Seal of the Prophets. There will be no others. This Prophet is the last in a long series of God's messengers, beginning with Adam. Traditional sources suggest that the total number is one hundred and twenty-four thousand, which makes for considerable diversity. The prophets most often mentioned in the *Quran* are Adam, Noah, David, Moses, and Jesus. All are worthy of the utmost respect. All were sent by God with a message particular to the people to whom it was directed: "For every people there is an apostle." (10:47) Islam is the final, perfected, and inclusive, but not the exclusive Truth.

From the beginning the Prophet began to attract followers. They were convinced by the sudden transformation of an otherwise unremarkable, though honest and good man, "by the incredible eloquence of his language" in a culture where the importance of the mastery of language cannot be overestimated, and "by the recognition that his message was something they had always known but somehow had stopped taking seriously."[26] That message, although subject to one thousand four hundred years of interpretations, is in essence simple and direct enough to be grasped by the simplest tribesman: There is one God, Allah, who must be obeyed. The reward for obedience is bliss in Heaven. The punishment for disobedience is damnation in Hell. And you cannot escape Judgement. There will come the Day of Judgement at the end of Time when Justice will be done.

But what is it that God demands? At the heart of the Islamic vision is the idea of wholeness, or the Unity and Oneness of God, *tawhid*. This is no abstract monism. Oneness for humans, the perfection of the soul that is the goal of the religious life, demands harmony, balance, and equilibrium. These are the primary characteristics of a life lived in accordance with the will of Allah. The three guiding concepts of the religion are *Islam*, *Iman*, and *Ihsan*. *Islam* is submission to God's will. This is the realm of action. *Iman* is faith in God, His Angels, His Books, His Prophets, and the Last Day. This is the realm of understanding. *Ihsan* is doing what is beautiful. This is the realm of intention, of bringing the soul into harmony with action and understanding.

To begin with then one must act in accordance with the rules articulated in the *Quran*. Muslims are united in adhering to the required practices of the "Five Pillars." These are the minimal requirements for complete acceptance of the religion. The first is the recitation of the *Shahadah*, which in its simplest form states only that "There is no God but God, and Muhammad is His Messenger." The second is the *salat*, the ritual prayer towards Mecca, performed five times a day. The third is the *zakat*, the donation of a portion of one's

---

26. Murata and Chittick, *The Vision of Islam*, xxii.

wealth to the needy. This is only required of those who can afford it. The fourth pillar is fasting, that is, refraining from food, drink, smoking, and all sexual activity, between dawn and dusk during the month of *Ramadan*. The fifth is the *Hajj*, the pilgrimage to Mecca at least once in a lifetime for those who have the means to do so. Some Muslims add a sixth pillar, the *Jihad*, or "Holy War." This is a poor translation of a practice that has been co-opted by extremists of all sorts. In essence it refers to the necessity of the struggle for freedom and justice in an unjust world.

But beyond these pillars of the faith, Islam has been characterized from the beginning by rules for right conduct that extend into every sphere of human activity. There is no aspect of life that is not included under God's purview. The compilation of laws is the *Shari'a*. An important branch of Islamic learning involves jurisprudence, the study of the required, recommended, indifferent, discouraged, and forbidden practices as laid out in the *Quran* and the records of the actions and sayings of the Prophet (the *Hadith*). The masters of jurisprudence are those to whom Corbin refers with unmistakable disdain as the doctors of the law. And yet he recognizes, in accordance with the foundational theology of Islam, that without an outer form, there can be no inner meaning.

But in all matters of the law, in all matters of life, it is always the Book that is central to the faithful. As Christ is to Christianity, so the *Quran* is to Islam. The word itself is usually taken to mean "to recite" or "to gather together." The Book is the direct unmediated Word of God. And it is for any Western reader an unusual book indeed. It is made up of one hundred and fourteen chapters or *suras*, which are arranged neither thematically nor chronologically in the order of their revelation, but by length. It is, in this at least says Brown, more *avant garde* than *Finnegan's Wake*.[27] Nasr writes,

> Many people, especially non-Muslims, who read the *Quran* for the first time are struck by what appears as a kind of

---

27. Brown, "The Apocalypse of Islam," 90.

incoherence from the human point of view. It is neither like a highly mystical text nor a manual of Aristotelian logic, though it contains both mysticism and logic. It is not just poetry, although it contains the most powerful poetry. The text of the *Quran* reveals human language crushed by the power of the Divine Word. It is as if human language were scattered into a thousand fragments like a wave scattered into drops against the rocks at sea. One feels through the shattering effect left upon the language of the *Quran*, the power of the Divine whence it originated. The *Quran* displays human language with all the weakness inherent in it becoming suddenly the recipient of the Divine Word and displaying its frailty before a power which is infinitely greater than man can imagine.[28]

To non-Muslims it is a difficult text to read. It seems allusive, disjointed, confusing, and illogical, with little or no narrative continuity. Early Western scholars dismissed it as unworthy of serious study. As Corbin comments, "It is commonly said in the West that the *Quran* contains nothing mystical or philosophical in nature... Our concern here...is to know what it is the Muslims themselves have actually discovered in it."[29] And as attested by centuries of commentary and by all of Islamic civilization itself, there is a great deal in it indeed. The Prophet said that the *Quran* has seven levels of meaning, and the last and highest is known only to God.

Much of its essential character lies in its language. The *Quran* is written in Arabic. That is the language in which God revealed it to Muhammad, and unlike the *Bible*, it is not the *Quran* when it is translated—the language is essential to its essence. Arabic, like Hebrew and Aramaic, is a Semitic language. These are consonantal languages: that is, in the early written form, vowels did not appear. In the later development of the scripts, they may be indicated by diacritical marks. Each word is based upon a three-letter root, which gives rise to a whole family of associated words, which are completely invisible

---

28. Nasr, quoted in Brown, "The Apocalyse of Islam," 90.
29. Corbin, *A History of Islamic Philosophy*, 1.

in translation. It is an allusive language that loses a great deal in translation, and the aura of associations around each word makes it subject to a variety of interpretations. Arabic is unlike English in another crucial respect: English is full of abstractions, and good philosophical prose is expected to be abstract, general, universal, and timeless. The language of the *Quran* and of Arabic in general is rooted in sensual particulars. This fundamental difference in outlook is of importance for understanding the meaning and the direction of Corbin's work. Chittick writes,

> An old joke among orientalists tells us that every Arabic word has four meanings: It means what it means, then it means the opposite of what it means, then it has something to do with sex, and finally it designates something to do with a camel. Part of the truth of the witticism is the way it indicates how Arabic is grounded in everyday human experience. The rational mind tends to push the meaning of a word away from experience to "what it means," but the imaginal mind finds the self-disclosure of the Real in the sex and the camel...it is in the world's concrete realities that God is found, not in its abstractions.[30]

It was the discovery and exploration of this imaginal mind and the cosmology that accompanies it that captivated Corbin.

The roots of social, political, and theological diversification within Islam are traceable directly to bloody and turbulent events that unfolded after the death of the Prophet in 632. His son-in-law Ali and his daughter Fatimah, along with a small group of their supporters, claimed that Muhammad had chosen Ali to be his successor. But the elders of the community appointed the Prophet's close friend Abu Bakr as the first Imam (leader). Ali acceded in this choice but did not give up his claim. Ali's partisans (the *shi'a*, partisans) were not satisfied until 656 when Ali won his place as Fourth Imam after the Battle of the Camel, fought against forces supported by the Prophet's wife Aisha. His reign as leader lasted

---

30. Chittick, *The Self-Disclosure of God*, xxxv-xxxvi.

only five years until he was murdered by a member of a rival group. There was still no agreement on how successors should be chosen. At length his son, Hussein, grandson of the Prophet, led an insurrection against the reigning Ummayad leader. In 680, on the plains of Karbala south of Baghdad, his small band of supporters was slaughtered by the Ummayad army. This defeat marks the break between the Sunnis (followers of traditional practice) and the minority Shi'ites (partisans of the house of Ali).

In the eighth century the Shi'ites themselves split, again over the question of rightful succession to the Imamate. Jafar al-Sadiq was the sixth Shi'ite Imam and the great-great-great grandson of the Prophet. He had named his son Ismail to be his successor, but Ismail died before Jafar himself died in 765. His second son, Abd-Allah, died soon after without leaving an heir. Most Shi'ites accepted another of Jafar's sons as Imam, but a minority believed that Ismail was the only true heir, whether on earth or in Heaven. They became the Ismailians or Sevener Shi'ites. But a crisis arose for the majority again in 873 when the Imam Hasan died without leaving a successor. Stories sprang up to explain the lack of an apparent heir. It became accepted that Hasan must have had a son, but that he had disappeared or been hidden to escape persecution. He would have been the twelfth Imam, and his followers became the *Ithna'asharis*, the Twelver Shi'ites. For the Ismailis it is the Seventh, for the Ithna'asharis it is the Twelfth Imam who is the eternal Hidden Imam who will reappear in the Final Days to bring victory to the faithful. Hodgson writes, "The imams, then, came to be invested with cosmic worth, and their lives reflected the sad vicissitudes of the divine cause among ungrateful mankind."[31] The political fortunes of the Shi'ites rose and fell over the centuries, but within Islam as a whole they were to remain a minority. The Ismailis were to establish the Fatimid dynasty (909-1171) in North Africa, whose capital at Cairo rivalled Baghdad as a center of commerce, art, and science in the eleventh century. Twelver Shi'ism became the official religion of Persia

---

31. Hodgson, *The Venture of Islam*, Vol. 1, 377.

in the sixteenth century. It is in Twelver and especially in Ismaili Shi'ism that Islamic esotericism developed to an extraordinary degree. It is this aspect of Islam that drew Henry Corbin most strongly.

The Sunni-Shi'ite schism raises a complex question concerning the relationship between Shi'ism and Sufism, usually regarded as the mystical branch of Sunni Islam or of Islam as a whole. Of the spirituals to whom Corbin refers, most, with the notable exception of Ibn 'Arabi, are Shi'ites. Both Sufism and Shi'ism express the esoteric side or, for Corbin and the esotericists, the inner core of Islam. Nasr, a Shi'ite, summarizes the relation succinctly:

> One can say that Islamic esotericism or gnosis crystallized into the form of Sufism in the Sunni world while it poured into the whole structure of Shi'ism especially during its early period. From the Sunni point of view Sufism presents similarities to Shi'ism and has even assimilated aspects thereof.... From the Shi'ite point of view Shi'ism is the origin of what later became known as Sufism. But here by Shi'ism is meant the esoteric instructions of the Prophet.... Shi'ism and Sunnism have their roots in the very origin of the Islamic revelation, placed there providentially to accommodate different psychological and ethnic types.[32]

Broadly speaking, "Sufism" is often the term used to refer to the esoteric approach to Islam as a whole, but one must be careful to notice what the context is and how a given author uses these terms. It should perhaps be pointed out that Sufism in this wider sense has in common with Christian monasticism a focus on the spiritual life, but it is really a very different phenomenon. Nasr writes,

> Since it is based upon the social and juridical teachings of Islam, Sufism is meant to be practiced within society and not in a monastic environment outside the social order. But the attitudes of monastic life are integrated with the daily life lived within the human community.... Sufism is the way

---

32. Nasr, "Shi'ism and Sufism," 105-06.

of integration of the active and contemplative lives so that man is able to remain receptive inwardly to the influences of heaven and lead an intense inner contemplative life while outwardly remaining most active in a world which he moulds according to his inner spiritual nature, instead of becoming its prisoner as happens to the profane man.[33]

The long history of disputes over rightful leadership of the society of the faithful points to a fact that is for Corbin one of the chief differences between the history of Christianity before the Reformation and the course of Islamic history. In Islam, there has never been a Church or a phenomenon akin to the Councils that established the dogmatic form of Christian doctrine. In Corbin's eyes, this absence of an official public and political hierarchy is in part responsible for the maintenance in Islam of an esoteric tradition that was quickly eclipsed by the official forms of Christian doctrine, since it threatened the power and authority of the clergy and the Church. In Islam there are no priests; each Muslim stands alone before God. Corbin writes, "What the 'gnostics' in Islam acknowledge is fidelity to the 'men of God,' to the Imams, (the Guides)."[34] Access to the heart of the religion requires a Guide, but such guides are not, for Corbin, primarily purveyors or protectors of public dogma. They are rather the guardians of the secrets of the most personal initiation into the secret core of Revelation.

Philosophy and Theology

Amid the tremendous political and social change that accompanied the spread of Islam, the continuity of the scholarly tradition can easily be overlooked. The work of translation undertaken by Islamic scholars of Greek texts or, much more frequently, from Syriac translations of these texts into Arabic, should be understood as a continuation of the work begun during the Sassanian period. Baghdad, for instance, was to become a major intellectual focus beginning in 832 with the

---

33. Nasr, "Shi'ism and Sufism," 37.
34. Corbin, *A History of Islamic Philosophy*, 21.

founding of a school there. Corbin comments, "All the technical vocabulary of philosophy and theology in the Arabic language was fashioned in this way during the course of the...ninth century."[35] But we must recall that we are embarked now on the study of that "other history of Being," which is written, thought, and lived in Persian and Arabic. Corbin cautions us to remember that "from this point onwards words and concepts possess a life of their own in Arabic. To resort to the Greek dictionary in order to translate the vocabulary used by later thinkers, who themselves were ignorant of Greek, can give rise to misunderstandings."[36]

In the tenth century, near Edessa, site of the original "School of the Persians," the Sabeans of Harran established another school. The syncretism of these thinkers is instructive:

> They traced their spiritual line of descent back to Hermes and to Agathodaimon [the tutelary angel of Hermeticism], as al-Suhrawardi did later. Their doctrines bring together the ancient astral religion of the Chaldeans, studies in mathematics and astronomy, and Neo-Pythagorean and Neo-Platonic spirituality.[37]

But as Corbin reminds us, syncretism is not a sin, and it may not result from an incoherent amalgamation of ideas, but rather spring from the perception of "pre-established harmonies" among various systems. The Sabeans, through their ability to perceive these harmonies, serve as an important link in the history of esotericism in the West as well as in Islamic culture.

Among the many translations done in the early years of the Islamic period, there are several of surpassing importance which are *pseudepigrapha*: works mis-attributed to one author or another. Of prime importance among these is the so-called *Theology* of Aristotle. This is in fact a paraphrase of the last three books of Plotinus' *Enneads*, that astonishing mystical work of the great

---

35. Corbin, *A History of Islamic Philosophy*, 16.
36. *Ibid.*
37. *Ibid.*, 17.

neo-Platonist. In a famous passage in this *Theology* of "Aristotle," in truth an account of the ecstatic experiences of Plotinus (*Enneads*, IV, 8,1), mystical philosophers in Islam saw a connection between Greek philosophy and the Celestial Ascent of the Prophet. Among the other works attributed to Aristotle is the *Book on the Pure Good*, which is in fact an extract from the work of Proclus, the fifth century Byzantine neo-Platonist. There was also in circulation a vast body of works attributed to Plato, Pythagoras, and many others that also served to confuse the Islamic view of Greek thought. Add to this the pre-existing conflation of the Greek sages with Christian monks and ascetics, due to the Syriac translators of the Sassanian dynasty, and the fusion of Abrahamic religion with Greek philosophy in its Platonic and neo-Platonic formulations begins to seem natural, if not inevitable.

In the eastern part of Islamic Persia, the Graeco-Oriental influences remained. Many scholars originated in Central Asia, Khiva, Merv, Balkh, and Bactria. We have already noted the heterogeneous nature of the cultures represented in these areas. The work of these scholars is the origin of many technical Persian terms in astronomy, astrology, and alchemy. This is evidence that the continuity between Greek alchemy and the later Islamic alchemical tradition was provided by the cultural centers of northern and eastern Persia and Central Asia.

This then is a rough outline of the complex matrix of influences that guided the subsequent development of theosophical speculation and religious experience in the Islamic tradition, especially in Persia, that median and mediating world in which Henry Corbin found a spiritual home very different from that provided by Christianity and the traditions of the Church.

CHAPTER THREE

The Modes of Knowing and the Levels of Being

Thought and Being

One of the most fateful characteristics of modern consciousness is our utter confusion concerning the nature of the relation between thought and being. As Heidegger said, we have forgotten even the meaning of the question "what do we mean by 'being?'" In our implicit metaphysics we are most immediately the heirs of Descartes: when we speak of being, we mean one of two kinds of "things," two kinds of "substance." On the one hand, there is the *res cogitans*, thinking substance, and on the other, *res extensa*, extended substance. And, like Descartes, we do not know how they are ever to be related except by reducing one to the other. Unlike Descartes, who could still call on God for a solution, we have as a culture largely opted for the materialist position. Thought, the elusive nature of which is recognized by allowing it the status of an emergent property, is nevertheless in practice understandable in terms of changes that take place in matter. For the evolutionary biologist, the higher order thinking skills are a perhaps surprising result of natural selection for traits that allow the development of optimal behaviors. For the neurophysiologist thinking occurs in the brain and can be understood and in the end perhaps controlled as a sophisticated form of electrochemistry. For the digital technologist, it is a complex kind of computation, differing only in complexity from what goes in a computer.

The situation resulting from this metaphysics is dangerous not least because of the effects it has on the distribution of power in the world at every level: psychological, spiritual, and political. The kind of knowledge that science pursues is entirely materialist, and we have been successful in the pursuit. We have the power to change things in the world of material causality, though we do not often understand the consequences. We have nearly lost the ability to conceive or speak of any other kind of power. All motion is change of location; all causes are material. To change the world, you do physics or engineering. To change people, you use biophysics and biotechnology: Prozac and gene therapy. Religion is sociology is psychology is biology is chemistry is physics: this produces in the end a cosmology that is the history of matter in quantitative space.[1]

The powers of materialist rationality, usually in the guise of Technology and The Economy, are opposed effectively rarely. The opposition seems to take two major forms, though the categories overlap. One is diffuse, small-scale, and democratic; the other focused, collective, and dogmatic. All the opposition is branded "irrational." On the one hand, there is a collection of groups, including among others, the renegade ecologists opposed to a monolithic view of the scientific enterprise, those promoting a spirituality based often upon a return to "pagan" ideals, and factions within the developing world who see all too clearly the dangers of industrial capitalism as another form of colonialism. These factions tend to agree upon the necessity of the local or regional distribution of power and wealth and to champion the democratic ideal of the importance of the individual. On the other hand, there are those whose opposition to Modern Western ideals takes the form of a dogmatic fundamentalism that is as rigid

---

1. The "New Sciences" of complex systems theory and the like claim to be post-Cartesian and post-Newtonian, and there is a real sense in which this is true; they are a remarkable advance over simple mechanical models of the world. But in the end, for all their advances upon Descartes and Newton, they remain at the same level of Presence, in the same mode of being, because the metaphysical cosmology in which they operate has not escaped materialism. It has only transformed it into energy or information or some other metaphor on the same level of being as before. In this sense Reimanian space or Lobachevskian space is, though not Euclidean, still Cartesian, that is, quantitative and continuous.

and focused as its opponent. Here we could include those Christian fundamentalists whose position is often complicated by the fact that they want to reject science but accept a free market economy.

The intensity of the conflict between the modern, eclectic, unstable West and a traditional, coherent, and stable Islamic culture has constellated the extremes on both sides. It is important to realize the magnitude of the encounter. Iran and the Islamic world have faced the task of coming to terms in a short time with a culture that is as radically alien to it as our world would be to someone living in the European Middle Ages. The traditional religious schools, in places like Qom in modern Iran, were until recently based upon study of the *Qur'an* and the tradition of commentaries upon it and on cosmological sciences such as astrology and alchemy. They were in fact "medieval," whether one means this as praise or criticism. Corbin was concerned about the destabilizing effect that modern agnostic and nihilistic culture would have upon such traditional societies and wanted to avoid the clash of dogmatisms which has in fact developed.

Scientific rationalism can degenerate into a fundamentalism just as dogmatic and fanatic as expressed within any religion but bolstered by rationality. It is sophisticated, organized, powerfully focused, and has tremendous economic, intellectual, and social prestige and power. Thus the conflicting powers are rooted in the dual dogmas of science and religion, and they share nothing like a common language or a common view of the world. The stage is set for fruitless conflict or standoff. And while the dogmatists battle, the economies of capitalism, itself given birth by a collusion between science and Protestantism, thunder over the globe unconstrained, wiping out diversities of every sort. What Corbin might have stressed is that what is lacking in any such conflict of dogmatisms is an understanding of the meaning of the transformative power of the spirit and any means of making this power effective in the world through the transformation of individual souls.

This situation is rooted in the way we grasp the relation between Thought and Being. This is the origin of that dualism of Spirit and

Matter that finds its most poignant contemporary expression in the conflict between science and religion. Here again Corbin claims the priority of metaphysics. It is our unacknowledged metaphysics that determines our ability to open ourselves to other modes of Presence. The Being that is involved here is ours, and the Thought in question is not pure Reason, since that assumes *res cogitans*, but rather thinking understood as expressive of the mode of being, the mode of Presence of the thinker, what in medieval philosophy was known as *intellectus*. Thought is not something that is somehow tacked onto some substance, whether that substance is Spirit or Matter. Thought is an expression of a mode of being, of a mode of Presence. Thought is not extrinsic to the thinker. If it were, then it would not matter to the thinker what the content of the thought is. We then would be computers. But we are not. Thought is essential; it reveals the essence of who we are. It is expressive of a moral and a spiritual mode of being. It is not something we do. It expresses what we are.

It is our particular history of Being, and thus the history of the language, that we use that which has bewitched us. For Corbin and Heidegger, because our language, our thought, and our mode of presence are all inextricably interwoven, the history of language is crucial for understanding who we are and how we have come to be the way we are. In the passage from Greek to Latin and beyond, the linguistic distinctions between the essence and the existence of a thing became correlated with "a fundamental dissociation between thought and being." But in the Islamic world, the story was different. Corbin says, "The Arabic words used to designate the action to be, to exist, and that of being, existing . . . cannot give rise to the same vicissitudes as in the modern Western vocabulary."[2] Iranian theosophers, thinking and writing in Persian and Arabic, could never fall prey to the same ontological mistakes as did the philosophers of the West.

What Corbin means by philosophy, by thinking properly understood, is a transformational activity, rooted in Language, which is conceived not as a human creation, or merely a means of communication, but as a funda-

---

2. Corbin, *The Voyage and the Messenger: Iran and Philosophy*, 207-08.

mental structural feature of the cosmos. *Philosophia* is a spiritual pursuit akin to depth psychology. This kind of thinking is Gnosis, "knowledge that changes and transforms the knowing subject."[3] Thinking need not leave the thinker unchanged, as does the "thinking" done by a computer. That kind of thinking is entirely restricted to the level of material causality. The kind of thinking that does leave the thinker unchanged is therefore abstract, in Corbin's sense, because it is ineffective in transforming the knower and the world. And, although it is perhaps useful for describing historical relations among things or ideas and for pushing things around in the world of objects, it is restricted to one mode of being and one mode of presence.

Yet more fundamentally the mode of presence required for this kind of thinking is in reality a mode of absence. That is to say, the objectivity of all the sciences is based on an impersonal, abstract, and distanced relation between the knower and the known. Only in this way can the object of knowledge be reduced, explained, or explained away, in terms of something else already known, already past. This means of understanding requires that anything that appears, that reveals itself to us in the present, must, in order to be understood, be regarded in terms of something else which is not present. Thus the thing we confront is erased, swallowed into a system already in place, and the possibility of Presence removed. Corbin is always thinking explicitly in terms of the humanities, of history, sociology, and study of religion. The same points are true to an even greater degree with respect to the natural sciences, since they have provided the template upon which the humanities are increasingly modeled.

As we will see later on, Corbin's deeper point concerns the nature of Time as an explanatory principle. To explain something new, something present, with respect to that which is already understood, already closed and distanced by the passage of time, and so past, is the essence of the reductionism inherent in the historical sciences. In this case "The notion of something spontaneous and original then appears as vaguely scandalous, since it is inexplicable."[4] And in that case the new

---

3. Corbin, "Eyes of Flesh and Eyes of Fire," 7.
4. Corbin, *The Voyage and the Messenger*, 54.

must be explained by precursors, influences, and causes. Again to think this way is to be this way, and to do so we and the world we inhabit must remain in Absence.

In order to come to grips with this way of thinking, we must overcome the modern rational skepticism that makes us think that metaphysics is something we have outgrown. Properly understood it is a necessary part of any transformative discipline, because as Heidegger has shown, far from being abstract and non-utilitarian, our metaphysical presuppositions provide the framework for our mode of being in the world. So it is through understanding our metaphysical presuppositions and the language in which they are embedded that we can see their limitations and so begin to free ourselves to move beyond them. This should sound like another, perhaps unfamiliar, way of saying the same kind of thing that Freud was trying to say within the essentially materialist framework that he adopted. The task for us is to free ourselves from a trap that we do not know we are in. The task is to become conscious, to reveal to ourselves our mode of being and our form of life. If our entrapment is caused by the nature of our most basic stance towards what Heidegger calls our being-in-the-world, then we must bring that very mode of being into light. Corbin writes,

> [T]he mode of presence assumed by the philosopher by reason of the system that he professes is what, in the last analysis, appears as the genuinely *situative* element in that system considered in itself. This mode of presence is usually concealed beneath the tissue of didactic demonstrations and impersonal developments. Yet it is this mode of presence that must be disclosed, for it determines...the personal genuineness of his *motivations*; it is these that finally account for the "motifs" that the philosopher adopted or rejected....[5]

The mode of presence is what situates us, what determines the quality of the space in which we live, and the nature of our relationship to the objects in our world, to what we can know. The mode of presence determines what can be understood: "like can only be known by like; every mode of understanding corresponds to the mode of

5. Corbin, *Avicenna*, 3-4.

being of the interpreter."[6] And to acknowledge only one such level, to sever "pure thought," conceived as a single abstract mode of presence, from the material world, as Descartes did, and to conceive that world as existing on a single plane of being is to be trapped in the "web of historical causality"—in the continuous, quantitative, impersonal space of historical time. It is, in fact, to be *a-gnostic*. It is the gnostic who knows there are other levels of Being corresponding to other modes of Presence. Only the gnostic can see these other levels of being: "Is it possible to see without *being* in the place where one sees?"[7] The a-gnostic will have nothing to do with a thinking that does not claim to be an analysis conducted within the framework of quantitative space and time, since such "intellecting" can only be powerless, useless, because there "is" the realm of Quantity. The defining characteristic of a-gnosticism is thus the divorce between Thought and Being and the consequent dominion of impersonal Knowledge.[8]

Civilization in the West has, since at least the twelfth century, been split by "the conflict between philosophy and theology, between faith and knowledge, between symbol and history," based on this deeper divorce.[9] In the Islamic world this was not the case. The gnostic tradition of the ontologically transformative power of intellect has lived on until today.[10] For the thinkers that are closest to Corbin's heart, there is no point to a philosophy that is not also a spirituality, which does not lead

6. Corbin, *Man of Light*, 145, n. 3. See also, Corbin's *En islam iranienne*, v. 1, 136ff.

7. Corbin, *Creative Imagination*, 93.

8. Corbin, *En islam iranienne*, v. 1, xviii-xix, for example. For Descartes the *res cogitans* did have the characteristics of intellect to some degree. But precisely because of the dualism he posited, it was only a matter of time before the *res cogitans* would disappear into the *res extensa* as they have done in modern neurophysiology.

9. Corbin, *Creative Imagination*, 13. The importance of the twelfth century for the subsequent history of the West cannot be overemphasized. Many scholars have recognized it as a turning point in the history of Western consciousness. For an analysis of the revolution in the concept of the individual, with particular reference to textual hermeneutics, see Cranz, Radding, and Illich, which also provide references to the literature. See below, Chapter 6.

10. For a presentation of the place of intellect in Islamic and Christian traditions, see Nasr's Gifford Lectures in *Knowledge and the Sacred*.

to a mystical vision. For Suhrawardi: "There is no true philosophy which does not reach completion in a metaphysic of ecstasy, nor mystical experience which does not demand a serious philosophical preparation."[11]

A Hermeneutics of Presence

The question becomes one of practice. How do we overcome these schisms, free ourselves from our self-imposed blindness, and move outward into a wider world? How do we reveal our mode of presence and open our souls to the Presences surrounding us? Corbin says that it was Heidegger who provided the key with which to open the locks closing him off from the other levels of being. "This key is, one might say, the principal tool equipping the mental laboratory of phenomenology."[12] The key is hermeneutics. "The immense merit of Heidegger will always be that he centered the very act of *philosophizing* on hermeneutics… It is the art or the technique of Understanding…"[13] This kind of "Understanding" already implies transformation. It is not concerned with language as it is conceived by linguists or analytic philosophers but with the Language of the Word of the theologians. This language is a cosmological phenomenon rather than a human creation. Language is a feature common to soul, to God, and to the world. Corbin stresses that the hermeneutic tradition that Heidegger continues stems from Wilhelm Dilthey and Friedrich Schliermacher and the theological practice of Biblical interpretation. Corbin comments that many contemporary Heideggerians are happy to forget this connection.[14]

In Heidegger's analytic the first task is the hermeneutics of itself—of the "act of presence." Corbin writes,

> Hermeneutics proceeds starting with the act of presence
> signified by the *Da* of *Dasein*; it has therefore as its task
> bringing to light how, in understanding itself, the human-
> presence situates itself, circumscribes the "*Da*," the *situs*

11. Quoted in Corbin, *Spiritual Body and Celestial Earth*, 110.
12. Corbin, *Henry Corbin*, ed. Jambet, 30.
13. *Ibid.*, 24.
14. See Corbin, *Henry Corbin*, especially "De Heidegger à Sohravardi."

of its presence and unveils the horizon which was up to then hidden from it.[15]

So far this seems to be a straightforward explication of Heidegger's analysis. In fact the notion of unveiling the hidden to reveal the Truth of Being plays a large part in his late work.[16] But Corbin is traveling in wider circles than most Heideggerians. His grasp of hermeneutics and of the phenomenology that it makes possible springs not from the undoubted originality of Heidegger or Husserl but from far older, traditional conceptions of Sufism and Shi'ism. Nasr, who taught with Corbin in Teheran for many years writes,

> Corbin...used to translate *phenomenology*...to the Persian speaking students as *kashf al-mahjub*, literally "rending asunder of the veil to reveal the hidden essence," and considered his method...to be spiritual hermeneutics (*al-ta'wil*) as understood in classical Sufi and Shi'ite thought."[17]

Without doubt Heidegger provided the foundation for a bridge between Western philosophy and Islamic theology, but Corbin crosses it without hesitation to move into a more spacious world. As we have seen already, he emphasizes that to use the key that Heidegger provided by no means requires us to adopt his mode of presence. "In Heidegger, arranged around this *situs* is all the ambiguity of human finitude characterized by 'Being-towards-death.'" But "this connection to the world, the pre-*existentiell* philosophical option...is itself a constitutive element of the *Da* of *Dasein*," which we need not take as our own. Once we have truly realized this and become conscious of our unconscious decision, and therefore of our freedom to decide otherwise, the real meditation on our situation can begin: "From then on there is only to grasp as closely as possible this notion of Presence. *To what is human presence present?*"[18]

---

15. Corbin, *Henry Corbin*, ed, Christian Jambet, 31.
16. See Avens, *The New Gnosis*.
17. Nasr, *Religion and the Order of Nature*, 26, n. 13.
18. Corbin, *Henry Corbin*, ed. Jambet, 31. My italics.

For the spiritual theosophers and philosophers of Islam, "the presence that they experience in the world...lived by them, is not a Presence of which the finality is death, a 'being-towards-death,' but a "being-*towards-the-other-side-of-death*...."[19] The transformation required for this kind of Presence to open up for us requires the discovery, or the recognition, of a space adequate for this Presence to reveal itself. The exploration of those spaces is the subject matter of Corbin's life work.

And so he will move beyond the confines of *Being and Time* by means of the very premises of that work itself. The "decisive moment" when he grasped the "historicality" of *Dasein*, its ability to stand apart from secular history, was so decisive because "it was also without doubt the moment when, taking the Heideggerian analytic as an example, I was led to see hermeneutic levels that his program had not foreseen."[20]

With this the world opens up, everything changes. The full existential importance of Heidegger's "question of the meaning of being" strikes home. Hermeneutics is the unveiling of modes of presence and of the worlds and the states of being to which they correspond. It is itself a transformative act, since the understanding accomplished through hermeneutics changes the mode of being of the knower and reveals the Hidden things. As we will see, the entire meaning of prophetic philosophy hinges upon the power of hermeneutics to lead the soul to new states of being. These modes of Presence correspond to the mystical Stations (*maqamat*) of Sufism and Shi'ism. Chittick writes,

> human beings...are infinitely diverse and ever-changing in their inward forms.... A human being comes into the world as a potential divine form, but he or she may leave it as practically anything at all—an angel, a saint, a prophet, a devil, an animal, a vegetable.[21]

---

19. *Ibid.*
20. *Ibid.*, 28.
21. Chittick, *Imaginal Worlds*, 33.

The Stations are modes of being, corresponding to specific virtues, which have their place in an ascending hierarchy leading to the Divine. There is no possible distinction between ontology and ethics: stations of the soul are both levels of being and moral virtues.[22] Within the Islamic tradition there are many descriptions of these Stations along the Way. As in climbing a mountain, "The beginning and the end are known as well as the major features on the way. But the actual number and the details of each step depend upon the climber as well as on the path and its beginning and end."[23]

The hermeneutic of presence frees the soul from the narrow confines of the world into which it had found itself. The mode of being of the soul must change in order that it can be free for the other levels of presence. And so their recognition and revelation mark a rupture with all that came before. Here we must turn to Suhrawardi, whose experience of the personal hermeneutics of the soul reveals the move beyond Heidegger. One night, during an intense period of meditation on the problem of knowledge, Aristotle appeared to Suhrawardi in a dream. He told him "Awaken to yourself." Corbin summarizes the mystic's account of this meeting:

> Then there begins a progressive initiation into self-knowledge as knowledge which is neither the product of abstraction nor a re-presentation of the object through the intermediary of a form, of a Species, but a Knowledge which

---

22. There is controversy concerning Heidegger's personal moral failings represented by his early connections with National Socialism. Entwined with this is the question of the moral status of his philosophical project as a whole and the fact that he never wrote any explicitly ethical treatise. That there is an implicit moralism in *Being and Time* is clear. His disdain for "*das Mann*" and the morality of the collective is clear. Such mixing of morality and ontology should not be surprising since his early phenomenology must take the whole being of *Dasein* into account—ethical considerations are there at the ontological roots. His later works suffer from an excessive abstraction, perhaps even an inhumanism, which explains the feeling that his work lacks any place for an ethics to take hold. For Corbin, as for the Sufis, it does matter for your philosophy what kind of a person you are, since it is the life that matters, not the theory. On the moral status of Heidegger's life and philosophical project, see Steiner's *Martin Heidegger*.

23. Nasr, "Shi'ism and Sufism," 77.

is identical to the Soul itself, to the personal, existential subjectivity, and which is therefore essentially life, light, epiphany, awareness of self. In contrast to *representative* knowledge, which is knowledge of the abstract or logical universal, what is in question is *presential*, unitive, intuitive knowledge...a presential illumination which the soul, as a being of light, causes to shine upon its object. By making herself present to herself, the soul also makes the object present to her. Her own epiphany to herself is the Presence of this presence.... The truth of all objective knowledge is thus nothing more nor less than the awareness which the knowing subject has of itself.[24]

It is the power of this Presence that breaks the frame in which the soul had been imprisoned.

---

24. Corbin, *A History of Islamic Philosophy*, 210. Corbin has interpolated the Arabic terms for many of these words into his text. I have not included them in this quote.

CHAPTER FOUR

Coming Home:
The Heart and Face of the Earth

Beyond the Cosmos

Everything in Corbin's thinking follows from the epiphany that reveals the soul to itself as a being of light whose presence illuminates the world. This radical change in a person's mode of being marks a critical point in the drama of the relationship between the knower and the known. From it flow all the major themes of Corbin's work and of the mystics and philosophers whose causes he took for his own. The hermeneutic of the "act of presence" of the philosopher or "spiritual," whose quest is Corbin's subject, is a process of becoming conscious.[1] Corbin says:

> Yet it is this mode of presence that must be disclosed, for it determines, if not always the material genuineness of the *motifs* incorporated in the philosopher's work, at least the personal genuineness of his *motivations*; it is these that finally account for the "motifs" that the philosopher adopted or rejected, understood or failed to understand, carried to their maximum of meaning, or, on the contrary, degraded to trivialities. But it is not very often that the philosopher attains such a consciousness of his effort that the rational

---

1. Corbin attended his first Eranos conference in 1949 where he would have met C. G. Jung. *Avicenna and the Visionary Recital* was published in 1954. The prevalence of terms from analytical psychology in that book reveals Corbin's knowledge of Jung's ideas and the fact that he saw certain commonalities in their work. However Corbin was always careful to dissociate himself from "psychologism."

constructions in which his thought was projected finally show him their connection with his inmost self, so that the secret motivations of which he himself was not yet conscious when he projected his system lie revealed. This revelation marks a rupture of plane in the course of his inner life and meditations. The doctrines that he has elaborated scientifically prove to be a setting for his most personal adventure. The lofty constructions of conscious thought become blurred in the rays not of a twilight but rather of a dawn, from which figures always foreboded, awaited, and loved rise into view.[2]

Thus begins his treatment of the visionary recitals of Avicenna[3] and of Suhrawardi. The recitals are "brief spiritual romances, narratives of inner initiations" which mark this rupture of plane with the theoretical and systematic treatises which form the largest part of the work of both thinkers and of others as well, including Ibn 'Arabi,[4] whose work also had a profound significance for Corbin. What makes a philosophical system and the universe it exposes come to life is that it is ultimately the place of "a dramaturgy," of a "personally lived adventure" of the soul. These dramas show us the universe of their authors

2. Corbin, *Avicenna*, 4. In this work Corbin lays out nearly all of the most central themes that we shall be treating. Pages 3-35 are particularly dense and complex and repay close study. He was fifty-one years old at the time of its first publication (1954), and it is no surprise that so much of his thought is present in this work.

3. Born near Bukhara (west of Samarkand in modern Uzbekistan) in 980 and died near Hamadhan, southwest of Teheran, in 1037. As a child he was "extraordinarily precocious," and he lived a life full of public and political activity as well as authoring two hundred and forty-two titles covering "the entire field of philosophy and the sciences studied at the time." Corbin, *A History of Islamic Philosophy*, 169. See also, Nasr, *Introduction to Islamic Cosmological Doctrines*.

4. Born in Murcia, Spain, in 1165, died in Damascus, in 1240. By all accounts one of the most influential mystical philosophers in Islam and among the greatest visionaries of all time. See Corbin's *Creative Imagination*; for an introduction, see Chittick, *Imaginal Worlds*, and for extended treatments of this subject, see Chittick, *The Sufi Path of Knowledge* and *The Self-Disclosure of God*. The literature on Ibn 'Arabi in English has grown at a rapid pace since Corbin wrote his study and includes annual publications of the Ibn 'Arabi Society. Bibliographies can be found in Chittick's books.

not as an abstract magnitude, transcended by our "modern" conceptions, but as the repository of the Image...[that each] carries in himself, as each of us also carries his own. The Image in question is not one that results from some previous external perception; it is an Image that precedes all perception, an a priori expressing the deepest being of the person, what depth psychology calls an Imago. Each of us carries within himself an Image of his own world, his *Imago mundi*, and projects it into a more or less coherent universe, which becomes the stage on which his destiny is played out. He may not be conscious of it, and to that extent he will experience as imposed upon himself and on others this world that in fact he himself or others impose on themselves. This is also the situation that remains in force as long as philosophical systems profess to be "objectively" established. It ceases in proportion to such an acquisition of consciousness as permits the soul triumphantly to pass beyond the circles that held it prisoner. And that is the entire adventure related, as personal experience, in [these recitals].[5]

By making conscious this Image of the soul, one steps "beyond the system of the cosmos" that rational thought has erected, and this cosmos is revealed as coming from the soul, as the soul's own, and now consciously integrated with it. The recitals are the record of an "exodus from this world.""[T]he Event carries us to the utmost limit of the world; at this limit, the cosmos yields before the soul, it can no longer escape being interiorized into the soul, being *integrated* with it."[6] This momentous Event, this spiritual birth, frees the soul from its entrapment in and subordination to an alien and external world. It marks an escape from the world of impersonal knowledge, from that Absence in which only objects can appear. There can be no more objects for with this exodus there arises the Soul of the World, the *anima mundi*, and all creation comes alive through the encounter with the *imago mundi*:

5. Corbin, *Avicenna*, 7-8.
6. *Ibid.*, 32.

G. T. Fechner tells how on a spring morning, while a transfiguring light cast a halo over the face of the earth, he was
struck not merely by the esthetic idea, but by the vision and
the concrete evidence that "the earth is an Angel, such a
gorgeously real Angel, so like a flower!"[7]

To be precise, "the telluric glory…is the liturgical creation, the
hierurgy of that Earth Angel whose features are perceived as a glori-
fied human image."[8] "What the soul suddenly visualizes is its *own*
archetypal Image, that Image whose imprint it simultaneously bears
within it, projects, and recognizes outside of itself."[9] This is the lived
experience of the "personification" of the world: "…the perception of
all reality becomes the perception or visualization of a concrete person."[10] All events, all abstractions by which we refer to events and
actions are referred back

> to the person of the *agent* who enacts the action or the event
> as the true reality of both. For all mental or ideal reality, every
> concept (*ma'na*) in the world of the universal has its counter-
> part in the world of the individual: a concrete person…outside
> of which this ideal or mental reality remains virtuality and pure
> abstraction. Everything takes place as though the question
> "Who is it?" were substituted for the question "What is it?"—
> as though to name the *person* were to define its *essence;* and it
> is to this person and not to the abstract, universal concept that
> the…[hermeneutic] leads back. We gain this impression by
> juxtaposing propositions such as these: "Paradise is a *person*
> (or a human being)." "Every thought, every word, every action
> *is* a person." And finally: "Every true thought, every true word,
> every good action *has* an Angel."[11]

---

7. Corbin, *Spiritual Body and Celestial Earth*, 3.

8. *Ibid.*, 4.

9. Corbin, *Avicenna*, 32.

10. Corbin, *Cyclical Time and Ismaili Gnosis*, 50.

11. *Ibid.*, 50-51. Here Corbin is quoting from Khwajir Nasir al-Din Tusi, born
in Tus in Khurasan in 1201, died in Baghdad in 1274. He was a Shi'ite philosopher,
mystic, astronomer, mathematician, and political advisor to Hulaghu Khan after the
Mongol invasion and a major figure in Shi'ite thinking.

COMING HOME

The soul can only be at home in a world ensouled, animated with presences, which are here conceived as Angels. Only by turning inward can the objectivity of the world of the *Anima Mundi* be found.

> [F]or all our esotericists, the interior world designates the spiritual reality of the supersensible universe which, while a spiritual reality, is that which encircles and envelopes the reality of the external world.... "To leave" that which we commonly call the exterior world is an experience not at all "subjective" but as "objective" as possible, but it is difficult to transmit this to a spirit wanting to be modern.[12]

Every birth requires the death of that which came before, and so it is here. The Prophet said, "You must die before you die!" Corbin writes: "For to leave this world it does not suffice to die. One can die and remain in it for ever. One must be living to leave it. Or rather, to be living is just this."[13] This death to the world of Absence is a birth to the Presence of the World and takes place by a kind of inversion; it is a process of turning inside out. In this blossoming, this triumph of the esoteric, the soul finds that it was a stranger in the world in which it had lived, and that now it has come home:

> [I]t is a matter of entering, passing into the interior and, in passing *into the interior* of finding oneself, paradoxically, outside.... The relationship involved is essentially that of the external, the visible, the exoteric..., and the internal, the invisible, the esoteric..., or the natural and the spiritual world. To depart from the *where...* is to leave the external or natural appearances that enclose the hidden realities.... This step is made in order for the Stranger, the gnostic, to return *home*—or at least to lead to that return.
>
> But an odd thing happens: once this transition is accomplished, it turns out that henceforth this reality, previously internal and hidden, is revealed to be enveloping, surrounding, containing what was first of all external and visible, since

---

12. Corbin, *En islam iranienne*, v.1, 82.
13. Corbin, *Cyclical Time and Ismaili Gnosis*, 58.

> by means of *interiorization* one has *departed* from that
> *external* reality. Henceforth it is spiritual reality
> that…contains the reality called material.[14]

In this treatment of the gnostic theme of the Stranger, there is no sense of
the pessimistic and world-denying kind of Gnosticism that seeks only to
escape to the Beyond. The escape occurs in this world, by the spiritual-
ization of this world, not by its rejection.

We encounter a strikingly similar phenomenology in David Abram's
description of the reanimation of the sensuous world. His work, like
Corbin's, is influenced by Heidegger as well as by direct contact with
traditional cultures, in particular those of Indonesia and Nepal. We find
in this comparison evidence for the universality of the experience of the
anima mundi. Abram too describes a process of "turning inside out." He
writes, in words that apply equally well to the phenomena that Corbin
presents to us:

> As we become conscious of the unseen depths that surround us,
> the inwardness or interiority that we have come to associate with
> the personal psyche begins to be encountered in the world at large:
> we feel ourselves enveloped, immersed, caught up *within* the sen-
> suous world. This breathing landscape is no longer just a passive
> backdrop against which human history unfolds, but a potentized
> field of intelligence in which our actions participate. As the
> regime of self reference begins to break down, as we awaken to
> the air, and to the multiplicitous Others that are implicated, with
> us, in its generative depths, the shapes around us seem to awaken,
> to come alive….[15]

---

14. Corbin, *Swedenborg and Esoteric Islam*, 6.

15. Abram, *The Spell of the Sensuous*, 260. The last chapter in his book is
called "Turning Inside Out." Abram is no Sufi, and his approach differs in many
important respects from Corbin's, particularly with respect to the status of spiritual
reality. Nonetheless they share a sense that imagination must be placed near the
center of reality, and their works are mutually illuminating. For another approach to
this Event, see Hillman's treatment of the phenomenology of interiorization in *Anima:
An Anatomy of a Personified Notion*.

Coming to consciousness in this way and thus realizing that the realities of the soul, or of the psyche, are objective, all-encompassing and ubiquitous, means that we are never alone. In fact it is only to the degree that we become conscious in this way that we can experience the light of that Presence which is the ultimate source of all personification, of all the presence required for the appearance of persons. Without some degree of this interiorization, without some sense for this *anima mundi*, we cannot experience persons at all. What we are then left with is a world of absence: of objects existing only in public space and historical time. Paradoxically the world of the objective public depends upon the gaze of no one. And so for Corbin a world without Presence becomes a world in which there can no longer be persons.

At this point Corbin makes an absolutely crucial move, and one that is peculiarly modern. The realization that all systems of the world, all cosmologies, are realities of soul, allows for the possibility of integrating not just this cosmos, but a plurality of such worlds, interiorizing them within oneself. One can in fact, Corbin says,

> "valorize"...[a plurality of spiritual universes] positively, and, without taking up one's abode in them, keep an abode for them in oneself.... In addition, it is necessary to understand the mode of perception proper to each of them, the *modus intelligendi* that is each time the direct expression of a mode of being, of a *modus essendi*. This task demands a whole spiritual "formation," and its results are in turn integrated into the sum of this formation. This is why the formation that it bestows on itself is the secret of a soul, just as it is the secret of its metamorphoses. *The more perceptions and representations of the universe each monad integrates, the more it unfolds its own perfection and differs from every other.*[16]

It is the spiritual formation of the individual soul that is the source and origin of all the systems of the world, and it is from this that they

---

16. Corbin, *Avicenna*, 9. My italics.

receive or fail to receive their meaning. The decision of the future is not "imposed by things." "The decision of the future falls to the soul, depends upon how the soul understands *itself*, upon its refusal or acceptance of a new birth."[17] The daring of Avicenna and living within the all-encompassing world view of Islam, was a daring to become conscious, to step to the edge of the cosmos in order to free themselves from exile in that cosmos conceived as exterior to the soul, the cosmos of "rational constructions." We moderns, on the other hand, historically conscious, confronted by a diversity of cultures and conflict, are in a different situation, not unlike that of the people of the Hellenistic world. We are faced with a plurality of conflicting worldviews, both of the past and of the present. The same often conflicting tendencies are at work: desperate and unthinking syncretism, pessimism, millenialism, and the hope for a final monolithic and unified world view, whether it be in a religious form or by means of the domination of science. Corbin provides an option which avoids the dangers of both fragmentation and of single vision.

By stepping outside of the time of history, we can become responsible for our lives. There is a remedy for our immersion in the terrors of history. We are not irremediably lost in a world of Absence. By freeing ourselves from our determined and determinative histories, we can make a future for other universes by giving them a place in us. And the only way to make even our own past come alive into the present is by freeing it from the current of objective history. In a world governed by history, where every present is determined by the past and where there is such a diversity of "presents" with no "objective" way to reconcile them, then it is small wonder that no one can be at home. The only escape from this trap is to free the past from the absence into which it has disappeared. "One cannot free *oneself* from the past without *freeing that past* itself; but to free it is to give it a future again, to make it significant."[18]

---

17. Corbin, *Avicenna*, 10.
18. *Ibid.*

Whether we are speaking of our own past worlds or those of other cultures, we must avoid the traps of either denying them entirely or clinging to them blindly. Dogmatism will not do: "But one transcends only by adopting; what one rejects outright or what one refuses to see remains as it is, not integrated into consciousness, a source of the most formidable psychoses."[19] It is by interiorizing other spiritual universes that one can see a solution to the conflicts presented by a diversity of worldviews. By standing simultaneously at the edge of two mutually exclusive worlds, one can perhaps transcend them both. Corbin comments on the situation of the comparative philosopher:

> The orientalist who lives in Iran, devoted especially to the philosophy of Ishraq, for example, feels that he is inwardly linked to his Ishraqi confrere, an Iranian contemporary, by the bonds of the same spiritual sympathy. Yet it is clear that their common sympathy has not quite the same meaning and direction. To seek the formula for the difference is of primary importance, for, in the last analysis, to do so is to make that effort toward acquisition of consciousness to which...the example of Avicenna invites us. I believe that, in broad outline, one may say: the Oriental philosopher professing the traditional philosophy *lives in* the Avicennan cosmos, or the Suhrawardian cosmos, for example. For the orientalist, it is rather that this cosmos *lives in him.* This inversion of the meaning of interiority at the same time expresses what, from the point of view of the conscious personality, is called *integration.* But to integrate a world, to make it one's own, also implies that one has emerged from it in order to make it enter into oneself.[20]

It is quite clear that Corbin is not suggesting what would amount to a process of unification. That would perhaps be subject to the same dynamics as the Hegelian Absolute Spirit, and that is far from Corbin's intent. There is a distinction between unification

---

19. Corbin, *Avicenna*, 11.
20. *Ibid.*, 15.

and integration, which depends upon a vision of the necessary plurality of perspectives. The integration of a world by the soul does not amount to its being engulfed by a dominant "*ego*," but rather to a releasing of that world into the power of its Presence to a soul for a time. This concept will return again in Corbin's work as the way in which he understands the plurality of theophanies of the One God. He will call it *kathenotheism*, from the Vedic view that each god in its turn is considered supreme and fully present, but that no single vision can be considered total—we cannot relate to the Totality in that way.[21]

This integration applies just as much to the rational system of the modern world, and here the relevance of the claim for the priority of the soul is particularly clear. The soul is in exile in the modern world—there is no place for it in the world of historical, material causality. The conflict between the past and the present occurs now in each of us. This past is not passed, it is present. All rational systems, whether of the philosophers or the scientists, are left behind when the soul is born to itself, when it comes to consciousness. Only then can the world be interiorized and reconquered by the soul as truly its own.

> It is only upon the condition of being thus reconquered as a world living *in the soul*, and no longer a world *into which* the soul is cast as a prisoner because it has not acquired consciousness of it, that this spiritual cosmos will cease to be liable to shatter into fragments at the contact of material or ideological advances fed from other sources. Otherwise, simultaneous "objective" experience of the Avicennan system of celestial orbs and of the Faustian space of our universe of limitless extension is certainly an experience difficult to conceive. The universe *in which* the soul had lived shatters into fragments, leaving the soul helpless and "disoriented," doomed to the most formidable psychoses. For it is then that the soul, delivered over defenseless and uncon-

---

21. See Chapter 5.

scious to the world of things, flings itself into all the compensations offered to it and alienates its being in them.... [We in the Occident are just at the moment when we are attempting], by various approaches (phenomenology, depth psychology, and so on)...to reconquer the soul that—as in the Avicennan *Recital of the Bird*—has fallen captive in the net of determinisms and positivisms.[22]

With these words Corbin makes plain his strategy and his recommendation for all those "literalists" or "fundamentalists," religious and scientific dogmatists alike, of any sort, in any land, who would struggle against the strictures and contradictions raised by the collisions among religions and between religion and science.

The rational systems are not to be denied their necessity. But they are inherently incomplete, since they are founded on a limited way of knowing. Though necessary, they can only lead so far. No exercise of rationality can achieve the goals which humans were made to strive towards. As we have seen, for Suhrawardi gnosis requires rationality, or better, intellect, as a prerequisite for mystical experience:

[W]ithout a solid philosophical foundation, the mystical experience is in danger of going astray and degenerating; yet it is equally true that a philosophical search which does not arrive at mystical experience, a personal spiritual realization, is a vanity and a waste of time.[23]

Yet neither does religious dogma provide a complete answer. Beyond all dogma lies the mystical experience. The Celestial Ascent of the Prophet Mohammad is the prototype of all mystical experience in Islam. There is "something in common between the vocation of the philosopher and the vocation of the Prophet."[24] This voyage beyond all systems, beyond all dogmas, and the vision in which it culminates, is the goal of the theosopher and visionary. The Event that we have described marks the beginning of that voyage.

---

22. Corbin, *Avicenna*, 15-16.
23. Corbin, *The Voyage and the Messenger*, 136.
24. *Ibid.*

Mundus Imaginalis

Two questions arise: where does the Event of "becoming conscious" occur? And who is the Angel that the soul meets? In
order to begin to answer the first and to investigate the nature of
this "place," we need to return to that primordial, mythic sense of
space that we encountered earlier as central to the notion of Presence. As we are not objects in historical time, so we are not
primordially in quantitative space. The human presence spatializes
a world around it in accordance with the mode of being of that
presence. As is the case for primordial time, the space of this primary presence is a qualitative, discontinuous space.

If we are limited to the quantitative space of the *res extensa*,
we will be unable to apprehend the objective reality of any other
kind of extension, any other kind of space. The limited space in
which the matter of the scientists exists, in which objects appear,
is the most limited and constricted of all the kinds of spaces there
are. It is restricted to the quality of the quantitative and to that
alone. It is the vast realm of spiritual or qualitative spaces that
provides the places of the events of the soul. These provide a kind
of limitless fourth dimension into which unfold the mysteries of
the soul. The realm of spiritual space is both more real and more
primordial than the abstract qualitative space of Descartes and
Newton. In the *Timaeus* Plato speaks of that out of which all things
are generated: the nurse, the receptacle "that we may liken to a
mother" or a womb "that partakes of the intelligible [but] is yet
most incomprehensible." Timaeus says: "of this receptacle and
nurse of all creation we have only this dream-like sense, being
unable to cast off sleep and determine the truth about it." It exists
only as "an ever-fleeting shadow." Ivan Illich comments: "In these
delightful lines Plato still speaks of the image-pregnant stuff of
dreams and imagination...as one who still has the experience of living
in precategorical, "founded" space."[25] That is, in the pre-Cartesian,

---

25. Illich, *H₂O and the Waters of Forgetfulness*, 17.

pre-Newtonian space of qualities. This Platonic and Neo-Platonic notion of spatiality, which Henry More and the Cambridge Platonists called *spissitudo spiritualis*, or spiritual condensation, describes the world of visionary events. It is the world of Immanuel Swedenborg's Heaven. These spaces indeed have extension, but are not evaluated according to that calculus. They are measured by the states of the soul.

> [S]paces which are measured by inner states presuppose, essentially, a qualitative or discontinuous space of which each inner event is itself the measure, as opposed to a space which is quantitative, continuous, homogeneous, and measurable in constant measures. Such a space is existential space, whose relationship to physico-mathematical space is analogous to the relationship of existential time to the historical time of chronology.[26]

This conception of space is based upon Presence, rather than upon any sort of quantitative framework, and in it alone is it possible to speak of personification. "For what would a world without face or features—without, that is to say, a look—actually be? (One thinks of the Islamic precept: never strike at the face!)"[27] It would be a world entirely lifeless, wholly mechanical, a world with no soul, no presence, whatever.[28]

This space, which is the location of visionary events, is called the *'alam al-mithal* in Arabic, which Corbin has translated into Latin as the *mundus imaginalis*, or the imaginal world. In his view much of the enormous philosophical merit of Suhrawardi lies in the fact that he was the first to attempt to provide an ontological foundation for reality.[29]

---

26. Corbin, *Temple and Contemplation*, 187.

27. *Ibid.*, 189.

28. The difficulty of attaining this degree of lifelessness is indicated by how naturally we personify machines. See Hillman's *Revisioning Psychology*, Part One.

29. A good deal has been written about the imaginal world, especially by archetypal psychologists. Without intending in any way to minimize the central importance of this notion for Corbin or his "spirituals," it is one *(continued next page)*

To provide such a foundation, there must be available a cosmology which disappeared from mainstream Western experience with the triumph of the Aristotelianism of Averroes[30] and the demise of the Neoplatonic cosmology of Avicenna, which Corbin dates to the twelfth century. This latter provides a tripartite cosmology with a corresponding epistemology, or as Corbin often calls it, gnosiology. There are in truth three worlds and three sources of knowledge. In the West, we admit only two of these: on the one hand, sense perception gives

(continued from the previous page) of the purposes of this essay to place it in its proper context. In this regard, it is worth noting the comments of William Chittick, student and translator of Islamic texts, most notably Rumi and Ibn 'Arabi. He studied in Teheran while Corbin and Seyyed Hossein Nasr were teaching there. He writes,

> Corbin performed the great service of introducing the Western world to many uniquely Islamic ways of expressing philosophical positions, but it is beyond the capacity of a single individual to bring out everything worthy of consideration. Moreover, in his zeal to revive the honor due to the imaginal realm, Corbin tended to de-emphasize the cornerstone of Islamic teachings, *tawhid*, the "declaration of God's Unity." It is as if Corbin was so entranced by the recovery of the imaginal that he had difficulty seeing beyond it.
>
> From the point of view of the Islamic intellectual tradition, the tendency to become transfixed by the multiple apparitions of the One represents a danger inherent in the current revival of interest in imagination. It is clear, for example, that certain varieties of Jungianism divinize the imaginal world, giving to the soul an autonomous status never granted to it by the great traditions. Man's own domain of microcosmic imagination is posited as the Real, since "God" is merely the soul's projection. But this—in the Islamic view—is to fall into the error of associating other gods with God (*shirk*), the opposite of *tawhid*. We are left with polytheistic multiplicity, and the "gods" are reinstated as real entities possessing insuperable differences.
>
> Corbin never fell into such a position, which would have betrayed the central teaching of the texts with which he was concerned. Nevertheless, if his approach to Islamic thought is to be understood as reflecting the concerns of his sources, it needs to be tempered by more attention to the ultimate Unity lying behind the theophanic facade of created existence. (Chittick, *The Sufi Path of Knowledge*, x).

30. Born in Cordoba, Spain, in 1126 and died in Morocco in 1198. Averroes' Aristotelianism had a major influence on Latin Scholasticism, and for a long time Averroes and Avicenna, in poorly understood summaries, represented nearly all that the West knew of Islamic thought. In Iranian Islam, Averroes' thought had little effect. See Corbin, *A History of Islamic Philosophy*.

us knowledge of the world of material objects, and on the other, concepts of understanding give us knowledge of the abstract laws governing these objects. *Res cogitans* can know *res extensa*, though how this can come about has been a source of extensive debate. But the knower limited in that way must remain forever trapped in one mode of presence and the objects of knowledge must remain in one mode of being.

> Yet the fact remains that between the sense perceptions and the intuitions or categories of the intellect there has remained a void. That which ought to have taken its place between the two, and which in other times and places did occupy this intermediate space, that is to say the Active Imagination, has been left to the poets.[31]

The cosmology that underlies the metaphysics of Presence and provides the ontological foundation for this intermediate world where visionary events occur gives a privileged place to Imagination. The kind of spirituality in question here is not empty of forms:

> While we encounter in other philosophies or systems a distrust of the Image, a degradation of all that properly belongs to the Imagination, the *mundus imaginalis* is its exaltation, because it is the link in whose absence the schema of the worlds is put out of joint.[32]

This intermediary world is an interworld because it shares aspects of both the world of sensation and the world of intellectual forms. The world of the imaginal is a place "'where the spiritual takes body and the body becomes spiritual,' a world consisting of real matter and real extension, though by comparison to sensible, corruptible matter these are subtle and immaterial."[33] It is a measure of the depth of the

---

31. Corbin, *Spiritual Body and Celestial Earth*, vii. And of course, as Corbin was well aware, by 1949 at least, to Jung and the Jungians. Jung's discovery of the power of active imagination is given a framework completely outside the Western tradition by Corbin's investigations.

32. *Ibid.*, ix.

33. Corbin, *Creative Imagination*, 4.

catastrophe to which we have succumbed that we have come to regard this realm as just a fantasy in our heads. It is a realm of Being with its own characteristics, its own laws, and to which we have access by an organ of cognition appropriate to just this realm. The organ of cognition that gains us access to this universe is the active Imagination. It has a cognitive function just as fundamental as sensation or intellection, and like them, it must be trained. Therefore there are a perfectly objective imaginative perception, an imaginative knowledge, and an imaginative consciousness.

The import of this realm can be grasped only when we see that in the absence of the fully functional active Imagination, all the phenomena of religious consciousness lose not only their meaning, but the very place of their occurrence: "[the active Imagination] is the *place* of theophanic visions, the scene on which visionary events and symbolic histories *appear* in their true reality."[34] The objective function of Imagination must be accepted in order for the phenomena of religious consciousness to have any meaning.

> Upon it depends...both the validity of visionary accounts that perceive and relate "events in Heaven" and the validity of dreams, symbolic rituals, the reality of places formed by intense meditation, the reality of inspired imaginative visions, cosmogonies, and theogonies, and thus, in the first place, the truth of the *spiritual sense* perceived in the imaginative data of prophetic revelations.[35]

The cognitive function of Imagination is neither passive reception, nor unconstrained fantasy. It is the organ of objective transmutation of intellectual forms or sensible form into symbolic forms.

> The active Imagination guides, anticipates, molds sense perception; that is why it transmutes sensory data into symbols. The Burning Bush is only a brushwood fire if it is merely perceived by the sensory organs. In order that Moses

---

34. Corbin, *Creative Imagination*, 4.
35. Corbin, *Swedenborg and Esoteric Islam*, 11.

may perceive the Burning Bush and hear the Voice calling him "from the right side of the valley"—in short, in order that there may be a theophany—an organ of trans-sensory perception is needed.[36]

Entry into this world is dependent upon the transmutation of the soul, through and by means of the transmutation of the objects of knowledge. It is the mediating function of active Imagination that couples the two realms of what would otherwise be the subjective and the objective. In this world knower and known can come to correspond. Without this world they remain divided. It is here that the connection must be made between thought and being; it is here and here alone that hermeneutics can take on its true function, escaping the confines of the quantitative space and time of objects by moving into a world "of mystical cities...where time becomes reversible and where space is a function of desire, because it is only the external aspect of an internal state."[37] Imagination

is the organ that permits the transmutation of internal spiritual states into external states, into vision-events symbolizing with those internal states...

...[It can perceive] concrete things whose existence, as it is actualized in its knowledge and in its imagination, constitutes *eo ipso* the very form of concrete existence of those things (in other words: consciousness and its object are here ontologically inseparable).[38]

This is the realm of the *imaginatio vera* of Paracelsus, the realm of subtle bodies transcending the limitations of the physical. Corbin follows Mulla Sadra Shirazi, the great sixteenth century Shi'ite theosopher, one of the pre-eminent "Platonists of Persia," in holding that the Imagination in us is a "spiritual faculty independent of the physical organism and consequently surviving it."[39]

36. Corbin, *Creative Imagination*, 80.

37. Corbin, *Swedenborg and Esoteric Islam*, 16.

38. *Ibid.*, 15.

39. Corbin, *Spiritual Body and Celestial Earth*, x. Mulla Sadra was born in Shiraz, Iran, in 1571 and died in that city in 1640. He was a *(continued on next page)*

The world of the imaginal is limitless, and to acknowledge its reality changes the face of everything. It requires a view of phenomenology very different from that of Husserl and of Heidegger as well:

> To say that the Imagination (or love, or sympathy, or any other sentiment) *induces knowledge*, and knowledge of an "object" which is proper to it, no longer smacks of paradox. Still, once the full noetic value of the Imagination is admitted, it may be advisable to free the intentions of the Imagination from the parentheses in which a purely phenomenological interpretation encloses them...."[40]

But while it is true that this "imaginal" frees us from the confines of the literal and dogmatic, it does not thereby automatically free us to some unconstrained Arcadia where our every wish is granted and happiness reigns, or even to some less happy relativist universe where whatever one thinks is true. In the modern world, where we are used to thinking in terms of Spirit/Matter dualisms, it is common to hear that the opposition between Realists and Idealists conforms to something like the distinction between engineers, politicians, economists, or businessmen, on the one hand, and artists, humanists, or poets on the other. The former of course know how the real world works and have no illusions. The latter can think or write whatever they feel and they somehow have whatever value they do because they can express their emotions so well. But everyone knows in whose hands the effective Truth lies.

(continued from the previous page) powerful synthesizer of the many intellectual currents active in his time. "Down to our time his thought has left a personal stamp on all Iranian philosophy, or more broadly speaking, on Shi'ite consciousness at the level of philosophical expression." Corbin, *A History of Islamic Philosophy*, 342. Corbin suggests that to gain some idea of his stature and position, we might think of his work as combining the qualities of St. Thomas Aquinas, Jacob Boehme, and Immanuel Swedenborg; a combination, Corbin says, perhaps possible only in Iran. See Corbin, *Creative Imagination*, 23.

40. Corbin, *Creative Imagination*, 3. This reference to "parentheses" is to Husserl's concept of "bracketing" by means of which he meant to ensure a kind of non-judgmental objectivity in his investigations of phenomena.

We must not misunderstand Corbin here. This is no toy cosmology. The power of the Imagination is enormous, more fateful even than the powers of rational or sensible cognition, since this power is creative too, but not of things independent of the knower. It is "ideoplastic," creative of forms that reflect and embody the essential truth of the person. Corbin is most emphatic:

> The seriousness of the role of the Imagination is stressed by our philosophers when they state that it can be "the Tree of Blessedness" or on the contrary "the Accursed Tree" of which the *Quran* speaks, that which means Angel or Demon in power. The imaginary can be innocuous; the *imaginal* never can be so.[41]

It is worth quoting Mulla Sadra:

> Of all the realities that man sees and contemplates in the world beyond, those which delight, like houris, castles, gardens, green vegetation, and steams of running water—as well as their opposites—the horrifying kinds of which Hell is composed—none of these is extrinsic to him, to the very essence of his soul, none is distinct or separated from his own act of existing.[42]

It is clearly of the utmost importance to the individual soul to understand the power of this faculty and to learn to exercise it in accordance with the laws of the Intellect and not according to that rationality which is wholly blind to the autonomy of the Imagination anyway. The Imagination is inherently ambiguous, and this because of its intermediary status and its dual nature. It has both a "sensitive-passive" aspect and an active aspect. We share the former with the animals, "but in humans it leads to judgments which violate the laws of the intellect. Reduced to this level, the active Imagination is only able to produce the fantastic, the imaginary, unreal, or even absurd."[43] But when the Imagination acts in accordance with the

41. Corbin, *Spiritual Body and Celestial Earth*, x.
42. *Ibid.*, 165.
43. Corbin, *The Voyage and the Messenger*, 127.

Intellect, it becomes capable of producing meditative thinking and visionary events that are true perceptions of realities in the imaginal worlds. We will come back to this later.[44]

In the doctrine of Ibn 'Arabi, as in Sufism in general, it is the heart which is the organ most closely linked to the functions of the Imagination. The power of this heart is *himma,*

> a word whose content is perhaps best suggested by the Greek word *enthymesis,* which signifies the act of meditating, conceiving, imagining, projecting, ardently desiring—in other words, of having (something) present in the *thymos* which is vital force, soul, heart, intention, thought, desire.... [It is t]he force of an *intention* so powerful as to project and realize ("essentiate") a being external to the being who conceives the intention, ...[45]

The representational, estimatory, or calculative faculty (*wahm*) is common to all men, and by means of it the Imagination creates perfectly real images, which are however not separable from the subject. For the gnostic, however, the force of *himma* is capable of creating objects and producing changes in the "outside world," which are only visible to other mystics. These events are taken to be the domain of parapsychology in the modern world.[46] And it is by means of the power of the *imaginatio vera* that the subtle body of each of us is formed and has its place. This body of light is the essential person:

> Its substance derives from all the soul's movements, that is to say from its habits and ways of being, its affections and behaviour, knowledge and wishes, aspirations, emotions, nostalgias and ardent desires. It is the body that the soul itself has formed and acquired for itself; it may be a body of dazzling light or of darkened light, a garden among the gardens of Paradise or a pit among the pits of Hell.[47]

---

44. Chapter 5. *Disciples of Khidr.*
45. Corbin, *Creative Imagination,* 222.
46. *Ibid.,* 223.
47. Corbin, *Temple and Contemplation,* 194.

COMING HOME

The modern world is unbalanced because, although these means of cognition still exist in us, we are largely unconscious of them, and we are at their mercies. Even if we do give some credence to the powers of the imagination, we cannot know what to do with them since we have no framework in which to understand their significance, their power, or their use. The chief characteristic of the metaphysical structures upon which Suhrawardi, Avicenna, and the mystics of Islam base their ontologies is their hierarchical ordering, leading from the material world through multiple levels of angel-souls and beyond to the realm of the Absolute Divinity. In all these schemes, a divine progression of creative Presences couples cosmology, angelology, and anthropology into an indivisible unity. In order to understand the significance and the place of the *mundus imaginalis* and of the Imagination in Islamic thought and in the work of Corbin, we must understand these metaphysical structures.

The cosmologies of Avicenna and Suhrawardi were among the most influential in the history of Islamic thought. A sketch of each will have to suffice to indicate the context for the spirituality that Corbin describes.[48] In Avicenna's system an emanation from the Divine Being thinking itself produces a being that is the First Intelligence, the First Archangel, or Cherub, and from this the multiplicity of all Creation proceeds in the following way. There is a triadic structure to the emanation. The First Intelligence "intelligizes" itself in three modes: as thought by the First Being; as necessitated, or empowered by the First Being; and as not necessary in itself, that is, as a kind of Shadow of its own possible non-being. From these actions there emanate three existents corresponding to Spirit, Soul, and Matter: a second Archangel, the first of the Celestial Souls (*Animae coelestes*) who are the moving forces of the heavenly spheres, and the Ninth and highest of those heavenly spheres. Each of the successive Archangels in the series this initiates

---

48. For a more detailed treatment of Avicenna's cosmology in the broader context of Islamic cosmologies as a whole, see Nasr, *An Introduction to Islamic Cosmological Doctrines.*

is defined by a quaternity: its own essence, as well as the Archangel, the Celestial Soul, and the Heaven that proceed from it. This flowering of creation proceeds eternally until it reaches the level of the tenth Archangel, the Soul that powers the heavens of our world and our world of "sublunary" matter itself. The creative, unifying power is diminished at this remove from the Divinity. "This Tenth Intelligence, at the farthest point of the cosmic procession in which the Shadow will reach its maximum, no longer has sufficient energy to engender *one* other Intelligence, *one* Soul, and *one* heaven."[49] And so, for lack of proximity to the One Divinity, the Creation shatters into a plurality of human souls and the multiplicity of matter.

And thus there are three realms, spirit, soul, and matter, in a repeating, ascending, and descending triad. The celestial souls are moved by and move the heavens by means of "an aspiration of love which remains forever unassuaged."[50] They long for return to the Archangel from which they emanate, and it is the desire and the nostalgia of their love that powers the heavens. They are all Strangers, and they long to return to the origin from which they descended. At each level there is a coupling, a syzygy between the angel-souls and the Angel that produced them. At the levels above ours, the Heavens are composed of "immaterial matter," and the *Animae coelestes* have no sensory perception, though they do live in real, concrete, extended space. They possess Imagination in the pure state, unconstrained by the requirements of material causality. Their space is the space of the *mundus imaginalis*.

From the point of view of modern Faustian space, the hierarchy of the worlds according to Suhrawardi shares many features in common with Avicenna's. Yet the cosmos of the Shayk al-Ishraq results from an "explosion" of that universe into an infinite expanse of "innumerable marvelous universes." In his youth, Suhrawardi was granted an ecstatic vision in the course of which he saw the closed spiritual universe of the Aristotelians explode "and was shown the multitude of

---

49. Corbin, *Avicenna*, 62.
50. Corbin, *A History of Islamic Philosophy*, 171.

those 'beings of Light whom Hermes and Plato contemplated, and the celestial beams which are the sources of the *Light of Glory*...heralded by Zarathustra....'"[51] This is the Transfiguring Light which the *Avesta* calls Xvarnah.

By means of this Light, the first of the Archangels emanates from the Light of Lights. The relationship between this first pair defines the "archetypal relationship between the first Lover and the first Beloved," and this pairing cascades through all Creation "establishing all beings in pairs."[52] The intelligible dimensions of these Beings of Light come in pairs such as dominion and love, illumination and contemplation, independence and indigence. These compound with one another and "by engendering each other out of their irradiations and reflections, the hypostases of Light become countless in number."[53] This constitutes the universe of the Primordial Ruling Lights who proceed from each other and are the causes of each other. They are the Archangels, the Supreme Sovereign Lights, who make up the world of the Mothers. From their positive dimensions, such as dominion, active contemplation, and independence, a new order of Archangel-Archetypes is produced, who are not each other's causes and who are of equal rank among themselves in the hierarchy. These beings are equivalent to the Platonic archetypes except that they are not abstract universals, but rather beings of Light. They include Gabriel, the Angel of Humanity as Active Intelligence. Taken together, the world of the Primordial Lights and the Archangel-Archetypes make up the world of the *jabarut*. From these Archangel-Archetypes in turn, there emanates another Order of Lights, through which the Archangel-Archetypes govern beings with bodies. These intermediaries are the Angel-Souls that correspond to the *Animae caelestes* of Avicenna's system. This is the world of the *malakut*.

From the negative dimensions of the world of the Mothers, such as dependence, passive illumination, and love as indigence, are produced the innumerable Heavens of the Fixed Stars, each corresponding

51. Corbin, *A History of Islamic Philosophy*, 208.
52. *Ibid.*, 211.
53. *Ibid.*

to one of the innumerable negative dimensions. These are composed of subtle matter and represent the materialization of the negative dimension of the beings of Light. This is the world of the *mulk*.

In Suhrawardi's scheme, there is a fourth world, intermediary between the worlds of the beings of Light, both the *Jabarut* and the *Malakut*, and the world of sensible perception, the *mulk*: this is the *'alam al-mithal*, the *mundus imaginalis*. Thus for Suhrawardi, creation is structured as a quaternity. However Corbin most often speaks of the triadic structure of reality, and this is due to the interpretation of Mulla Sadra, according to whom the *mundus imaginalis* corresponds to the world of the *Malakut*. This is the world of Forms and Images appropriate to the Active Imagination. It is the world where symbols are True.

Given this metaphysical structure, the connection between human souls and celestial souls becomes clear:

> Celestial Souls and human souls share the modality of not being purely intelligential or intellective...; they have in common the function of ruling and governing physical bodies. To do this, they must *imagine*. The whole immense world of the imaginable, the universe of Symbol...would not exist without the soul.... The body with which they [the Angels] are furnished...is made of a "celestial matter."... For this reason, and because, unlike human imaginations, theirs are not dependent on sensible knowledge, their imaginations are *true*.[54]

To make any sense of the active Imagination, to place it in its proper context, an entire cosmology is required. It will not do to attempt to stress the importance of Imagination in human life by simply adding it on to a modern view of reality as a kind of appendage and speaking naively of the importance of the role of Art in out lives. It must be understood as an integral part of the whole of the cosmos if there is to be any chance of grasping its full import. Without an appropriate cosmology we are subject to illusion, error, and spiritual catastrophe:

---

54. Corbin, *Avicenna*, 74.

If we do not have available a cosmology whose schema can include, as does the one that belongs to our traditional philosophers, the plurality of universes in ascensional order, our Imagination will remain *unbalanced*, its recurrent conjunctions with the will to power will be an endless source of horrors. We will be continually searching for a new discipline of the Imagination, and we will have great difficulty in finding it as long as we persist in seeing in it only a certain way of keeping our *distance* with regard to what we call the *real*, and in order to exert an influence on that real.... [I]t is always the word *fantasy* that appears as the excuse: literary fantasy, for example, or preferably, in the taste and style of the day, social fantasy.[55]

That is, we who see Imagination as a human faculty cannot help but regard it as in some sense distinct from the Real. Thus we project our wishes and desires upon the world and try to change the world in accordance with our projections. We have an idea, and we try to exert an influence on the real. This may take the form of social or biological engineering. Or it may be merely artistic: we may only make art. This engineering or this art may be in accordance with a spiritual effort for the transformation of society and the soul, or it may not. The connection between Imagination and the World is extremely problematic if Imagination is in us in precisely the same way that the connection between *res cogitans* and *res extensa* is unclear if we understand thinking as something that we do. The schism is there in both cases: Thought or Imagination on the side of the Subject and the stuff of the world out there as Objects to be pushed around willy-nilly in accordance with our desires. And, in either case, the schism is in reality an illusion, since there is really nothing in us, because the subject inevitably disappears into the social, the material, and the historical. For without Intellect or Imagination understood as coming from a divine source beyond the *ego*, the only desires we can have are those forced upon us by history.

---

55. Corbin, *Swedenborg and Esoteric Islam*, 19-20.

Corbin decries the secularization of the arts and, by extension, of any discipline of the imagination, including science, which cannot rise above the level of the merely sensible to the level of symbols, which alone are real. Even our dreams have become decadent.[56] Without access to the world of visionary reality, all art and science must remain leveled out metaphysically and doomed to the perpetual futility of one-dimensional man cleverly rearranging objects in space, never entertaining the notion of spiritual birth and therefore doomed to decay into the status of the monstrous and the less-than-human. All the disciplines of the Imagination, and it is hard to conceive of any human activity as being exempt, are in reality possible means of transformation of the soul and the soul of the world. But the secularization of Imagination prevents us from realizing this:

> [I]t is impossible to avoid wondering whether the *mundus imaginalis*, in the proper meaning of the' term, would of necessity be lost and leave room only for the imaginary if something like a secularization of the *imaginal* into the *imaginary* were not required for the fantastic, the horrible, the monstrous, the macabre, the miserable and the absurd to triumph. On the other hand, the art and imagination of Islamic culture in its traditional form are characterized by the hieratic and the serious, by gravity, stylization and meaning.[57]

The hierarchical cosmos leads upwards to the light. Corbin and his mystical theosophers are not inclined to give any positive evaluation to the darker aspects of the imaginal. They are to be transcended. Their triumph in the modern world is the result of the very unbalance caused by the ignorance of the world of the soul.[58] Because of the dangers for the soul

---

56. Corbin, *Creative Imagination*, 224.

57. Corbin, *Swedenborg and Esoteric Islam*, 20.

58. Archetypal psychologists will note here a considerable difference between Corbin's essentially theological approach and that of Hillman's psychological use of the *mundus imaginalis*. Hillman comments explicitly on this divergence:

> Clearly the pathologizings of the image do *not* belong to the *mundus imaginalis* as [Corbin] has given us this word. But in the soul-making of actual psychotherapy, pathologizings are *(continued on the next page)*

inherent in the Imagination and the *mundus imaginalis*, they must be understood in this metaphysical context, and Corbin warns against any misuse of the term *imaginal*:

> If this term is used to apply to anything other than the *mundus imaginalis* and the imaginal Forms as they are located in the schema of the worlds which necessitate them and legitimize them, there is a great danger that the term will be degraded and its meaning be lost.... If one transfers its usage outside this precisely defined schema one sets out on a false trail and strays far from the intention which our Iranian philosophers have induced us to restore in our use of this word. It is superfluous to add...that the *mundus imaginalis* has nothing to do with what the fashion of our time calls the "civilization of the image."[59]

The unbearable constriction of the Real that accompanies the loss of the hierarchical cosmos and the realms of the Imagination is impossible to underestimate. The Western world has been vainly struggling to escape the terror of that claustrophobia ever since. This goes a long way towards explaining our drive towards the Future and towards the New World, whether that is America, the Moon, or the

---

pathologizings are often the *via regia* into the imaginal.... The refinement of our imaginal sensibility must begin where sensibility itself begins. From the gross to the subtle is an operation, not an ontology. The ontological priority of Corbin's world is nonetheless arrived at via the operational priority of Jung's method—because we must begin where we have fallen, flat on our backs in personal pain. The difference between Jung and Corbin can be resolved by practicing Jung's technique with Corbin's vision; that is, active imagination is not for the sake of the doer and *our* actions in the sensible world of literal realities, but for the sake of the images and to where they can take us, *their* realization.

Hillman, "On the Necessity of Abnormal Psychology," 33, n. 5.

    For Corbin, however, it is true that "from the gross to the subtle" is both an operation and an ontology. Jung and Jungians are regarded with some suspicion by many of those who interpret Corbin's work from within an Islamic framework (Nasr and Chittick, for instance), and much of the difference in outlook hinges on the significance of the imagination. Detractors of the psychological approach tend to be more wary of the dangers of the imaginary than the "psychologizers" who celebrate it.

    59. Corbin, *Spiritual Body and Celestial Earth*, xviii-xix.

virtual realities of the Internet. We can never after such a loss have enough space. In our drive to recover the spaces of the Imagination, we have taken refuge in the Image. Television, movies, video screens in every classroom, magazines, billboards—the world is full of Images, all coming to us from Outside, according to someone else's agenda. They are immeasurably powerful. The Free Market has known that for a long time. But this is precisely the opposite of that Interiorization of the world that is the goal of gnosis. It is in fact the latest, perhaps the last, step in the exteriorization and total objectification of the soul. We are driven to it by a kind of perverse necessity: the more we need space for the things of the soul, the more we seek images to fill the space that we no longer create for ourselves. And yet fewer and fewer of us know the source of this panic or where to turn in response. And so we continue to search for new disciplines of the imagination and are caught by each in turn, disoriented and confused in a world that will not cohere.

The Imagination is then "a median and mediating power" between the sensible and the intellectual. Without this mediation, any relationship between them is blocked, and neither can stand on its own. The lack of this mediating function is the source of the "catastrophe of the spirit" which split the West. The Imagination provides access to the world where "the conflict between theology and philosophy, between faith and knowledge, between symbol and history, is resolved."[60] It provides, in other words, the place for the resolution of the split between thought and being, subject and object, humanity and nature. It provides the only place where the soul can find a home.

Finally, we must complete this discussion by indicating where to look for the crowning Jewel in this cosmology, which is ultimately the source of the power which links these worlds together and which points out clearly the central mystery of Being that runs through all of the hierarchies. In a crucial passage in which he discusses the relation of Jacob Boehme's theology to that of the mystical theosophers of Iran, Corbin makes clear that the world

---

60. Corbin, *Creative Imagination*, 13.

of "intellectual forms," the *Jabarut,* is not merely the world of abstract understanding, as we might be misled into thinking, for it points beyond itself to something more distant yet:

> Between the intellectual and the sensible, or expressed more precisely still, between the transcendent and hidden Deity, the *Deitas abscondita,* and the world of man, Boehme places an intermediary which he calls the sacred Element, a "spiritual corporeity" which represents the Dwelling, the Divine Presence, for our world.[61]

This Dwelling is the Soul of the World, and it is Boehme's equivalent to the *mundus imaginalis.* Without the Soul of the World to provide a living connection between the hidden Deity and the world of creation, it was only a matter of time before agnosticism and nihilism would triumph, culminating in the Death of God proclaimed by Nietzsche. It is the very hiddenness of this Deity, forever receding into the Beyond, which provides the motive force for the upward spiral of the cosmic hierarchies. Without it the world would cease to exist; it would perish in immobility in a final act of Absence. We will return to this central theme again later. In stepping beyond the physical world, we have discovered the world of the imaginal, which is the place of the Presence of the Angel. It is this world into which we "turn inside out" and that must be present for the spiritual birth that this signals. We have said that at this limit the soul perceives its Imago. Nonetheless the second question raised above must be addressed in more detail. Who precisely is this Angel, and what is its significance?

---

61. Corbin, *Spiritual Body and Celestial Earth,* xiii.

CHAPTER FIVE
The Angel and Individuation

The Celestial Twin and the Metaphysics of Individuation

Here we are near to the heart of Corbin's concerns. We are in a position to answer the ques-tion posed by Corbin: "To what is human presence present?" Around this question of the Angel of Humanity revolve the central motivations of the spiritual Voyager, and here lies the ultimate significance of the Personal God of all of the Religions of the Book: Mazdaism, Judaism, Christianity, and Islam.[1] It has been a long time since philosophy (and even theology in the West) has taken angels seriously. But to understand Corbin we must readmit them into philosophical discussion. According to Corbin without them there is no chance of our ever understanding ourselves. We have seen the kind of hierarchic, personified cosmos that is the objective result of the interiorization of the world. This limitless cosmos is full of Presences, full of Persons—full of Angels. We have to discard all our trivialized and anthropocentric conceptions of the nature of such beings. They are personified metaphysical presences, the movers of worlds, and they provide the connection between ourselves and divinity. There is no ques-tion of anthropomorphism. The personality of these beings is not derived from ours; ours is only a dim reflection of theirs. The charge of anthropo-morphism has a certain force while the world is "wrong side out." But it is only by turning the world right side out again that we can see this.

---

1. Corbin, *A History of Islamic Philosophy*, 1. Corbin's *Spiritual Body and Celestial Earth: From Mazdean Iran to Shi'ite Iran* addresses the relations between Mazdean Persia and the later Islamic tradition.

85

It is not too much to say that Corbin's entire work revolves around the ontological priority of the individual. It is the Presence of the Angel that provides the conditions for the possibility of the experience of the Person. Any of the various secular cosmologies of the modern world are incompatible with the existence of persons. That category of beings has no place in a world that excludes Presence from the beginning. And it is not the post-Cartesian world that is the problem, as one might suppose. We must go back further than Descartes. It is from the time of the triumph of the Aristotelianism of Averroes in the West that we must date the rise of the modern impersonal universe. For Averroes the principal of individuation is matter: "[T]he human soul receives its individuality only through its union with the body, and this individuation is the 'service' that the body renders the soul."[2] Averroes

> accepts the existence of a human intelligence independent
> of the organic world, but this intelligence is not the indi-
> vidual. The individual is identified with the perishable; what
> can become eternal in the individual pertains exclusively
> to the separate and unique active Intelligence.[3]

The history of a civilization hinges on the interpretation of this active Intelligence. To see this we must look briefly at Aristotle's conception of knowledge. For Aristotle "the soul is somehow all beings,"[4] at least potentially, for only so can the soul know them. Thus he can say, "In what is without matter, what thinks and what is thought are the same."[5] When "mind" or *nous* exercises its power of knowing, it moves from potentiality to act (*energeia*), and through this *energeia*, it becomes the intelligible form of what is known. In a short but pregnant passage in *de Anima*, Aristotle distinguishes two faculties in the soul, one of which is passive and one of which is active. When *nous* is activated, it must be

---

2. Corbin, *Avicenna*, 82.
3. Corbin, *Creative Imagination*, 12.
4. Aristotle's *de Anima* III, 8: 432b20 f. Quoted in Cranz, unpub. ms, "The Reorientation of Western Thought."
5. *Ibid.*, *de Anima* III, 5: 430a2 f.

activated by something else: the movement from potency to act always requires a mover—something must be already in act. And so there must be two faculties in the soul: one passive (the *nous pathetikos*), and one active (the *nous poietikos*). The passive intellect is perishable. The active Intellect "is a kind of positive state like the sun [or light]"[6] and is eternal, unmixed *energeia*. For Aristotle, this eternal *nous* has nothing in it of the individual. It is a kind of cosmic Intellect in which we participate, but which is a light shining equally for all. And for Aristotle our knowledge of the sensible world comes from the sensible world itself, as seems so evident to us now. The intelligible forms of the sensible world are derived by extraction, or as we would call it—abstraction— from the world of matter. *Nous* perhaps provides the forms of right thinking, but the sensible world provides the content.

In the strongest possible contrast to this are the Neoplatonic "angelologies" of Avicenna and Suhrawardi, which on the contrary assure "a secure foundation for the radical autonomy of the individual."[7] The crucial difference lies in the nature and function of this *nous poietikos*. For Averroes, as for Aristotle, we participate in some way in this universal and eternal mind, but this has nothing to do with our accidental, particular uniqueness. This doctrine of the active Intellect was adopted in various forms by the Neoplatonists. As we saw earlier, in their emanationist schemas, there is a hierarchy of intermediary Intelligences descending from God as the Unmoved Mover and ending in the active or agent Intellect. All knowledge is the result of illumination from above, not of abstraction from below. And in the mystical angelologies of Avicenna and Suhrawardi, that active Intellect, which is merely conceived by abstract theorizing, is actually encountered in the Event "at the limit of the Cosmos," as personified and individualized in a Celestial Person, who is in each case unique. Each human soul has a counterpart in Heaven, who is the eternal and perfected

6. Aristotle's *de Anima*, III, 5: 430a15 f, quoted in Cranz, unpub. ms, "The Reorientation of Western Thought."

7. Corbin, *Creative Imagination*, 12.

individuality of that soul:

> At the moment when the soul discovers itself to be a stranger and
> alone in a world formerly familiar, a *personal* figure appears on its
> horizon, a figure that announces itself to the soul *personally* be-
> cause it symbolizes *with* the soul's most intimate depths. In other
> words, the soul discovers itself to be the earthly counterpart of
> another being with which it forms a totality that is dual in struc-
> ture. The two elements of this *dualitude* may be called the ego
> and the Self, or the transcendent celestial Self and the earthly Self,
> or by still other names. It is from this transcendent Self that the
> soul originates in the past of metahistory; this Self had be-
> come strange to it while the soul slumbered in the world of ordinary
> consciousness; but it ceases to be strange to it at the moment
> when the soul in turn feels itself a stranger in this world. This is
> why the soul requires an absolutely individual expression of this
> Self, one that could pass into the common stock of symbol-
> ism (or into alegory) only at the cost of its painfully won
> individual differentiation being repressed, leveled, and abol-
> ished by ordinary consciousness.
> ... [T]he idea of the integration of the *ego* with its Self be-
> comes the recital of an Event that...is real to the highest degree....
> The Self...is, "in person," the heavenly counterpart of a pair or a
> syzygy made up of a fallen angel, or an angel appointed to
> govern a body, and of an angel retaining his abode in heaven....
> [This syzygy] individualizes the Holy Spirit into an individual
> Spirit, who is the celestial *paredros* of the human being, its guard-
> ian angel, guide and companion, helper and savior.
> ...This relation of the soul to the Angel...differentiates [Gnos-
> ticism] from any premystical or nonmystical monotheism that
> situates souls as each equidistant from the divine Unity, and it
> establishes the connection...between angelology and
> mysticism.[8]

For Avicenna and Suhrawardi, the active Intelligence is the
"Angel of Humanity" and is identified "with the Holy Spirit, that

---

8. Corbin, *Avicenna*, 20-22.

is, with the Angel Gabriel as the Angel of Knowledge and of Revelation."[9] There is a consistency among the various gnostic and esoteric angelologies within the Abrahamic tradition:

> Whether it be Metatron as the *protos Anthropos* and Active Intelligence, or the Active Intelligence as Holy Spirit and Archangel Gabriel, or as Holy Spirit and Angel of Humanity in the philosophy of Ishraq, the same figure never ceases to manifest itself to mental vision under this angelophany.[10]

The same figure appears in Hermetic thought as the Perfect Nature, and it corresponds to the idea of the Paraclete in the Gospel of St. John. Corbin's ecumenical vision, based upon the homologies and pre-established harmonies among the religions of the Book, centers upon this Figure of the Celestial Self. "In the perspective of the *Paraclete*, the three Abrahamic faiths can come together in the same city-temple."[11]

For instance the mystery of the Pentecost is that it does not occur in time but is forever available to those with access to the *mundus imaginalis*. And it is through the encounter with the Angel of the Holy Spirit, the Angel of the Face, through that encounter which is the result of a Quest and a struggle, that each individual is in fact promoted to the rank of person.[12] And herein lies the significance of Suhrawardi's revival of Mazdean angelology in alliance with Platonic metaphysics. This philosophical anthropology is traceable back to the Mazdean Fravarti:

---

9. Corbin, *Creative Imagination*, 10. As we have seen, the details of Suhrawardi's cosmology differ from those of Avicenna in certain crucial respects. For Suhrawardi, there is a distinction to be made between the celestial *alter ego* and the Angel Holy Spirit. The former is on the level of the Angel-Souls, the latter of the Angel-Archetypes. It is the latter that allows the soul to find its own unique "Perfect Nature." See Corbin, "Epistle on the State of Childhood, by Sohravardi," 57-58.

10. Corbin, *Avicenna*, 67.

11. Corbin, *Temple and Contemplation*, 338. See also Corbin's "L'idee du paraclet en philosophie iranienne" in *Face de Dieu, face de l'homme: hermeneutique et soufisme.*

12. Corbin, *Le paradoxe du monothèisme*, 250.

> Every physical or moral entity, every complete being or group
> of beings belonging to the world of Light...has its Fravarti.
> What they announce to earthly beings is, therefore, an
> essentially dual structure that gives to each one a heavenly
> archetype or Angel, whose earthly counterpart he is.[13]

This is more than an "anthropology." The unity, individuality
and Presence of "every being...belonging to the world of Light," depends upon the connection with the Angel, the archetype in Heaven.
This guarantees that every such being can be more itself, more real,
more alive, to the degree that it is in contact with this celestial Presence. We misunderstand Presence if we restrict it to human persons,
though they can express it more perfectly than any other beings. It
is a potential lying within all created things of the world of Light. But
it is also true that we can perceive this quality in the world around
us only to the degree that we have come to live it ourselves. The
ultimate source of this Living Spirit is the same for all the beings
of Light.[14]

This ontology of individuation was given a further crucial determination in the philosophy of Mulla Sadra where the process of
"Personification" is explained in terms of a metaphysics of existence.
He replaced a static conception of the essence of the soul with an
active ontology that emphasizes the qualitative alterations caused by
activity on the part of the person:

> Before him the essences or quiddities were thought of as
> priorities and immutable. Whether existence were
> superadded to them or not, nothing changed in the consti-
> tution of these essences. Mulla Sadra, on the contrary, gave
> priority to existence. It was the act and mode of existing that
> determined what an essence was. The act of existing was

---

13. Corbin, *Spiritual Body and Celestial Earth*, 9-10.
14. The architect Christopher Alexander calls this Presence "the Quality without a name" and has devoted his life to reviving in us the ability to perceive and
create it in the world of art and architecture. See Alexander, *A Timeless Way of
Building* and *A Foreshadowing of 21st Century Art*.

indeed capable of many degrees of intensification or degradation. For example, to the metaphysics of essences, the status of man or the status of the body is a constant. But to Mulla Sadra's existential metaphysic, being a man is possible in many degrees, from being a demon with a human face to the sublime condition of being the Perfect Man. What is called the body passes through a multitude of states from being a perishable body in this world to being a subtle or even a divine body (*jism ilahi*). These changes always depend upon intensifications or attenuations (that is, degradations) in the act of existing. The thought that intensifications of being give life to our idea of the forms of being, of essences, is one of the main characteristics of his metaphysics. In itself it initiates a phenomenology of the act of existing.[15]

It does not require a large leap to connect this phenomenology of modes of Presence with Heidegger's conception of human being as *Dasein*. But Corbin warns against any facile identification of "existentialisms" East and West. Mulla Sadra's metaphysics is deeply rooted in the hierarchic structure of being, in the levels of hermeneutics that Heidegger "had not foreseen."

The phenomenology of the intensities of existence corresponds exactly to the qualitative space of the *mundus imaginalis*, because it is only there that these qualitative differences, these intensifications and degradations of being, can occur. They are not visible as such in the world of matter. Even the creations of the powerful *himma* of gnostic masters are visible only to other gnostics. Moral and spiritual advances or failures create the worlds in which the soul moves, by virtue of the intensity of existence, the act of Presence, and the degree of individuation of that soul. This intensification of being is accomplished in the *mundus imaginalis*, through the struggle of the human person with and for the angel of its being.

---

15. Corbin, Henry, "The Question of Comparative Philosophy: Convergences in Iranian and European Thought," *Spring*, trans. Jane Pratt (1980), 11-12.

> The intensification of the acts of *existing*, as professed by
> the metaphysics of Sadra Shirazi, raises the status of the
> body to the state of spiritual body, in truth the divine body
> (*jism ilahi*). The organ of this transmutation, this generation
> of the spiritual body is, in Boehme as in Mulla Sadra,
> the power of the *imaginatrix*, which is the magical faculty
> par excellence (*Imago-Magia*), because it is the soul itself
> "animated" by its "Perfect Nature," its celestial role.[16]

But if we are not in possession of and able to live within the
corresponding cosmology, there is no way this contact with the
Angel can occur. However much we might struggle, there will be
no direction in which to turn. We may well know we are lost, but
there is quite literally no way home in a world without the Place
where this encounter can occur. The history of the modern West is
the history of "*l'homme sans Fravarti.*"[17]

> It is this fravarti which gives its true dimension to the
> person. The human person is only a person by virtue of
> this celestial dimension, archetypal, angelic, which is
> the celestial pole without which the terrestrial pole of
> his human dimension is completely *depolarized* in vaga-
> bondage and perdition.[18]

The cosmos of Averroes, lacking this personal connection between
the individual soul and its archetype, is based upon an abstract connection between heaven and earth that denies the cosmic role of
Presence, individuality, and personal, revelatory knowledge. The intelligible forms became impersonal and universal. For a while, the sensible
forms retained their personal force, because they are closest to us in
this cosmology, since it is matter that individuates. But in the end they
faded, lost their animation, their life, and inevitably descended to the level
of objects. And the soul descended with them, turning increasingly towards the world of matter as the living connection with Heaven faded.

---

16. Corbin, *Le paradoxe du monothèisme*, 253.
17. *Ibid.*, 246.
18. *Ibid.*, 243-44.

THE ANGEL AND INDIVIDUATION

This makes more precise the sense in which the cosmology of Avicenna and Suhrawardi is both an angelology and an anthropology. Human knowledge, human destiny, and the existence of persons depend upon the presence of the angelic hierarchy and upon the search for a realization of the connection to this realm by means of the active Imagination. And the central spiritual fact of this great structure is its focus upon the individuality of each soul. It is this celestial Pole which is the source of that Orientation without which humanity is irremediably lost in the world of Absence.

Corbin says,

> if the Prophet received his revelations from the Angel Gabriel, it is none the less true that, for each mystical Sage, joining himself with the Active Intelligence (which is but the speculative name of the Angel Holy Spirit) is each time equivalent to becoming the "seal of prophecy."[19]

This experience is the foundation of prophetic philosophy. This claim appears heretical in the extreme to the literalists and the dogmatists in all the Abrahamic religions, because this relationship takes precedence over any public doctrines or sectarian affiliations. The personal yet objective nature of the experience is expressed by Corbin in reference to the Gnostic *Acts of Peter*:

> Here, then, the Apostle Peter evokes the event of the Transfiguration. Of this event, which was visible only to some and, even then, not to their bodily eyes, he can say but one thing: *Talem eum vidi qualem capere potui* (I saw him as I was able to receive him)... Each time, the soul has attained, or is on the way to attaining, its state of perfect individuation.[20]

But this cosmology also implies that we are engaged in a cosmic drama. We are not observers but must be active participants on pain of losing our true Life. Neither the salvational attainment of individuation

---

19. Corbin, *Avicenna*, 75.
20. *Ibid.*, 92-93.

and the birth of the soul in heaven, nor the concomitant vision of the Guide or Lord to whom the Guide may lead, are to be regarded as given. They must be won. We are engaged in a battle for the Angel, for our Lord, for ourselves, and it is all the same battle. On the one hand,

> It may befall a soul to "die" as a soul can die, by falling below itself, below its condition of a human soul: by actualizing in itself its bestial and demonic virtuality. This is its hell, the hell that it carries in itself—just as its bliss is elevation above itself, flowering of its angelic virtuality. Personal survival cannot then be thought of as purely and simply prolonging the status of the human condition, the "acquired dispositions." The latter doubtless concern what we call the "personality." But…the *essential person*, in its posthumous becoming and in its immortality perhaps immeasurably transcends the "personality" of so-and-so son of so-and-so.[21]

We can aspire to the meeting with the essential person, or we can fail to do so. If we fail to make ourselves fit companions for the Angel, we are barred from the immortality of the essential person. The powers of Darkness are real. The wholeness that Corbin seeks through the encounter with the Angel is based upon the Light of the essential Person:

> The totality represented by their bi-unity is therefore "light upon light"; it can never be a composite of Ohrmazdian light and Ahrimanian darkness, or in psychological terms, of consciousness and its *shadow*.[22]

Thus Corbin differentiates this doctrine from Jung's conception of wholeness. There is to be no integration of the Shadow but victory over the forces of Darkness.

Suhrawardi stresses the positive reality of Ahrimanian negativity in its struggle with the Forces of Light. His doctrine is marked by a kind of Manichean dualism. The Darkness of evil is not a mere absence of Light; it is its contrary and would exist even in the

---

21. Corbin, *Avicenna*, 116.
22. Corbin, *The Man of Light in Iranian Sufism*, 31.

absence of Light. We ally ourselves with one side or the other. While we cannot destroy the Angel, we can turn away from it, from our responsibility to ourselves, and to what is best in us:

> It is not in the power of a human being to destroy his celestial Idea; but it is in his power to betray it, to separate himself from it, to have, at the entrance to the Chinvat Bridge, nothing face to face with him but the abominable and demonic caricature of his "I" delivered over to himself without a heavenly sponsor.[23]

But the cosmic struggle is not one-sided. In a theme which stretches from Mazdean Iran to contemporary Shi'ism, "the God of Light has need of the aide of all [of his fravartis]" because the "menace of active nihilism" is terrifying.[24] As in pre-Eternity, the Fravartis chose to give up their purely celestial existence and incarnate as Angel-Souls, so we must choose to help combat the horrors of Ahriman. There is a mystical solidarity between the paired beings who comprise the cosmic hierarchy: between God and His Fravartis, in the ranks of the Archangels with their bonds of love and devotion, and between the human soul and its Angel. This bond is what the Shi'ites call "spiritual chivalry."[25] If this reciprocal bond is broken, then "[t]hey face each other as Master and Slave. One of the two must disappear."[26] The personal God, as the supreme determination of the Absolute, can only appear as and to a Person. If the possibility of encountering the Angel, the Lord, is eliminated, the human individual has no longer any celestial pole, no orientation, and thus no direction for its moral compass and nothing to guarantee its unique being—"there will no longer be persons," only units in a totalitarian or totalizing regime of one form or another. Whether that regime is political, economic, or scientific, the

---

23. Corbin, *Spiritual Body and Celestial Earth*, 42.

24. Corbin, *Le paradoxe du monothèisme*, 246.

25. See Corbin, *En islam iranienne*, v. 4. This chivalry is a crucial concept for Corbin and in Islamic mysticism. It was Corbin's hope that this may be ultimately what can unite the followers of the three Abrahamic religions in a single diversely determined purpose. See especially pages 410-40.

26. Corbin, *Le paradoxe du monothèisme*, 246.

result is the same. We are powerless, lost in anonymity, rolled along like the foam in the torrent, and completely at the mercy of the social, biological, and political environments. This is the Abyss, the final loss of the soul in bitterness and helplessness, knowing ourselves to be only objects in a world where, in Charles Darwin's famous phrase, "there is no higher or lower."

It is revealing to see that Darwin in his later years was intensely aware of the impact of historical reductionism, of that Fall into history, which turns Nature into a collection of objects:

> Poetry of many kinds…gave me great pleasure… [F]ormerly pictures gave me considerable, and music very great, delight. But now for many years I cannot endure to read a line of poetry… I have also lost almost any taste for pictures or music… My mind seems to have become a kind of machine for grinding general laws out of large collections of fact… The loss of these [higher] tastes is a loss of happiness, and may possibly be injurious to the intellect, and more probably to the moral character, by enfeebling the emotional part of our nature. [27]

From the viewpoint of these traditional cosmologies, it is not the emotional part of us that degenerates but the imagining part.

So the cosmic charge laid on us is "to make ourselves capable of God;"[28] for ourselves—to achieve our eternal individuality by struggling with and for the Angel; and for God—not the Absolute, the *deus absconditus* beyond all knowing, but God as revealed through the Creation experienced as the revelation of Divine Being, as a personal theophanic form appearing simultaneously as and to a Person. This common bond of sympathy gives meaning and direction to the most important struggle in which we can engage. One thinks here not only of Jung and his emphasis on individuation, but of the poets as well: Robert Frost—"The most important thing is to find your voice." And Diane di Prima—"The most important war is the war against the Imagination." Or again, H. D.—"What can be seen is at stake."[29] We

---

27. Cited in Bly *et al.*, *The Rag and Bone Shop of the Heart*, 192.
28. Corbin, *Creative Imagination*, 290, n. 10.
29. Rothenberg and Joris, *Poems for the Millennium*, v. 2, 449, v. 1, 378.

have relegated the imagination to the realm of the poets and with it the struggle for Individuation, for one's Angel. This is not certainly the struggle to be an *ego* of an "Angel-less" soul, but the struggle to enact the reality that all our knowledge, our action, all our "*passion* is the *action* of the Donor," that our soul "receives the illumination that emanates upon it, floods its being, ... [T]o recognize this *action* of the *Active* Intelligence or Holy Spirit is the 'Oriental knowledge,' the knowledge that is the *Orient*, the *origin* of all knowledge."[30] The struggle is to become whole, and this requires uniting with the other half of our being. The highest form of being is the Person and the Presence that this entails, and our most profound and essential function is theophanic: "to manifest God, to be the *theophore*," the bearer of the Divinity.[31]

There are in these philosophies of esoteric Islam, entire ontologies and phenomenologies of individuation and of the active Imagination which require an anthropo-cosmology so grand in its conception, so all-encompassing in its vision that little in modern thought can rival it. It is no wonder that Corbin, much as he may borrow from the vocabulary of C. G. Jung (a fellow lecturer at Eranos), in discussing these issues is always careful to say that there must be no question of psychologizing the meanings of these cosmologies and ontologies. As Jung well knew, a scientific or rationalistic context for the events of the soul is insufficient at best and damaging at worst. In order to heal the wounded, disoriented soul, it will not do to propose remedies that are crippled in their effectiveness by their implicit presumption that the prison in which the soul is trapped is the whole of reality. But the escape from this prison is not easy. Re-orientation requires a revolution of consciousness so profound that it may well threaten the sanity of an unguided *ego*. The *ego* must be wholly and painfully transformed in order for the encounter with the Angel to occur. Spiritual birth requires the death of the *ego*. As Jung would have it, "A victory for the Self is always a defeat for the *ego*."

---

30. Corbin, *Avicenna*, 263-64.
31. Corbin, *Le paradoxe du monothèisme*, 241.

Disciples of Khidr

The meeting with the angelic Guide, which marks the dawn of consciousness, is only the beginning. The voyage has just begun to free itself from the unconsciousness of ignorance of the soul

> must pass through the Darkness; this is a terrifying and painful experience, for it ruins and destroys all the patencies and norms on which the natural man lived and depended —a true "descent into hell," the hell of the unconscious.[32]

To attain to the Water of life, this passage must be made. But what can be done to guard against the dangers? "Sohravardi considers that anyone who sets out on the spiritual way without a serious philosophical training, lays himself open to all the traps and illusions, all the troubles that nowadays go by the name of schizophrenia."[33] As we have seen Corbin, like Paracelsus, warns "against any confusion of the *Imaginatio vera*, as the alchemists said, with fantasy, 'that cornerstone of the mad,'"[34] and this requires access not merely to rationality but to the true intellect. Therefore it is necessary to distinguish between the two different facets of the imaginative faculty.

> Our visionary theosophers...are no less aware than we are of the perils of the *imaginary*... [For] the Imagination possesses a twofold aspect and fulfils a twofold function. On the one hand there is the passive imagination, the imagination that "re-presents" or "re-produces" (*khayal*). As such the imagination is, quite simply, the storehouse that garners all the images perceived by the *sensorium*, this latter being the mirror in which all the perceptions of the external senses converge. On the other hand there is the active Imagination (*mutakhayyilah*). This active Imagination is caught between two fires. It can submit docilely to the injunctions of the estimatory faculty (*wahmiyah*), in which case it is the

---

32. Corbin, *Avicenna*, 159.
33. Corbin, "Epistle on the State of Childhood," 56.
34. Corbin, *Swedenborg and Esoteric Islam*, 17.

rational animal that assesses things in a way related to that of animals. The *rational animal* can and in fact does fall prey to all the deliriums and monstrous inventions of the imaginary, obstinately rejecting the judgment of the intellect. Yet the active Imagination can...put itself exclusively at the service of the intellect—of, that is to say, the *intellectus sanctus* as this functions in both philosophers and prophets. ...

The whole task consists in purifying and liberating one's inner being so that the intelligible realities perceived on the *imaginal* level may be reflected in the mirror of the *sensorium* and be translated into visionary perception. We have, I think, already gone a considerable distance beyond the limits imposed by psychology.... [T]he vision of the angel...does not emerge from the negativity of an *unconscious*, but descends from a level of a positively differentiated *supra-consciousness*.[35]

There is a difference between the hell of unconscious ignorance and the differentiated supra-consciousness from which the angel descends. It is not easy to distinguish them. The Master of Hades is always a deceiver. And so there arises the question of the Guide in every living spiritual tradition.

For the task of liberation and purification, Corbin provides little in the way of explicit, concrete, methodological guidance. He is wary of any answer that is general, collective, or dogmatic. His emphasis is on the personal and individual nature of the quest, and he tends to be suspicious of human spiritual masters. He says, not without humor, "Unlike modern philosophers of History, visionary theosophers always have someone—a personal messenger—who comes to give them instruction and to be their guide."[36] Always. He cites with approval the Iranian Sufi Master Abu'l-Hasan Kharraqani, "I am amazed at those disciples who declare that they require this or that master. You are perfectly well aware that I have never been taught by any man. God was my guide, though I have the greatest respect for all the masters."[37] It is because of Corbin's attraction to the

35. Corbin, *Temple and Contemplation*, 265-66.
36. *Ibid.*, 264.
37. Corbin, *Creative Imagination*, 33. Abu'l-Hasan Kharraqani, d. 1034.

notion of the invisible personal guide that the Shi'ite doctrine of the Hidden Imam has such appeal for him. He speaks favorably of those among the Shi'ite esotericists who look with a certain disfavor on those Sufis who require a human master.[38]

This question of the relationship between the Voyager and his Guide is of the first importance, practically speaking, and is perhaps the central question of method in the spiritual sciences. Here Corbin takes a position that, not surprisingly, is at odds with many of the more dogmatically minded. Corbin always favors the individual over the collective and over anything that threatens to collapse downward into dogma.

Here it is pertinent to raise the question of Corbin's relation to what is known in the West as Traditional Philosophy or Neotraditionalism. There is a large literature on Tradition, or *philosophia perennis*, much of which is relevant to the understanding of Islam in the West. Corbin's Iranian colleague and friend, Seyyed Hossein Nasr, must be counted among the Traditionalists allied with the school of Coomaraswamy, Schuon, Lings, and Burckhardt.[39] Many of the Western expositors of Traditional philosophy trace their roots in the West to René Guénon. Their emphasis tends to be upon what they see as the "immutabilities" of traditional religion as it has been expressed in the major religions of the world, as well as on what Schuon has called the Transcendent Unity of religions. Their outlook is ecumenical but has a rather rigid feel to it, especially the work of Guénon. Corbin refers disparagingly to "a certain Tradition" made up, as it were in the West and opposes to it the freedom of thought and Imagination that he found attractive. It is certainly true that Corbin shared not at all Guénon's distaste for the modern Western world. Kathleen Raine has commented on their differences:

> "Tradition" as understood by followers of Guénon, for all their
> insistence on "revealed" knowledge and the metaphysical order,
> seems unconnected to the living source itself and highly suspi-

38. See, for example, Corbin's *En islam iranienne*, Vol. 1, 18.

39. See, for instance, S. H. Nasr, *Knowledge and the Sacred*, Chapters 2 and 3; Frithjof Schuon, *The Essential Writings of Frithjof Schuon*, ed. S. H. Nasr; and for a survey, Antoine Faivre's *Access to Western Esotericism*.

cious of those very inner worlds from which it ultimately derives.
That inner world both Blake and Jung affirm, and both appreci-
ated the value of the alchemical symbolism and the alchemical
"work" of self transformation.... I find what is missing from the
work of Guénon and his followers in the writings of Henry
Corbin...whose term, the "imaginal" describes the order to which
Blake's Prophetic Books belong—as it does Jung's world of psyche
and its archetypes. Corbin understands that sacred tradition is
itself without meaning outside that context.... Corbin thus harmo-
nizes what one might call the Protestant vision of Blake and Jung,
their insistence on discovering the truth "within the human
breast," and the recognition of a tradition of sacred knowledge
embodied in every civilization and all mythologies."[40]

However it is quite clear that Corbin would never advocate abandon-
ment of traditional religious doctrines. He is too aware of the dangers of the
Darkness and of the necessity for the exoteric formulation of esoteric truths.
The inner Guide is a goal to be sought but not by falling into the Formless.
Guidance and initiation are required in some form. Corbin's relation to
Traditionalism remains somewhat ambiguous but perhaps can be clarified by
Arthur Versluis' comment that, "Christianity is so radical precisely be-
cause it offers a direct or immediate relation to God in the Trinity." This is
particularly true of the German Protestant tradition to which Corbin was
so attracted.[41]

It will be helpful to provide an account of the meaning of initiation
and the status of the Guide in the esoteric traditions of Islam, both Sunni
and Shi'ite, in order to help place Corbin's discussion in an Islamic context.[42] In the Islamic view all genuine religions have their origins in
Revelation. It may be the Primordial Revelation of nature itself, or it

---

40. Kathleen Raine, *Golgonooza: City of Imagination. Last Studies in William Blake*, 4.

41. Versluis, *Theosophia: Hidden Dimensions of Christianity*, 12. Versluis provides a good
summary of the esoteric Protestant tradition which Corbin knew so well: Jacob Boehme, Friedrich
Christoph Oetinger, Franz von Baader, and others, though he does not treat Martin Luther and
Johann Georg Hamann in that work.

42. This account is based on Nasr, *Knowledge and the Sacred*, "Shi'ism and
Sufism," and *Religion and the Order of Nature*.

may come through a prophet sent to carry a divine message. Though many may be satisfied with the outer form of the religion—the *Shari'a*—it is the deepest purpose of human existence to journey from the outward to the inward and so "return creation to its origin." This requires a spiritual Path—a *Tariqah*. In order to penetrate to the inner meaning of Revelation, the seeker must first of all conform to the outer requirements of the particular religion in question but in addition must have access to the grace (*barakah*) that has its source in that Revelation. In Islam the source of that grace is Muhammad. In order for that grace to effect the transmutation of the soul, which is the essence of esoteric birth, several things are necessary. An initiation is required that attaches the disciple to a master, who must in turn be connected with the Prophet by means of an initiatic chain of transmission (*silsilah*). The master will by definition have command of a method for training the soul. And the disciple must gain sufficient knowledge of the doctrine of the nature of things to be an aid during the journey.[43] Both the Sunnis and the Shi'ites recognize Ali as the first recipient of the esoteric meaning of Revelation. The Prophet said: "I am the city of Knowledge, and 'Ali is its gate." In Sunni Sufism the grace of the Prophet passes from master to master. In Shi'ism the power of initiation and spiritual guidance (*walayah*) passed through Ali and Fatimah to the lineage of the Imams. Although Muhammad was the Seal of Prophecy and closed the cycle of Prophecy, the cycle of initiation remains open through the eternal presence of the Imams. It is the function of the Imams to protect and bear the esoteric meaning of Revelation and through their own presence to make possible the continued presence of the Muhammadan grace in the world. For the Shi'ite the Quest is to seek the encounter with the figure of the Hidden Imam as the inner spiritual Guide, who may appear to each disciple as the individualized Imam of the soul. It may happen in rare cases that the seeker can find this inner, personal Guide in a wholly, inward way. But for the

---

43. Nasr, "Shi'ism and Sufism," 17.

majority of disciples, a master in earthly form is required. It is dangerous to experiment with the development of the soul. Lacking a living connection to a Tradition, to an established Path, the isolated soul is easily lost in a wilderness of dangers.

The stakes could not be higher. The question is to whom do we entrust our souls? To the Church? To the Master? To the Imam? Certainly not to the *ego*. But when the *ego* falls apart, who will provide the vessel in which transformation can occur? In the modern West it increasingly has become the role of the psychoanalyst. For Freudians this is a secular figure; for some Jungians, a quasi-religious initiator.[44]

In *Creative Imagination in the Sufism of Ibn 'Arabi*, Corbin devotes considerable attention to the topic of the invisible guide. In a characteristic move he suggests that whether one has or does not have such a guide depends upon "a crucial existential decision." This decision

> —prefigures and conditions a whole chain of spiritual development with far-reaching consequences. For it announces either that each human being is *oriented* toward a quest for his personal invisible guide, or that he entrusts himself to the collective, magisterial authority as the intermediary between himself and Revelation.[45]

The echoes of Luther's condemnation of the Church are clear.

For Corbin Ibn al'Arabi is a symbol (as important perhaps as Suhrawardi) of the triumph of the individual soul over the servitude to rational philosophy and equally to the "God created in

---

44. Some of the vitriol aimed at Jung by the Traditionalists (and others) is explained by his perceived usurpation of a legitimate religious function. It seems to me that Jung for the most part understood the dangers of this, and that explains much of the ambiguity in his own perception of his role as Doctor/Priest. The problems of initiation for Protestants were quite clear to him—he commented that he hardly ever had a patient who was a practicing Catholic, but plenty who were Protestants.

45. Corbin, *Creative Imagination*, 33.

dogmas."[46] Ibn al'Arabi's triumph "is the fruit of a long quest, the work of an entire lifetime...."[47] And this is because of his orientation towards the personal face of the Lord.

> Ibn 'Arabi was, and never ceased to be, the disciple of
> an invisible master, a mysterious prophet figure to whom
> a number of traditions, both significant and obscure, lend
> features which relate him, or tend to identify him, with
> Elijah, with St. George, and still others. Ibn 'Arabi was
> above all the disciple of Khidr (Khadir).[48]

In a real sense the central questions for Corbin's Voyager are "Who is Khidr?", and "What does it mean to be a disciple of Khidr?" It is the answer to these questions that will determine the course of a spiritual voyage. In Norman O. Brown's analysis, what Corbin and Massignon have shown us is that these are the central questions for the Prophetic Tradition after Mohammad, and these questions are the legacy of Islam for the Western, post-Christian world.[49] They stand at the center of Corbin's work.

Corbin outlines the *Qur'anic* source for this Person. In *Sura XVIII* the figure that came to be interpreted as Khidr, appears in an enigmatic episode. Moses and his servant travel to "the meeting place of the two seas." There he meets an unnamed messenger:

---

46. Corbin's interpretation of Ibn 'Arabi is controversial. Regarding Corbin's *Creative Imagination in the Sufism of Ibn 'Arabi*, Chittick writes: "Corbin's rhetorical flourishes and passion for his subject put his work into a unique category... [He] is concerned with his own philosophical project... Any reader of *Creative Imagination* soon begins to wonder where Ibn al-'Arabi ends and Corbin begins. The lines are not clear, especially if one does not have access to the Arabic texts. Certainly we come to realize the Ibn al-'Arabi is a precious larder from which all sorts of delicious vittles can be extracted. But most people familiar with the original texts would agree that Corbin has highly individual tastes." Chittick, *The Sufi Path of Knowledge: Ibn 'Arabi's Metaphysics of the Imagination*, xix.

47. Corbin, *Creative Imagination*, 44.

48. *Ibid.*, 32.

49. Brown, "The Prophetic Tradition."

He is represented as Moses' guide, who initiates Moses "into the science of predestination." Thus he reveals himself to be the repository of an inspired divine science, superior to the law (*shari'a*); thus Khidr is superior to Moses in so far as Moses is a prophet invested with the mission of revealing a *shari'a*. He reveals to Moses precisely the secret, mystic truth (*haqiqa*) that transcends the *shari'a*, and this explains why the spirituality inaugurated by Khidr is free from the servitude of the literal religion.[50]

The function of Khidr as a "person-archetype" for both Suhrawardi and Ibn 'Arabi is

to reveal each disciple to himself.
    ... He leads each disciple to his own theophany...because that theophany corresponds to his own "inner heaven," to the form of his own being, to his eternal individuality... Khidr's mission consists in enabling you to attain to the "Khidr of your being," for it is in this inner depth, in this "prophet of your being," that springs the Water of Life at the foot of the mystic Sinai, pole of the microcosm, center of the world, etc.[51]

And speaking of the study of Ibn 'Arabi's work itself, Corbin writes,

It goes without saying that the form in which each of us receives the master's thought *conforms* to his "inner heaven"; that is the very principle of the theophanism of Ibn 'Arabi, who for that reason can only guide *each* man individually to what he alone is capable of *seeing*, and not bring him to any collective pre-established dogma....[52]

Recall the statement from Corbin's work on Avicenna: "The more perceptions and representations of the universe each monad [soul] integrates, the more it unfolds its own perfection and differs from every other." Here we encounter this expansive ideal of the fundamental freedom of

    50. Corbin, *Creative Imagination*, 55.
    51. *Ibid.*, 61.
    52. *Ibid.*, 75-76.

unity through plurality again. If the soul attains to the "Khidr of its being," to its perfection, then "you can indeed do what Khidr *does*."

> And this is perhaps the secret reason for which the doctrine of Ibn 'Arabi was so feared by the adepts of the literal religion, of the historical faith...of the dogma imposed uniformly upon all. He...who is the disciple of Khidr possesses sufficient inner strength to seek freely the teaching of all masters.[53]

This unwavering emphasis on spiritual freedom in Corbin's work should not be misunderstood. The personal Guide is not chosen by the *ego*. The dangers of subjective dilettantism or of an ill-prepared soul are clearly laid out: psychosis and schizophrenia have already been mentioned. It does not suffice to want Khidr as a Guide, and souls as strong as Ibn 'Arabi are rare. In any case such an event as the meeting with the Guide can be so private, so intensely personal, that it cannot really be spoken of or revealed. Shayegan, who knew Corbin well, comments, "Whether Corbin...may have been personally initiated by the hermeneutic Angel whose pedagogical function he never ceased to valorize, we will never know."[54]

Certainly Corbin knew well that Islam, as any religion, requires a doctrine, a literal outside, a Law, which must exist in order for there to be anything in which to conceal the hidden meanings. Nonetheless it is clear where his sympathies lie. The Ismailis have long been known among detractors and supporters both for the priority which they give to the esoteric at the expense of the exoteric. Corbin calls to our attention more than once, with a kind of longing, another symbolic event of that epochal twelfth century—the Ismaili Declaration at Alamut.

> Alamut! The stronghold lost in the high solitary summits of the Elburz mountain chain, to the southwest of the Caspian Sea, where, on 8 August 1164, the Great Resurrection was proclaimed.... Undoubtedly, though, a proclamation of this type pertains to that spiritual history, the events of which

---

53. Corbin, *Creative Imagination*, 67.
54. Shayegan, *Henry Corbin: La topographie spirituelle*, 14.

occur unnoticed by external official history, because their
implications cannot be suspected by historians whose
attention is given exclusively to the latter. In any case,
the proclamation of the Great Resurrection was intended
to be the triumph of absolute spiritual hermeneutics,
since it purely and simply abolished the *shari'at* and its
observances, in order to permit the reign of the spiritual
Idea...alone to subsist.[55]

But, he continues,

Here again, the impatience of the soul provoked a pre-
mature anticipation of eschatology... [The major Shi'ite
traditions] continued carefully to maintain...the coexist-
ence of the esoteric and the exoteric, for as long as the
human condition remains what it is in the present world,
the soul cannot manifest itself without being contained
in a material body.[56]

As much as we might long for spiritual freedom and emanci-
pation from all external laws, all public decrees, we cannot be
entirely freed from "the outer" without falling into chaos. That
condition is for the Angels alone, as we shall see.[57]

The question of the inner Guide versus the human Master
raises the question of the relation of the spiritual and the political.
It is often not at all clear in reading Corbin that there is any politically important component in the history of the Shi'ites. In fact he
often remarks that it is when Shi'ism does come to political power
that it is most in danger of betraying its inner trust. Success on the
political front is the "most formidable and paradoxical ordeal that
an esoteric religion may undergo."[58] It is in fact just the "sacral-
ization" of institutions that is the prime symptom of metaphysical

55. Corbin, *Swedenborg and Esoteric Islam*, 95.

56. *Ibid.*, 95-96.

57. For an extended account of the significance of the events at Alamut
according to one of Corbin's most illustrious students, see Jambet, *La grande
résurrection d'Alamût*.

58. Corbin, *Swedenborg and Esoteric Islam*, 95.

"secularization."[59] He goes so far as to say, "The very idea of associating such concepts as 'power' and the 'spiritual' implies an initial secularization." In the West the failure of the priesthood to gain secular power was the cause of the projection of "a fiction of that same power into the supernatural."[60] His exclusively spiritual view of things makes him a poor guide to political or social history. Brown remarks that, "Corbin, indispensable in other ways, refuses to see any political dimension whatsoever" in Ismaili or Shi'ite history.[61] It is perhaps unfair to accuse him of being politically naïve when his purpose is not to write political history. Yet it is wise to be aware of the limitations inherent in an exclusively spiritual perspective on history, particularly in view of the fact that the issue here is the source of legitimate authority in matters of soul. A spirituality that is blind to political realities is in danger of falling into folly.[62]

And yet it may be that this is precisely the point we can take from his work. Whatever his shortcomings as a social historian, Corbin's writings can be understood as political. By showing that a metaphysics of individuation is necessary to counter the threat of totalitarianisms, he makes it clear that any spirituality that holds itself aloof from the temporal is doomed to the ineffectuality of the abstract. Through his attempt to reinstate the Image in its rightful place in the scheme of things, Corbin attempts to restore balance to the lives of each of us and thereby to the social world as well. James Hillman has seen this aspect of his work

---

59. See e.g., Corbin, "Du message de la philosophie iranienne," from *Philosophie iranienne et philosophie comparée*, 132.

60. Corbin, *Creative Imagination*, 16-17.

61. Brown, "The Prophetic Tradition," 66, n. 15. Corbin did not, it seems, share the activist political sensibilities of his mentor Massignon. It was in fact the latter's refusal to abide by the stated but unwritten rule of the Eranos Conferences that politics should not be discussed that led to his not being invited back after the 1955 *Tagung*.

62. The interested reader should see the biased Steven M. Wasserstrom, *Religion After Religion: Gershom Scholem, Mircea Eliade, and Henry Corbin at Eranos*. Wasserstrom raises politically correct questions concerning the relation of Corbin's mysticism to contemporary politics. Wasserstrom's assessment of Corbin's position and his importance is at odds with mine, although a thorough discussion would require considerable space.

clearly. In reference to the nightmares of terrorism in the contemporary Islamic world he says:

> Corbin said to me one time, "What is wrong with the Islamic world is that it has destroyed its images, and without these images that are so rich in its tradition, they are going crazy because they have no containers for their extraordinary imaginative power." His work...can be seen as political action of the first order: it was meeting terrorism, fanaticism, nihilism right at its roots in the psyche.[63]

It is the ideal of the balanced life that is at the heart of the Islamic vision. Mohammad was simultaneously mystic and warrior, philosopher and statesman. And the biographies of many of the spiritual figures who Corbin represents tell a story of political engagement, not only scholarly, spiritual retreat. We have already heard Nasr on just this point: Sufism enables one to "lead an intense inner contemplative life while outwardly remaining most active in a world which he moulds according to his inner spiritual nature, instead of becoming its prisoner..."[64]

While Corbin's passionate defense of the centrality and the cosmic function of the individual is not in question, there may remain uneasiness about the relation between esoteric doctrines and the democratic ideals that of the West.[65] Esoteric spiritual disciplines have never been given over to the masses in theory. The hidden mysteries cannot be public. Recall the remarks of the Sixth Imam: "as for the rest, they are as the foam rolled along by the torrent." Our democratic ideals have sometimes been interpreted as meaning that all men are created equal. What this should signify is that all people must be free to find their Angel. If all people were truly equal, then the reign of totalitarian regimes, whether political, reli-

---

63. Hillman, *Archetypal Psychology: A Brief Account*, 142-3.

64. Nasr, "Shi'ism and Sufism," 37.

65. The question of how one might be both a Platonist and democratic is treated by Hillman in *The Soul's Code: In Search of Character and Calling*.

gious, or scientific, based on denial of individuality, would be unavoidable. Corbin presents an entire cosmology that guarantees an ontology of the unique.

Yet this individualism cannot mean that we are reduced to nihilistic relativism. Corbin is no relativist. The subtle body does bear the signs of a life well or poorly lived. There are consequences. You do make your own Heaven and your own Hell. There are absolute demands made upon us all. But this does not require a public dogma: this absolute is based upon the necessity for multiple faces of Divinity appearing differently to each person. Each of us must encounter our own Angel. This doctrine derives in part from Ibn 'Arabi, who, in Chittick's words,

> affirms an ultimate ground that must present itself through relativity and, more important for human destiny, he stresses the personal dimension of this absolute ground, a dimension that is oriented towards human happiness. In short, the Shaykh provides a way of seeing religious teachings as both historically relative and as personally absolute.[66]

A Sufi saying has it that "there are as many paths to God as there are human souls."[67] This is clearly in the spirit of Corbin.

This perhaps explains how Corbin can say that Averroes was

> inspired by the idea that not all minds have the same degree of discernment: to some men the literal aspect…is addressed, while others are capable of understanding the hidden meaning… He knew that if what only the latter can understand were revealed to the former, the result would be psychoses and social disasters.[68]

We democrats can see the dangers of monarchy and fascism with some clarity. We understand the dangers of democracy less well. A democracy which exists within the Faustian space of the modern world and has thereby lost any sense of the modes of being and levels of knowing can no longer know either what a person is or what wisdom is. We have been taught

---

66. Chittick, *Imaginal Worlds*, 11.
67. *Ibid.*, 4.
68. Corbin, *Creative Imagination*, 13.

that knowledge will make us free. But at the same time, we have come to confuse knowledge with wisdom, to believe that all knowledge is equally valuable, that anything we can do we should do, and that by making all knowledge available to everyone, our problems will be solved. The metaphysical perspective that gives priority to facts is blind to persons.

There is a fine line between the repression of individuality by totalitarian regimes (or totalizing discourses) and its evaporation into nihilism through the triumph of relativism, spiritual confusion, and the domination of the dis-Oriented. It is the virtue of Corbin's work to indicate how we might understand ourselves in order to avoid both Orwell's *1984* and Huxley's *Brave New World*.

CHAPTER SIX

Ta'wil and Prophetic Philosophy

The Key to the Soul and the Key to the World

Prophetic philosophy is based upon the occurrence of Revelation, the descent of the Divine Presence into Creation. A prophet is not a someone who foretells the future. A Prophet is a Messenger, a carrier of the Divine Word. In the Abrahamic Tradition as conceived in Islamic thought, there are many degrees of prophecy, ranked by their nearness to God, and there have been a multitude of prophets. Only a few of these had the task of establishing new religions: Noah, Abraham, Moses, Jesus, and Mohammad. In Judaism, Christianity, and Islam, as well as Mazdaism (though the religion of Zoroaster is not mentioned explicitly in the *Qur'an*), the Revelation is tied in various ways to a Book. The central fact for the prophetic philosophers of Islam is the existence of the Sacred Book. The Revelation of a text makes the idea of understanding its true meaning and the hermeneutic situation that this implies the central issue for human life. But in the context of Divine Revelation, "text" takes on a meaning not generally available to modern philosophies of language.

The hermeneutic key to understanding prophetic philosophy came to Corbin through Heidegger, but the prelude to this lies in Luther, and through him, in the Scholastic tradition of speculative grammar in which the notion of *significatio passiva* was crucial. Luther's insight into its meaning is foundational for Corbin:

> In the presence of the Psalm verse *In justitia tua libera me,* [Luther] experienced a movement of revolt and despair: what can there be in common between this attribute of justice

and *my* deliverance? ...[He] perceived in a sudden flash (and his entire personal theology was to result from this experience) that this attribute must be understood in its *significatio passiva*, that is to say, *thy* justice whereby we are made into just men, *thy* holiness whereby we are hallowed, etc.... Similarly...[for Ibn 'Arabi] the divine attributes are qualifications that we impute to the Divine Essence...as we experience it in ourselves.[1]

Corbin says that this insight provided the key for understanding the meaning of mystical philosophy in Islam. It provides the connection between the Divine attributes and those attributes as they appear in the created world. Upon the *significatio passiva* hinges an entire cosmology, an entire metaphysics of creation. It provides another way of understanding the connection between metaphysics, the intellect, and the transformation of the soul:

One simple example: the advent of being in this theosophy, is the placing of being in the imperative: KN [Arabic], *Esto* (in the second person, not *fiat*). This is primary, it is neither *ens* nor *esse*, but *esto*. "Be!"[2] This imperative inauguration of being, is the divine imperative in the active sense...but considered in the being that it makes be, the being that we are, it is the same imperative, but in its *significatio passiva*....

One could say, I think, that this is the triumph of the hermeneutic as *Verstehen*, to know that what we understand in truth, is never that which we experience and submit to, that which we suffer in ourselves alone. Hermeneutics does not consist in deliberating on concepts, it is essentially the unveiling of that which takes place in us, the unveiling of that which we make issue from ourselves, a conception, a vision, a projection, when our *passion* becomes *action*, an active suffering, prophetic-poietic.[3]

1. Corbin, *Creative Imagination*, 300, n. 25.
2. *Soit*! in French.
3. Corbin, *Henry Corbin*, ed. Jambet, 25.

Hermeneutics is an unveiling. It is not an operation on a text in anything like the modern sense of criticism, whether historical or literary. It is not a linguistic exercise at all in the usual sense or a conceptual manipulation based upon reasoning. It is an uncovering, a process by which we participate in the blossoming not of ideas or words, but of images. It occurs in the imaginal space between the soul and the text. From the perspective of the metaphysics of Presence, ideas and words as we have come to understand them occupy a space equivalent to that which is occupied by objects. They are the dead shells of the images, the visions which take place in us and which it is the task of hermeneutics to unveil. By conjoining hermeneutics and the Imperative to Be!, Corbin forces the insight upon us that understanding as unveiling is our most passionate mode of being.

The imperative to "Be!" is the source of the intensification of existence upon which is the basis of Mulla Sadra's metaphysics of individuation. The command is not from the *ego*, but from the Lord. And this be-ing is neither thinking nor acting, but a prophetic-poietic passion that combines both: it is imagining. Here is the connection between the merely human and the divine. Without this active movement in us we remain trapped in subjectivity. Corbin writes,

> But that implies that this person is an *agent* only in a superficial and metaphoric sense. More active than the person himself is the thought that is thought through him, the word that is spoken by him (and personified in him). And this thought of his thought is precisely what Nasir Tusi calls the Angel of his thought (or of this word or action). This Angel endows the soul with the aptitude for thinking it and rising by it; he is the Archetype, the finality without which a cause would never be a cause. He is the "destiny" of that soul.... The act of thinking is simultaneously a "being-thought" (*cogitor*) by the Angel.... [These propositions] describe a hermeneutic circle which fuses the schema of *angelology* with the process of *angelomorphosis*....[4]

---

4. Corbin, *Cyclical Time and Ismaili Gnosis*, 52-53.

This hermeneutic circle has a far larger circumference than that of agnostic philosophy: it includes the more-than-human. It is up to us, through our passion, to unveil it.

Of the utmost importance is Corbin's elision of prophetic and poetic. It is this connection with the Divine, realized through spiritual birth, or angelomorphosis as a never-ending process, which is impossible without the ontological reality of the Imagination, the spark of divine creativity in us *par excellence*. This Divine spark, personified as the Paraclete, is for Corbin the primary point of contact and communication among the Peoples of the Book. He is searching, in all his work, for the living source of prophetic religion in the Abrahamic tradition. It is found in part in the primordial and eternal reality of the individual, which defines the quest common to the three major monotheisms. In the end, this commonality rests upon the relation between these two modes of being: the prophetic and the poetic. "A *tradition* lives and transmits life only if it is a perpetual *rebirth*."[5] In this creative movement of the spirit lies the key to esoteric metaphysics. It is the pivot point around which all of Creation is ordered.

It is in this way that we must understand the transformational nature of hermeneutics and Corbin's use of the term phenomenology. "Hermeneutics is the proper form of the task of phenomenology."[6] This spiritual hermeneutics is the centerpiece of any philosophy worth pursuing. As Seyyed Hossein Nasr comments, Corbin's identification of phenomenology as a hermeneutics that has as its aim the disclosure of the hidden levels of being is at variance with the usual meaning of the term in Western philosophy. In the first place, it requires a belief in the reality of these other levels of being.[7]

For the Peoples of the Book, the primary fact is the existence of a revealed text, the word of God. In Islam the *Qur'an* occupies the place that Christ does in Christianity. For Christianity Christ is the Revelation, the Word. In Islam it is the Book itself.

---

5. Corbin, *History of Islamic Philosophy*, 366.
6. Corbin, *Henry Corbin*, ed. Jambet, 26.
7. Nasr, *Islamic Art and Spirituality*, 280.

> By its nature, at the heart of a prophetic religion—that is, a
> religion that professes the necessity of superhuman mediators
> between the divinity who inspires them and humanity as a
> whole—there is the *phenomenon of the Sacred Book* that
> every prophet who has the quality of a Messenger...brings
> to man. This phenomenon preeminently creates a "hermeneu-
> tic situation," the great issue being to know and understand
> the *true meaning* of the Book.[8]

But on this view of hermeneutics, it is impossible to interpret the
text without at the same time transforming the reader. Reading
becomes a liturgical act of transformation.

> But the mode of understanding is conditioned by the
> mode of being of him who understands; correspondingly,
> the believer's whole inner ethos derives from his mode
> of understanding. The lived situation is essentially
> *hermeneutical*, a situation, that is to say, in which the
> *true meaning* dawns on the believer and confers reality
> on his existence.[9]

Hermeneutics, far from being a critique of texts, results in
the conferral of reality on the believer, and ultimately, through
the encounter with the Angel, "promotion to the rank of Person."
It is only by virtue of this dual hermeneutic of the inner meaning
of the text and simultaneously of the soul that the Book lives in
the present. Without this, the literal letter of Revelation is only

> a dead body, an absurd husk.... [Without this inner
> sense] the *Qur'an* would have been dead for a long time;
> the *Qur'anic* Revelation would have long been only a
> museum of theological curiosities, which in fact is what
> it truly is in the eyes of the agnostics.[10]

---

8. Corbin, *Swedenborg and Esoteric Islam*, 37.
9. Corbin, *A History of Islamic Philosophy*, 1.
10. Corbin, *En islam iranienne*, Vol. 1, 128.

The kind of reading that is at issue here is far from unknown in the Christian tradition, but it faded from view along with the cosmology and the anthropology that support it. Ivan Illich has shown that during the 12th century in the Latin West a transition occurred from one kind of reading, one kind of hermeneutical situation, to another. And, in confirmation of Corbin's thesis, this is correlated with an alteration in the very experience of the self, of what it means to be an individual. In his study of the *Didascalicon* of Hugh of St. Victor, Illich details a change in the phenomenology of reading which is most striking in the present context. He takes Hugh as representative of the monastic approach to the Holy Book. He writes, "Reading, as Hugh perceives and interprets it, is an ontologically remedial technique."[11] It "is a remedy because it brings light back into a world from which sin banned it."[12] In the world of monastic readers, huddled over their parchment texts and reading aloud to themselves, the study of a text was an embodied activity, a challenge to the student's "heart and senses even more than to his stamina and brains."[13] "Study" meant something more akin to "sympathy" than to the abstract intellectual pursuit that it has become, and the enlightenment that is the end result of this study is not the light of Reason as the rationalists understand it. "The light of which Hugh speaks here brings man to a glow." Wisdom could shine through the pages of the Book, bringing the letters and symbols to light, "and kindle the eye of the reader."[14] Wisdom is not only in the heart, but in the object itself, in the world perceived with sympathy.

Illich, as an historian of technologies, argues that an essential part of this phenomenology lies in the physical act of reading itself that is closely tied to the literal presentation of the words on the page and on the necessity of oral reading of the Carolingian minuscule. Reading is a carnal, rhythmic, synaesthetic activity. David Abram, building on these insights, themselves built upon those of students of oral traditions, notably W. J. Ong and

---

11. Illich, *In the Vineyard of the Text: A Commentary to Hugh's Didascalicon,* 11.

12. *Ibid.,* 20.

13. *Ibid.,* 14.

14. *Ibid.,* 17-18.

M. Parry, points out that in Semitic languages the lack of written vowels requires a kind of participation on the part of the reader which is not necessary in the fully alphabetic script developed by the Greeks. To experience the consonantal language of Hebrew or Arabic, it must have the life literally breathed into it. This is still true today for the *Qur'an*. It is recited aloud. The letters must be activated by the breath. Not only this, but which vowels are chosen to be breathed is left to the reader. Neither the words nor their meanings simply lie there inert upon the page. Barry Holtz writes of the sacred texts of Judaism:

> We tend usually to think of reading as a passive occupation, but for the Jewish textual tradition, it was anything but that. Reading was a passionate and active grappling with God's living word. It held the challenge of uncovering secret meanings, unheard-of explanations, matters of great weight and significance....
> ...Torah called for a living and dynamic response...[and] remains unendingly alive.... For the tradition, the Torah *demands* interpretation.[15]

All of this applies equally to the Islamic tradition.[16] Abram's central claim and Illich's as well is that for such a phenomenology of reading to exist, the text must not be abstract and disembodied: it must remain connected to the body, the breath, and the world. According to Corbin, such a phenomenology and the hermeneutic it requires maintains in existence a relation of the soul to the text of the Book and to the Cosmos, which we have lost. What arose with the alphabetic technology invented by the Greeks and inherited by us was an abstract use of language and a sense of the text as fixed, final, and finally public that we take for granted today. All texts are exoteric for us, including the text of Nature. And at the same time, by a kind of symmetry, the fixation of the public text is accompanied by the implosion of the self into a private interiority that is understood as

---

15. Quoted in Abram, *The Spell of the Sensuous*, 243-44.
16. See, for instance, Nasr, "Oral Transmission and the Book in Islamic Education."

subjective. And so, thanks to our "history of being," we confound the esoteric with the subjective (and therefore the "unreal") and the exoteric with the objective (and therefore the "real.") Paradoxically, by severing the inner and the outer, by banishing all sense of interiority from the world and losing connection to the Word, language is increasingly experienced as occurring in the head, a wholly human creation. If only humans speak, then there is no Word, no Text.[17]

---

17. In a strikingly similar interpretation of the history of the West, especially of the 12th century, F. Edward Cranz put forward the thesis that the transition from "ancient" consciousness to our "modern" one is a transition from the "extensive self" to the "intensive self." For Aristotle, as we saw above, "the soul is somehow all things." Cranz writes:

> The ancients—and by the ancients I mean the Greeks, the Romans, and the Graeco-Roman Christians—the ancients experienced an awareness open to what lay around them, and they experienced no sense of dichotomy between their awareness and everything else. What they found in their own minds or intellects was of like character with much of what was outside it; what they found in the world could in large part move directly into their minds and be possessed by it. There was an ontological continuity between what happened in their intellects and what happened in the kosmos or world. Cranz, unpub. ms, "Reorientation of Western Thought."

This "extensive self" "was in the fullest sense part of a single realm of being and indeed, potentially identical with it." The kind of knowledge that is open to this self is, in Cranz's terms, "conjunctive." During the 12th century in the Christian West a reorientation (Cranz's term, but notice the consonance with Corbin) of the categories of thought and experience occurred. The new categories of the intensive self include dichotomous forms of knowing ("disjunctive" knowing), that is a split between the knower and the known, a distinction between meanings and things (language as a human system as opposed to the "things themselves" outside of language), and a rationality which depends upon coherence within language. Knowledge comes to "lack all immediacy." This 12th century reorientation gave birth to the modern self and all that comes with it. Cranz himself was dubious as to whether one could ever "go back." Corbin, of course, believes one can.

Cranz's brief but seminal writings remain largely unpublished. The quotes *supra* are from "The Reorientation of Western Thought c. 1100 A.D.: The Break with the Ancient Tradition and Its Consequences for Renaissance and Reformation," delivered at the Duke University Center for Medieval and Renaissance Studies, March 24, 1982. See also Cranz, "1100 AD: A Crisis for Us?" from *De Litteris: Occassional Papers in the Humanities*; and for a short discussion of his work, see Charles Radding, *A World Made by Men: Cogition and Society, 400-1200.*

The story that Illich and Abram tell of the phenomenology of the text is perhaps only one way in which the connection to the Word may be lost. In whatever form it takes, the loss of connection between the external, public form of the Book and the meaning hidden within it gives rise to a drama common to all the religions of the Book:

> If the true meaning of this Book is the interior meaning, hidden under the literal appearance, from the moment that men fail to recognize or refuse this interior meaning, from that moment they destroy the integrity of the Word, of the Logos, and then begins the drama of the "Lost Speech."[18]

From the moment we refuse the interiority of the text or of the world, then the world is turned inside out. The task of hermeneutics is to recover this living, integral Word and, through this, to make possible the Event at the edge of the exoteric cosmos which is the Great Inversion.

Corbin's understanding of Islamic spirituality, and in the end any spirituality, is centered on a characteristically Shi'ite notion of hermeneutics, spiritual exegesis, or *ta'wil*:

> [It] is the most characteristic mental operation of all our Spiritu-als, Neoplatonists, Ishraqiyun, Sufis, Ismailian theosophists.... [I]t finally appears as the mainspring of every spirituality, in the measure to which it furnishes the means of going beyond all con-formisms, all servitudes to the letter, all opinions ready-made.[19]

While it is not tied to the formulations of official exoteric dogma, this *ta'wil* is neither arbitrary nor unconstrained:

---

18. [French: "*Parole Perdue*"], Corbin, "Harmonia Abrahamica," preface to *Évangile de Barnabé*, 81.

19. Corbin, *Avicenna*, 28. Chittick points out that Corbin's conception of the term *ta'wil* is exclusively Shi'ite and that this led him to misconstrue Ibn 'Arabi's position, as well perhaps as that of Sunni Islam in general. See Chittick, *The Sufi Path of Knowledge*, 199-202 and notes. In this context it is useful to read Adams' for the most part laudatory review of Corbin's work in "The Hermeneutics of Henry Corbin," where he strongly emphasizes Corbin's Shi'ite orientation and cautions against reading Corbin as an "impartial" historian of religion.

> [W]e are concerned with spiritual hermeneutics that rigorous,
> systematic, and highly complex, in full possession of method,
> and vivified by a spirituality that cannot be ignored if there is a
> true desire to interpret (for that is the actual meaning of the Greek
> word *hermeneia*, hermeneutics).[20]

Ta'wil does not construct anything. Rather, a multidimensional world is discovered "by virtue of a principle of equilibrium and harmony."[21]

> In Islamic gnosis, the Balance signifies the equilibrium
> between Light and Darkness.... The visible aspect of a
> being presupposes its equilibration by an invisible and
> celestial counterpart; the apparent and exoteric (*zahir*)
> is equilibrated by the occulted and esoteric (*batin*).[22]

All things visible are kept in harmony by the counterweight provided by the correspondences between the spiritual and corporeal worlds. And the Science of the Balance is the *ta'wil*. It is akin to alchemy, for "the Balance is the principle that measures the intensity of the Soul's desire during its descent through matter." It is the alchemist's task to "measure the desire of the Soul of the World." The Science of the Balance affirms the ontological necessity of the counterweight provided by the other world through an analogical form of knowledge that raises up the beings it perceives, following the gradations of the hierarchy of the worlds.[23] "It is not theory; it is an initiation to vision."[24]

The experience of this hermeneutics is interior, but not subjective, since it is just by means of the spiritual birth which *ta'wil* signals that the world opens to reveal its Divine Face. *Ta'wil* is a kind of meditative, imaginative thinking that proceeds by means of images, not concepts.

---

20. Corbin, *Swedenborg and Esoteric Islam*, 39.
21. Corbin, *Creative Imagination*, 93.
22. Corbin, *Temple and Contemplation*, 57.
23. *Ibid.*, 55-57.
24. Corbin, *Creative Imagination*, 93.

The way of reading and of comprehending to which I refer presupposes, in the strict sense of the word, a *theosophia*, that is, the mental or visionary penetration of an entire hierarchy of spiritual universes that are not discovered by means of syllogisms, because they do not reveal themselves except through a certain mode of cognition, a *hierognosis* that unites the speculative knowledge of traditional information to the most personal interior experience, for, in the absence of the latter, technical models alone would be transmitted, and these would be doomed to a rapid decline.[25]

It is the basis of prophetic philosophy as a whole, for without this living Word, in the presence only of the literal letter of the Law, there can be no true philosophy:

From the very beginning...Shi'ite thinking has given sustenance to a prophetic type of philosophy which corresponds to a prophetic religion. A prophetic philosophy presupposes a type of thought which does not allow itself to be bound either by the historical past, or by the letter of the dogmatic form in which the teachings of this past are consolidated, or by the limits imposed by the resources and laws of rational Logic.[26]

This freedom of the poiesis of spiritual birth in a kind of counterpoint to the constraints of the letter of prophetic revelation is emphasized again and again in Corbin's writings, and it is only by holding firmly to this that we can come to understand the meaning of a true prophetic philosophy for him.

Everything depends upon the interiorization and true interpretation of Revelation. And this in turn depends upon the cosmic correspondences revealed by the science of the Balance. Visible reality has its complement, its completion, in the other world. *Ta'wil* must be understood as one half of a pair: *Ta'wil - Tanzil*.

Tanzil properly designates positive religion, the letter of the

---

25. Corbin, *Swedenborg and Esoteric Islam*, 38.
26. Corbin, *History of Islamic Philosophy*, 24-25.

> Revelation dictated to the Prophet by the Angel. It is to *cause*
> *the descent* of this Revelation from the higher world. *Ta'wil*
> is, etymologically and inversely, to *cause to return*, to lead
> back, to restore to one's origin and to the place where one
> comes home, consequently to return to the true and original
> meaning of a text.[27]

The phenomenologies of harmony and equilibrium expressed by
descent and return are expressed in other ways by other conjoined terms
of fundamental importance:

> *Majaz* is figure, metaphor, while *haqiqat* is the truth that is
> real, the reality that is true, the essence, the Idea.... But let us
> note well that the spiritual meaning to be disengaged from the
> letter is not to be thought of as constituting a metaphorical
> meaning; it is the *letter* itself that is the *metaphor*.... The *ta'wil*
> causes the letter to *regress* to its true and original meaning....
> The same is true of the pair of terms *zahir* and *batin*. *Zahir*
> is the exoteric, the apparent, the patency of the letter, the
> Law, the text of the *Qur'an*. *Zahir* holds the same relation-
> ship to *Batin* as *Majaz* does to *Haqiqat*; the *Ta'wil* must
> lead it back to the Hidden Reality, to the esoteric truth, with
> which it symbolizes.[28]

To enter into this cosmology we must see that the most fundamental premises which underlie the modern meaning of "reading"
and of "text" are no more valid here than a narrowly linguistic use of
the term "hermeneutics." "Metaphor," "hermeneutics," and the "literal" meaning are not literary concepts for the same reason that the
angelic hierarchies are not anthropomorphic. Our presence is a dim
reflection of the Angel, and poetic metaphor derives its truth and its
energy from the levels of meaning and the correspondences within a world
perceived as symbol, from the powers of the Angels to draw beings
upward: from the Desire of the Soul of the World. *Ta'wil* applies not only
to reading the text of a Book, but to the interpretation of the cosmic text

---

27. Corbin, *Avicenna*, 28-29.
28. *Ibid.*, 29-30.

as well, since the Cosmos itself is the Primordial Revelation.[29] The idea of the world as itself a divine Book is central to Islamic cosmology. Nasr writes,

> The order of nature is seen in the Islamic perspective to derive according to Divine Wisdom from the prototype of all existence in the Divine Order, the prototype which is identified according to the language of *Quranic* cosmology with the Pen...and the Guarded Tablet.... God wrote by means of the Pen, which symbolizes the active Principle of Creation, the realities of all things, upon the Guarded Tablet, which remains eternally with Him, while through the cosmogenic act, the realities written upon the Tablet were made to descend to lower levels of existence and finally to the world of nature.[30]

The *ta'wil* only effects transformation because it transmutes the world into symbols which by their very nature transcend the distinction between the outer and the inner, the subject and the object, and by interiorizing the cosmos, by revealing the *Imago mundi*, transform and lead the soul beyond the literal understanding of the world and to its truth, to its meeting with the Angel.

> Beneath the idea of exegesis appears that of the Guide (the *exegete*), and beneath the idea of an *exegesis* we glimpse that of an *exodus*, of a "departure from Egypt," which is an exodus from metaphor and the slavery to the letter, from *exile* and the *Occident* of exoteric appearance to the *Orient* of the original and hidden Idea.[31]

The fundamental structure of Reality takes the form of Descent and Return. The world is distant from the Divine to the extent that it is trapped in the dogmatic, the fixed, the literal, to the extent that we can only see the apparent, the letter. When the soul can stand at the

---

29. *Ibid.,* 31.
30. Nasr, *Religion and the Order of Nature,* 60. See also Chittick, *Self-Disclosure of God.*
31. Corbin, *Avicenna,* 29.

edge of the cosmos and see that cosmos and everything in it as symbolic of that which is hidden, of the inner meaning that leads to a flowering of the world, then the true meaning of the text has been seen, and the Return has begun. And this experience is in each case unique. And in each case the Guide, the *exegete*, is the Angel, the "Khidr of your being."

If this is true for each knower, then a prophetic theory of knowledge or gnosiology must understand all true knowledge as homologous to the Revelation to the Prophet and all mystic returns as mimetic of the Night of the *Mi'raj.* For Mulla Sadra, this culminates in a full-blown epistemology, which "...embraces simultaneously the knowledge of the philosophers, of those who are inspired, and of the prophets, as graduated variations of one and the same Manifestation."[32] All true knowledge is theophany. The Angel of Knowledge and the Angel of Revelation are ultimately the same. And it is this same Angel who is individualized in a way that is in each case unique and through whom the prophetic-poietic couple is joined.

> Because what is involved is the same Manifestation at different levels of eminence, whether by means of the senses or in some other way—a Manifestation whose highest form is the vision of the Angel "projecting" knowledge into the heart in a waking state, in a vision *similar* to the vision of the eyes—it could be said that...the philosopher does not see the Angel, but "intelligizes" through him, to an extent which depends upon his own efforts. The...Imams hear him through spiritual audition. The prophets see him.[33]

This knowledge as theophany is necessarily hidden, occulted. That is what ensures that it is in each case unique, because it concerns each soul individually, and that is what protects its very nature as sacred. What safeguards the sacred nature of this knowledge is precisely that it is hidden. In our time the Divine Presence is veiled, "and because it is *incognito*, it can never become an object or a

---

32. Corbin, *History of Islamic Philosophy*, 54-55.
33. *Ibid.*, 55.

thing, and it defies all socialization of the spiritual."[34] That which is common to all cannot be sacred, it can only point to it, as symbol to symbolized.

Falling into the World

An entire cosmology of Fall and Redemption, Descent and Return, of Creator and Creation, depends upon this action which is passion, this hermeneutics of Imperative Being. The consequences for the interpretation of the status of the world after the Fall, of the Incarnation of God in Christ, and of our understanding of time, space, and matter, are profound.

We should begin at the beginning. A symbolic expression of these doctrines is provided in an exegesis of the Fall given by Ismailism.[35] Adam is created on earth, from clay:

> In esoteric terms, clay signifies knowledge that is external or exoteric, opaque, material. Now the angels were created in a state of subtle knowledge, of esoteric, internal, spiritual science, a knowledge that did not depend upon initiatory instruction...and that was exempt from ritual obligations and observances of the Law. In brief, "the human being created on earth" signifies the condition of a being who cannot thenceforth attain to the esoteric, to hidden spiritual reality, except through the intermediary of the exoteric, that is by means of the knowledge of symbols.[36]

---

34. Corbin, *History of Islamic Philosophy*, 72.

35. Corbin, "Comparative Spiritual Hermeneutics," in *Swedenborg and Esoteric Islam*, 100ff. This is a version of the exegesis of the Fall set forth by Qazi No'man (d. 974), philosopher and jurist of Fatimid North Africa, also author of a monumental system of *Shari'a* law, whose works are recognized by both Ismailis and Twelve-Imam Shi'ites. See also Corbin's *En islam iranienne*, v. 1, 97ff., for a similar version according to Twelve-Imam Shi'ism. Here, as in other places, Corbin stresses the similarities between the esotericism of Shi'ism and Swedenborgian hermeneutics. For a comparative study, see Corbin's *Swedenborg and Esoteric Islam*; see also his *En islam iranienne*, v. 1. On Corbin's relationship to Swedenborg, see Roberts Avens, "The Subtle Realm: Corbin, Sufism and Swedenborg."

36. Corbin, *Swedenborg and Esoteric Islam*, 103.

Now Iblis (Satan) refused to bow down before Adam, as God commanded, because he knew that Adam was made of clay and less excellent than any angel, and so he was cursed. Iblis was one of the twelve angels, spiritual leaders, who had been chosen to surround Adam and help him. These are symbolized by his twelve ribs. But Iblis cut himself off from Adam and thus betrayed him.

> Iblis, by refusing to admit that the esoteric may be organically linked to the exoteric, betrayed Adam; he deprived Adam of that esoteric and forbade him the perception of symbols....
>
> ... Eve is given to Adam in compensation for Iblis, and that is why Adam transmits to Eve, invests in her, all his knowledge of the esoteric. Thenceforth, Eve assumes and bears the esoteric....
>
> ... Something emerges here that is highly significant for the spiritual world of Ismai'ilism: namely, that the esoteric is essentially the Feminine, and that the Feminine is the esoteric (the Self that is deep and hidden from man...).
>
> ... It is this masculine-feminine couple, Adam-Eve, that God established in the garden, the earthly paradise, "the most sublime thing that God has created."[37]

And therefore in this world both aspects are required in a delicate balance which, if upset, results in catastrophe:

> [T]here are two (complementary) ways of effecting an irreparable scission between the sensory and the spiritual, between the exoteric and the esoteric: namely, by an exclusive attachment to one or the other; the catastrophe is the same in either case. Esoterism degenerates into a purely abstract knowledge, that of the forces of nature, for example, or else succumbs to spiritual libertinage...the exoteric, deprived of its theophanic function, degenerates into a covering, a hollow cortex, something like the corpse of what might have been an angelic

---

37. Corbin, *Swedenborg and Esoteric Islam*, 104-06.

appearance, if this would be conceivable. Everything, then, becomes institutionalized; dogmas are formulated, legalistic religion triumphs; the science of Nature becomes the conquest and possession of Nature.... Certainly once the mystical Sword of the Word is broken into pieces, nothing less than the *quest* of a Galahad is needed to reunite them. All the effort in the West from Robert Fludd to Goethe, from Boehme to Swedenborg, takes on this meaning....[38]

This is the esoteric explanation of the imbalances of the modern sciences of power. They are the result of taking as ultimate the truths of abstract, quantitative Pure Reason, rather than the result of the exercise of *intellectus*, which is precisely not abstract because it is the thought of the soul, the thought of the heart. The opposite error, "spiritual libertinage," we might see in the follies of any spirituality which is based on the desires and attachments of the *ego*. On the one hand, the truths of Nature are taken literally—those Abstractions of the Will to Power the inflationary effects of which on the soul are wholly destructive. These are the realities of the sciences of Absence that reject the Balance and refuse the reality of the Celestial counter-weight. On the other hand, are the whims of the *ego*, unconstrained, fantastic: the result of an Eros disoriented, grasping and desperate for Presence, abandoned and alone.

In the Ismaili exegesis, God then places Adam and Eve in this garden, tells them not to eat of one of the trees, and warns against Iblis, who will tempt them. Notice what the temptation of Iblis is: he will try to make them renounce the exoteric, that is the "public" world, "which is, however, the 'place' of the flowering of symbols." Iblis is not tempting them with the carnal desires of the fleshly realm. On the contrary. The devil in this story tries to make them renounce this world, to destroy its balance. That is the hubris of Adam. The over-reaching is to destroy the complementarity between the hidden and the revealed. The forbidden tree represents the hidden things that are necessarily inaccessible to man until the Resurrection. Iblis succeeds in the end

---

38. Corbin, *Swedenborg and Esoteric Islam*, 107.

by awakening in Adam the memory, the nostalgia, for the angelic state that he enjoyed in the previous cycle of existence, but which is now the prerogative of the Angels alone. The "attempt on the part of man, Adam-Eve, to do away with the exoteric was equivalent to laying bare the esoteric…since it deprived the latter of its garment…. [But] Adam had neither the possibility nor the power."[39]

The difference between this reading and that of what became dogmatic Christianity is stunning. Here the expulsion from the Garden is not from a purely spiritual Paradise to an anti-world of worthless matter, occupying the lowest rung on the Great Chain of Being. The Exile amounts to the occultation of the esoteric, the Feminine, which had been in balance with the exoteric in Paradise, but is no longer. Access to the hidden, to the symbolic dimension, will now be cut off—but not entirely. In this story, the punishment for the disobedience is ameliorated by the possibility of gnosis:

> The entire human drama is played out on the plane of gnosis and gnostic consciousness. It is a drama of knowledge, not of the flesh….
> … [T]he end of the episode…has none of the somber resonance to which the religious man of the West has become accustomed over the centuries. It is said that Adam did not persist in his error and that God returned to him. … Adam departed from paradise, but thenceforth, by means of gnosis, he effected a return to the "potential paradise" which is the *da'wat* [the Convocation of spiritual beings embracing all the visible and invisible universes].[40]

And in this sense, the *ta'wil* that is the Return to the spiritual earth of this virtual paradise is the ever-repeatable return out of the Exile from the Garden.

In another version of the story of the Fall and the expulsion from the Garden, a different valorization of the world outside the Garden is given. In an exegesis provided by Twelve-Imam Shi'ism, it is empha-

---

39. Corbin, *Swedenborg and Esoteric Islam*, 109.
40. *Ibid.*, 110-11.

sized that without a Descent, there can never be a Return, and so the glories of Creation are in fact dependent upon the Fall from Heaven. Shayegan relates a story that indicates as much about Corbin's attitude towards Shi'ite spirituality as it does about that spirituality itself. In Teheran, when Corbin was in his early sixties, he once asked Shaykh Muhammad Hossayn Tabatabai, the influential Shi'ite theologian and professor at the Theological School at Qom, if Islamic gnosis admitted the idea of original sin as does Christianity:

> The Shaykh had a voice so low one could hardly understand him, and murmuring as if to himself, he responded: "The fall is neither a lack, nor a defect, even less a sin; if it had not been for the forbidden fruit of the tree, the inexhaustible possibilities of Being would never have been manifested." I will never forget Corbin's approving smile.... "It is because the Occident has lost the meaning of *ta'wil*," Corbin said, "that we can no longer succeed in penetrating the hidden things of the Holy Scriptures, and that we demythologize the sacred dimension of the world." This was the first time that I realized the unsuspected extent of the term that Corbin often used and which remained...the keystone of all his meditation.[41]

The esoteric vision of the world after the Fall clearly is not based upon the existence of a chasm between a transcendent God in a spiritual Heaven and a world of despair and darkness into which we have been cast as wretched sinners. The material world as an autonomous realm, belonging either to Science or to Caesar, possesses what little reality it does only by virtue of our blindness to the esoteric aspects of all things. It is this blindness that is the real punishment and the real Fall. So we are trapped in a world that falls apart into the Empirical and the Ideal that can only be sensed and thought about, leaving us devoid of the inner spaces and times of the Imagination, with no exit, no way to imagine ourselves into the world of the Real.

---

41. Shayegan, "Le Sens du Ta'wil," *Henry Corbin: La topographie spirituelle*, 84-85.

This means that the Western Christian and post-Christian views of the relation of Spirit and Matter do not hold. By opening up the question of the status of the world of the Flesh, we reopen the ancient debate about the ontology of the Incarnation of God in Christ. It is the Imaginative passion, putting our being in the Imperative, and hermeneutics as the ontologically remedial act of reading the text of the Word which will provide the key for understanding the primordial relations among Space, Time, and Matter.

The Word and the World: Time, Space, Matter, and Prophecy

Islamic cosmology is ahistorical and based upon a mythic sense of time. The meaning of history and of the Sacred Book has nothing to do with the unfolding of events in time and everything to do with what Corbin calls "hierohistory," with events in the eternal time of the soul. For Corbin, it is this conception of the meaning of history and time that is the most important difference between the official Christianity of the Councils and Islamic spirituality. Islam has simply never had to confront the problems of historical consciousness.

Corbin correlates the rise of historical consciousness in the West with the doctrine of the Incarnation: the appearance of God, in a body, at a moment in time. In his view the consequences of the official dogma of the Incarnation and the resulting interpretation of the relation between God and Creation are immense:

> The coming of historical consciousness is concomitant with the formation of dogmatic consciousness. In the official form given to it by the definitions of the Councils, the fundamental dogma of Christianity, that of the Incarnation, is the most characteristic symptom of this, because the Incarnation is a unique and irreversible fact; it takes its place in a series of material facts; God in person was incarnated in a moment in history; this "happened" within the framework of a set chronology. There is no more mystery, consequently esoterism [the doctrines of the hidden meanings] is no longer necessary.... Such

132

an Incarnation of "God in person" in empirical history, and, consequently, the historical consciousness that goes hand in hand with it, are unknown to the traditional Orient.[42]

The crucial fact is that the matter into which God is incarnated and both the space and the time in which this matter by definition must exist are all exoteric, public, and revealed. The official dogma of the Incarnation requires the literal space-time that was to be finally given an explicitly and exclusively quantitative formulation only much later.[43]

This Corbin contrasts in the strongest terms with the docetism of gnostic religion. Docetism was the doctrine, denounced by the early Christian Councils, that Christ was not fully flesh and blood, that he was "merely an appearance." From the point of view of what was to become orthodoxy, redemption was only possible through the full humanity of Christ, who at the same time must be fully God. But from the point of view that Corbin defends, this doctrine of the Incarnation precludes a unique and personal relationship between God manifesting as a person and the unique individual to whom He manifests and on whom He thereby confers personhood.

It is the most profound characteristic of the West that we have lost the phenomenology that accompanies the original meaning of the

---

42. Corbin, *Creative Imagination*, 83-84.

43. A counter current to this dogmatic formulation exists. Corbin points to Nicolas Oresme, who in the 14th century proposed a geometry of the intensities of existence, which is often regarded as a prelude to analytical geometry, but which Corbin compares to the ontology of Mulla Sadra. Corbin writes of Oresme, "He considers the corporeal quality as being made up of a double corporeality. There is the one resulting from the extension of the subject in the three dimensions of space, and there is another which is only *imagined* and which results from the intensity of the quality multiplied by the multiplicity of surfaces which one can detect in the inner nature of a subject." Corbin, *The Concept of Comparative Philosophy*, 23. This "fourth dimension" completes itself in the *mundus imaginalis*. We might compare this intuition to the claim of Ortega y Gassett: "So many things fail to interest us, simply because they don't find in us enough surfaces on which to live, and what we have to do then is to increase the number of planes in our mind, so that a much larger number of themes can find a place in it at the same time." Quoted in Bly (ed.) *Leaping Poetry*, v. In these ideas, we can see the outline of an entire philosophy of education. On Oresme, see Corbin, *The Concept of Comparative Philosophy*, 19-24.

word *dokesis* and thus have cut ourselves off from the foundation of religious experience itself. A docetic, gnostic understanding of this primary personal relation would put the worlds back into order by revealing the necessity of the *mundus imaginalis*. This relation

> between God manifested as a person (biblically, the Angel of the Face) and the person that it promotes to the rank of person in revealing itself to it is fundamentally an existential relation, never a dogmatic one. It cannot be expressed as a *dogma* but as a *dokhema*. The two terms derive from the same Greek word *dokeo*, signifying all at once, to appear, to show itself as, and believe, think, admit. The *dokhema* marks the line of interdependence between the form of that which manifests itself, and that to whom it manifests. It is this same correlation that can be called *dokesis*. Unfortunately it is from this that the routine accumulated over the centuries of history of Occidental dogmas has derived the term *docetism*, synonym of the phantasmic, the irreal, the apparent. So it is necessary to reinvigorate the primary sense: that which is called *docetism* is in fact the theological critique, or rather the theosophical critique, of religious consciousness. A critique which, questioning what is visible to the believer but invisible to the non-believer, questions the nature and causes of this invisibility. Nature and causes which hold to the event which has place and consists in the correlation of which we speak, that have their place neither in the world of sensible perception, nor in the abstract world of understanding. Another world is necessary therefore to us to assure ontologically the clear right of this relation which is not logical, conceptual, dogmatic, but a theophanic relation, constitutive of a visionary realism where the *apparent* becomes *apparition*.[44]

In Corbin's analysis, Christian and post-Christian history move always in exterior, literal, material Time—in the temporality characteristic of quantitative space. And this space-time has no vertical

---

44. Corbin, *Le paradoxe du monothèisme*, 250-51.

dimension. The "now" of this space-time has only the dimensions of the vanishing moment, emerging from the causal past and disappearing forever into the future. That is to say: there is nothing Present. In the space-time of literal matter, the past is passed, the future is not yet, and the present is Absence. And so there really is nothing— nihilism, the Abyss: The attack of Ahriman.

Western secular Utopian eschatologies of all sorts, including Marxism, the Utopias of science, science fiction, and capitalist economics are all the result of the secularization of this Christian historical consciousness. They all seek salvation from Nothing in that which is to come. Since there is only the Not Yet, they are all always of the Future and have their public place in literal time.

The two radically different cosmologies and the kinds of consciousness they require, the historical and the gnostic, are not only in conflict, but mutually exclusive, and develop from wholly incompatible formations of the soul:

> Perhaps one could say that the aptitude to perceive forms
> in irreversible chronological succession, to situate them in
> a moment of this succession and explain them as a function
> of this moment, is in inverse proportion to the aptitude for
> seeing them and situating them in space, in a space, that is,
> which is no longer physical, quantitative and homogeneous,
> and to explain them by their rank in a *qualitative, perma-
> nent and hierarchic space.*[45]

A true prophetic philosophy is based on the ever-present possibility of the irruption of the meaning of the Word into the soul of the believer, in the present, in the form of a spiritual birth, of gnosis. The meaning of the moment is just its flowering upward into Eternity. The negation of the significance of exterior time is the hallmark of esoteric religion.

---

45. Corbin, *En islam iranienne*, v. 1, 138.

> Such a prophetic philosophy moves in the dimension of a
> pure theophanic historicity, in the inner time of the soul;
> external events, cosmologies, the histories of the prophets,
> are perceived as the history of the spiritual man. Thus it
> obliterates the "historical trend" with which our epoch is
> obsessed. Prophetic philosophy looks for the meaning of
> history not in "horizons," that is, not by orienting itself in
> the latitudinal sense of a linear development, but vertically,
> by a longitudinal orientation extending from the celestial
> pole to the Earth, in the transparency of the heights or depths
> in which the spiritual individuality experiences the reality
> of its celestial counterpart, its "lordly" dimension, its
> "second person," its "Thou."[46]

The intensification of being as the goal of gnosis can have no ontological foundation without this vertical dimension.

An historical consciousness entirely bound by material causality is therefore incompatible with spirituality. The "cause" of the hermeneutic vision originates in the imaginal world not bounded by quantitative space and time, in a realm not subject to the laws operative there. The time of the soul, of the sacred, is qualitatively other, as is the space, and in the end perhaps the two are not easy to differentiate. The Nurse of all things in the *Timaeus* is perhaps both space and time, or the space out of which time is born. For the ancient Persians, Zervan is "sometimes Space, sometimes Time." Even in the great cosmogonic myth of modern physics, the primordial eruption of Being gives birth to space and time together.

This a-historicism is tied to the claim that we moderns can, indeed must, make a future for the past; by retrieving the past and its mythic cosmologies that are not of our time, we make it Present once again and so connect ourselves to the Divine. The past is not gone, it has not passed— it can yet be Present. The coordinates of the space-time of the world of Matter are the coordinates of Absence. In his late work, Heidegger meditated too about the structure of time in terms of presence and absence.

---

46. Corbin, *Creative Imagination*, 81.

He came to understand that past and future are both absent, but in different ways: but the former *refuses*, while the latter *withholds*.[47] In the context of Corbin's analysis, we can say that the spaces and times of Presence deny the refusal of the past, as well as the withholding of the future.

Here too lies the deepest meaning of the *significatio passiva*. By opening ourselves to the spaces of the soul, we "make ourselves capable of God." All of these themes come together in a passage in which Corbin speaks of the histories related in the Book:

> [I]f the past were really what we believe it to be, that is, completed and closed, it would not be the grounds of such vehement discussions.... [A]ll our *acts of understanding* are so many recommencements, re-*iterations* of events still unconcluded. Each one of us, willy-nilly, is the initiator of events in "Hurqalya" [the *mundus imaginalis*], whether they abort in its hell or bear fruit in its paradise. While we believe that we are looking at what is past and unchangeable, we are in fact consummating our own future.... It follows that the whole of the underlying metaphysics is that of an unceasing recurrence of the Creation...not a metaphysics of the *ens* and the *esse*, but of the *esto*, of *being* in the imperative. But the event is put, or put again, in the imperative only because it is itself the *iterative* form of *being* by which it is raised to the reality of an event. Perhaps, then, we shall glimpse the full gravity of a spiritual event and of the spiritual sense of events "perceived in Hurqalya" when at last consciousness rediscovers the Giver of what is given.[48]

The past and the future are indeed contained within and defined by a Present, the reality of which is a function of the experience of the intensity of being "given" as a passion of and by the Angel. And so the event of the Great Resurrection, the *parousia* of the Paraclete, the expectation of which is in common between Islam and Christianity and which

---

47. See Abram, *Spell of the Sensuous*, 211.
48. Corbin, *Spiritual Body and Celestial Earth*, xxix.

137

is symbolized for Shi'ism in the person of the Hidden Imam of the present time,

> is not an event which may suddenly erupt one fine day; it is something that happens day after day in the consciousness of the Shi'ite faithful....
>
> ... The Advent-to-come of the Imam presupposes...the metamorphosis of men's hearts; on the faith of his followers depends the progressive fulfillment of this *parousia*, through their own act of being....

> The *parousia* of the awaited Imam signifies a plenary anthropological revelation, unfolding *within* the man who lives in the Spirit."[49]

> The Imam has said: "I am with my friends wherever they seek me, on the mountain, in the plain and in the desert. The man to whom I have revealed my Essence, that is to say the mystical knowledge of myself, has no further need of my physical proximity. And this is the Great Resurrection."[50]

These events annihilate continuous, quantitative time in a way completely analogous to the shattering of language by the Divine Word as it flowed into the *Qur'an*:

> On each occasion, what occurs is a *re-assumption* by the soul, a decision, a *reconquest*. These unities of discontinuous time...irrupt into our own time and confer the dimension of eternity upon the scissions they produce. It is through this rupturing of time that the truth of all history can finally shine forth; for through it, history is liberated and transmuted into parable.[51]

These revelations apply not to the soul alone. They apply to the world. Here again in another context we discover that "magical faculty" of the soul born to its own Perfect Nature. For Corbin, the Incarnation

---

49. Corbin, *History of Islamic Philosophy*, 71-73.
50. *Ibid.*, 102.
51. Corbin, *Temple and Contemplation*, 268.

is not a mystery; it is the denial of mystery through the literalization of the sacred. Mystery requires the magical faculty of the Image of the Angel. The awaited Imam, as the Paraclete, the Holy Spirit, "enables all things to speak, and, in becoming alive, each thing becomes a threshold of the spiritual world."[52] And this finally is the plenary meaning of the hermeneutics of the Word become Flesh: all things speak. Only through the Word can the cosmos be released from the world of literal matter, quantitative space, and historical time. Without this Presence the world is mute, faceless, collapsing forever downward to the level of object. With it, not just the human soul, but the world itself exists in a perpetual state of Resurrection. In this "spiritual alchemy"[53] we may find the antidote to agnosticism and nihilism:

> if one of the destructive aspects of nihilism appears to us in the "disenchantment" of a world reduced to utilitarian positivism, without finality in the next world, we catch a glimpse perhaps of where to raise the ramparts against this nihilism.[54]

We can now understand the saying of the Sixth Imam, "Alchemy is the sister of Prophecy."[55] A prophetic philosophy properly includes a theosophy of Nature, which is consummated in alchemy, and the alchemical work fulfills the requirements of cosmic salvation. Alchemy expresses the ultimate meaning of the world as symbol, and a phenomeological hermeneutics properly has as its task the transmutation of the world by means of unveiling the Word in all things.[56] It is to the question of a prophetic philosophy or theosophy of Nature that we now turn.

---

52. Corbin, *History of Islamic Philosophy*, 72.
53. See e.g. Corbin, *Spiritual Body and Celestial Earth*, 98-100.
54. Corbin, *Le paradoxe du monothéisme*, 253.
55. Corbin, *Creative Imagination*, xi.
56. Corbin, *History of Islamic Philosophy*, 331. It is in the contributions that he made to the understanding of alchemy that Corbin finds the greatest importance of Jung, particularly with reference to the doctrines of the subtle body. See Corbin's "*Post-Scriptum à un entretiens philosophique*" in *Henry Corbin*, ed. Jambet.

CHAPTER SEVEN

The Angelic Function of Beings

Idols and Icons

Corbin held in high regard a figure nearly forgotten in Western philosophy except among specialists. The Neoplatonist philosopher Proclus, born in Constantinople in 412 C.E., had an enormous influence on Platonist thought both East and West. Nicolas of Cusa and Hegel may be counted among his admirers.[1] In his Commentary on Plato's *Parmenides,* he discusses the symbolic meaning of the dramatic setting of that dialogue. Corbin condenses this as follows:

> On the one hand there are the philosophers of the school of Ionia; [they] have studied every aspect of Nature, but they have scarcely given thought to spiritual matters... And there are, on the other hand, philosophers of the Italian School, represented above all by Parmenides and Zeno. These are exclusively concerned with things of the intelligible order. Between the two is the Attic school, which holds a middle position, because, under the stimulus of Socrates and Plato, a synthesis has been made between the findings of the other two Schools.... [T]he middle ground is symbolized by Athens, by whose mediation awakened souls ascend from the world of Nature to that of *nous,* intellect...
>
> These [Ionians] are types of those souls who have descended into this world who are really in need of the aid of

---

1. Morrow and Dillon, *Proclus' Commentary on Plato's Parmenides,* ix.

the *daimons*.... This is why they abandon their house, the
body: they emigrate to Athens.... [T]hey set out on the way
from ignorance to knowledge, from *agnosis* to *gnosis*.... They
come for the Goddess, whose sacred *peplum* is carried in the
theoria, or procession of the Panatheneia in celebration of
victory over the Titans who unloose chaos. The aim of the
Parmenides is precisely to unite everything to the One, and to
demonstrate how all things proceed from the One.... To come
[to Athens] is, for them, to know that it is within the soul that
the battle of the giants takes place, in which [Athene] is victo-
rious.... Athens is an *Emblematic City.*[2]

The battle takes place in the soul. And it is a battle for the soul as
the necessary intermediary, without which nothing coheres and there is
chaos. And more than the individual soul is at stake: "Our western
philosophy has been the theatre of what we may call the 'battle for the
Soul of the World'."[3] This Soul of the World is the Divine Presence, the
Dwelling, Wisdom itself as Sophia, which has its place only in the world
of the soul, the *mundus imaginalis.* What we find instead in the modern
understanding of the world is the analogue in Nature of the "absurd husk"
of the Book. This is Nature as a merely literal, historical artifact. Just as
the Letter of the Revealed text must be freed from the death of dogmatic
literalisms, so must the text of Nature.

The philosophy of Nature described by Corbin exhibits none of the
dualism or materialism characteristic of science in the West. Nature can
only be understood in the context of Creation as a whole.[4] We are micro-
cosms of this divine Creation. Nasr says of this cosmology: "At every
moment the universe is absorbed in the Divine Center and manifested
anew in a rhythm of contraction...and expansion...which the rhythm of
human breathing resembles."[5] We have already seen, in the gnosiology

2. Corbin, "Emblematic Cities: A Response to the Images of Henri Steirlin,"
11-12.
3. Corbin, *Spiritual Body and Celestial Earth,* xiv.
4. For a treatment of the philosophy of nature in the major religions of the
world in comparison with modern secular natural science, see Nasr, *Religion and the
Order of Nature.*
5. Nasr, *Religion and the Order of Nature,* 62.

that regards true knowledge as illumination from the Active Intellect, that epistemology and ontology are inseparable. The seamless passage from Above to Below and back again is not restricted to the human intellect. All the cosmos participates in this movement. An adequate philosophy of Nature is based upon Sympathy, Love, and Beauty.

Corbin draws on Proclus again, in passages where he describes the movements of the flower, the *Heliotrope*, as it keeps its face turned towards the sun. Proclus writes,

> For, in truth, each thing prays according to the rank it occupies in nature, and sings the praise of the leader of the divine series to which it belongs, a spiritual, or rational or physical or sensuous praise; for the heliotrope...[produces] a hymn to its king such as it is within the power of a plant to sing.[6]

Proclus saw clearly "the essential community between visible and invisible things." Corbin writes,

> This common essence...is the perception of a *sympathy*, of a reciprocal and simultaneous attraction between the manifest being and his celestial prince.... But taken as a phenomenon of sympathy, this tropism in the plant is at once *action* and *passion*: its action...is perceived as the action...of the Angel...whose name for that very reason it bears.... And this passion...is disclosed in a prayer, which is the act of this passion through which the invisible angel draws the flower toward him....
>
> But since sympathy here is also a condition and mode of perception...we must also speak of the poetic or cognitive function of sympathy....[7]

The cognitive function of sympathy is necessary for the elevation of the soul to a mode of being which transcends the literalisms

---

6. Quoted in Corbin, *Creative Imagination*, 105-06.
7. Corbin, *Creative Imagination*, 106-07.

and dogmas in which we so easily become trapped and entangled. It is only through such sympathy that we can recognize "the angelic function of a being,"[8] the angelic function of the Angel's mediation. It is this function of the Angel, acting through sensible things, and of beings so experienced, which makes possible "a life in sympathy with beings, capable of giving a transcendent dimension to their being, to their beauty, to the forms of their faith...."[9] A spiritual life is not therefore a life turned away from this world. Rather it is only through this world that such a life can be lived. For Suhrawardi,

> the sensible species does not divert from the Angel but leads to the "place" of the encounter, on the condition that the soul seeks the encounter.
> For there are various ways of turning towards the sensible. There is one that simultaneously and as such turns towards the Angel. What follows is the transmutation of the sensible into symbols....[10]

In one of the most vital passages in his book on Ibn 'Arabi, Corbin tells us that the primary importance of the angelic function of beings is that it protects us against Idolatry,

> that two-faced spiritual infirmity which consists in either loving an object without transcendence, or in misunderstanding that transcendence by separating it from the loved object, through which alone it is manifested. These two aspects spring from the same cause: in both cases a man becomes incapable of the sympathy which gives beings and forms their transcendent dimension.[11]

It is sympathy that is the prerequisite of *ta'wil*. Likewise in the hermeneutics of Hugh of St. Victor, "study" meant something like "sympathy." It is the ability to open oneself to the presence of things and of

---

8. The phrase is Etienne Souriau's. Corbin devotes a long note to his work in *Creative Imagination*, 290-94. See also, 155ff.

9. Corbin, *Creative Imagination*, 134.

10. Corbin, *Avicenna*, 116-17.

11. *Creative Imagination*, 133-34.

persons. The inability to experience such sympathy may come from two sources: On the one hand, it may come from a fear of the infinite vastness of Reality and the powerlessness of the *ego* to dominate and control it:

> The cause may be a will to power, dogmatic or otherwise, which wishes to immobilize beings and forms at the point where man has immobilized himself—perhaps out of a secret fear of the infinite successions of perpetual transcendences...and [the knowledge that]...to be faithful to the Angel is precisely to let ourselves be guided by him towards the transcendences that he announces.[12]

We moderns have come to believe that the pre-Copernican, pre-modern world of the angelic hierarchies was anthropocentric, cramped, and stifling; in truth a closed world. But it is not so. It is our world of endless material extension, dominated by a merely human reason, that is the snare and the deadly delusion.

On the other hand, Corbin says, the failure of sympathy may be due to a pious "asceticism or puritanism," "with all its furies and rejections." Such a soul, because it is itself frozen, can see in that "dialectic of Love," by means of which the soul is led from human love towards the celestial Image of the Beloved itself, only the "unconditional investiture" in the sensible being. It can see, that is, only idolatry, only profane love, and so, "isolating the sensible or imaginable from the spiritual, divests beings of their *aura*."[13]

In either case, it is literalism, the paralysis of persons and objects into ontological immobility, that prevents the perception of transcendence and produces the death, the hell, of idolatry.

> Idolatry consists in immobilizing oneself before an idol because one sees it as opaque, because one is incapable of discerning in it the hidden invitation that it offers to go beyond it. Hence, the opposite of idolatry would not consist

---

12. *Ibid.*, 134.
13. *Ibid.*, 134 and 290ff.

in breaking idols, in practicing a fierce iconoclasm aimed
against every inner or external Image; it would rather consist
in rendering the idol transparent to the light invested in it.
In short, it means transmuting the idol into an icon.[14]

In the Garden, everything was an icon. After the Fall only the
gnostic has the sympathy which allows perception of the angelic
function of beings. Everyone else sees idols.

The theosophy of Nature is an iconology of a transformed
world. Far from the static, human-centered world imagined and
parodied by modern historical consciousness, this hierarchic,
Neoplatonic, and medieval cosmos is in perpetual motion towards
infinite suprahuman divinity. There is nothing claustrophobic about
this vision of the world. On the contrary, it may induce a kind of
spiritual dizziness, an intoxication of the heart.[15] It is based on a
unending open-ness which prevents the hardening of the heart so
characteristic of fundamentalisms of all kinds. This is unsettling to
those seeking fixity and the armor of unfeeling certitude. In this
world, Corbin says, the movement of the soul is perpetual: "[O]thers

---

14. Corbin, "Theophanies and Mirrors," 2. Corbin's treatment of this issue is in
many ways similar to the analysis of Owen Barfield in *Saving the Appearances: A Study
in Idolatry* (1988), and a comparison would be worthwhile. Also pertinent are connections with both Heidegger and Jung. In a profound study of the relationship between
Jungian psychology and philosophical phenomenology, Roger Brooke comments that
"what analytical psychology calls images, phenomenology, following Heidegger, calls
things." Brooks, *Jung and Phenomenology*, 149. He also relates archetypes to the notion
of Presence: "Thus the archetype is not extraneous to the image but is that quality of
presence which leads to the depths of its own interiority." *Jung and Phenomenology*,
144. This is in the spirit of Corbin. At the same time it needs to be stressed that the
connections here are complex. I am convinced by George Steiner's contention in *Martin
Heidegger* that Heidegger's phenomenology is an attempt to produce an ontology
entirely without recourse to categories of transcendence, and this is antithetical to Corbin's
entire opus. See also Roberts Avens, *The New Gnosis*.

15. This aspect of the mystic vision is well represented in Sufi poetry. See, for
instance, Inayat Khan and Coleman Barks, *The Hand of Poetry: Five Mystic Poets of
Persia*; Barks, *The Essential Rumi*; Michael Sells, *Early Islamic Mysticism*; and for an
extended treatment of the language of mysticism, including that of Ibn 'Arabi,
see M. Sells, *Mystical Languages of Unsaying*.

have spoken of the necessity of a 'permanent revolution,' I preach the necessity of a 'permanent hermeneutics.'"[16]

This "cosmology in gothic style" is a "continual exaltation" that depends upon a perpetual alchemy of Resurrection, a formation and unfolding of the spiritual body.[17]

> [I]t may happen, just as we have learned to understand alchemy as signifying something quite different from a chapter in the history or prehistory of our sciences, that a geocentric cosmology will also be revealed in its true sense, having likewise no connection with the history of our sciences. Considering the perception of the world and the feeling of the universe on which it is based, it may be that geocentrism should be meditated upon and evaluated essentially after the manner of the construction of a *mandala*.
>
> It is this *mandala* upon which we should meditate in order to find again the northern dimension with its symbolic power, capable of opening the threshold of the beyond.[18]

It is clear now how Corbin can say, "Psychology is indistinguishable from cosmology; the theophanic Imagination joins them into a psycho-cosmology."[19] Knowledge of the Imaginal world is simultaneously knowledge of the knower and the known, and in the last analysis, since idolatry is the result of blindness, all knowledge, even of the "physical world," is "imagination."

> Let us emphasize then, that this does not mean knowing things as abstract idea, as philosophical concept, but as the perfectly *individuated* features of their Image, meditated, or rather, pre-meditated, by the soul, namely, their archetypal Image. That is why in this intermediate world there are Heavens and Earths, animals, plants, and minerals, cities, towns and forests....

---

16. Corbin, *Henry Corbin*, ed. Jambet, 36.
17. Corbin, *Cyclical Time and Ismaili Gnosis*, 54-56, and n. 98. Corbin is here speaking of the cosmology of Nasir Tusi.
18. Corbin, *The Man of Light in Iranian Sufism*, 3.
19. Corbin, *Creative Imagination*, 215.

> [U]ltimately what we call *physis* and the physical is but the
> reflection of the world of the Soul; there is no pure physics,
> but always the physics of some definite psychic activity.[20]

This is why Blake could say that the world imagined was more
real, more detailed, more perfectly formed than the merely sensible
world. And this means that the quantitative, literal space/time of
opaque matter is only one form, although the most limited, of the
infinite array of spiritual spaces and times.

There is, strictly speaking, no end point to the upward motion of
this meditative, imaginative, and sympathetic knowing, which is a
movement towards Paradise, drawn on by the Love of Beauty as the
supreme Theophany and by the desire of that Love. Each level is "Paradise" to the level below. But the "beyond" is not radically opposed to
"this world," though there is indeed a world "beyond the grave." Rather,

> Even while one is materially present in this world, there
> is a mode of being in Paradise; but it goes without saying
> that this *mode of being*, Paradise, can be realized, can
> exist "in the true sense," only in a person who precisely
> *is* this Paradise—that is to say, who always personifies
> this mode of being.[21]

Access to this world requires that true Imagination which is the
intermediary *locus* "at the meeting place of the two seas," where Moses
meets Khidr, the *mundus imaginalis*.

The Pathetic God

That for the most part we do not live in sympathy with beings is
obvious, and we have seen some of the ways in which this reveals
itself. But it remains to examine from another point of view a crucial
characteristic of the dominant form of Christianized consciousness
that is in large part responsible for this lack of sympathy. We have
come to misunderstand the meaning and significance of transcendence.

---

20. Corbin, *Spiritual Body and Celestial Earth*, 81.
21. Corbin, *Cyclical Time and Ismaili Gnosis*, 51-52.

148

The transcendent God is so transcendent that it has disappeared entirely from the modernist consciousness. For Corbin, the disappearance of God, the process of secularization, was almost inevitable from very early in the history of official Christianity, from the moment when the doctrine of the Incarnation was given its dogmatic form. But this doctrine itself is symptomatic of a deeper metaphysical problem. It is to the concept of Creation itself that we must now turn.

The Christian understanding of the relationship of the Creator to Creation is a source of deep confusion about the status of the world after the Fall. Christians were to be "in the world, but not of it." The stresses set up by the way this requirement has been understood have resulted in various kinds of madness and the sundering of human wholeness. On the one hand, for secular technology, "in the world" has been totalized, and any sense of limit is abandoned: whatever can be done, will be done, in fact must be done.[22] On the other, for many kinds of modern Christianity, "not of it" takes precedence in such a way that everything after the Fall is fouled with sin and the filth of the earth. Sex is demonized, as are women; wild, "virgin" Nature is to be feared and subdued, and the whole of Creation is merely a testing ground, a platform of sin and temptation, and all our energies must be turned towards attaining escape velocity.[23] In the end, modern technology, the economics of perpetual progress, and

22. "It is a profound and necessary truth that the deep things in science are not found because they are useful, they are found because it was possible to find them." Robert Oppenheimer, leader of the Manhattan Project, quoted in Robert Rhodes, *The Making of the Atomic Bomb.* For Oppenheimer this perhaps signified an almost mystical connection between the mind and nature. For Corbin and his spirituals, the Prometheanism implied is the significant and sad, deeper meaning. One also thinks of the proponents of the robotization of humanity, represented well by Marvin Minsky who proposes the eventual replacement of our biological bodies and brains with more permanent, reliable, and rational cybernetic improvements so that we may live longer and more rationally and thus have the time to become wise. See Minsky, "Will Robots Inherit the Earth?"

23. On these issues, see Carolyn Merchant, *The Death of Nature: Women, Ecology and the Scientific Revolution* and *Ecological Revolutions: Nature, Gender and Science in New England*; Anne Baring and Jules Cashford, *The Myth of the Goddess: Evolution of an Idea*; Max Oelschlager, *The Idea of Wilderness: From Prehistory to the Age of Ecology*, and references therein.

a certain kind of world-denying fundamentalist religion all come to the same end: the meaning of earthly life lies in Escape, and it is only the conception of the Destination which divides them. All of this is what Corbin means by post-Christian eschatology. And we are so accustomed to it, especially in the United States, a country founded upon dispersal and expansion, that it may be difficult to see that what Corbin offers is different. A living experience of transcendence is the foundation for Corbin's sense of the world, but it is transcendence of a different sort.

The origin of the specifically Western impulse towards The Elsewhere lies in the idea of creation *ex nihilo*. There is at the root of Christian dogma,

> the theological opposition between *ens increatum* and an *Ens creatum* drawn from nothingness, an opposition which makes it doubtful whether the relationship between the *Summum ens* and the *nothingness* from which He causes creatures to arise has ever been truly defined.... [This notion of a *creatio ex nihilo* opens] up a gulf which no rational thought will ever be able to bridge because it is this profoundly divisive idea itself which creates the opposition and distance....[24]

Creation conceived this way lies outside of and external to the Creator. This sense of reality, if not sufficiently compensated by a living connection between creature and Creator, is a powerful source of conflicts and of a desperate frenzy in the search for that severed umbilicus. To be sure, there is much in Christian tradition that seeks to bridge the gulf, and it is this to which Corbin is always drawn. This is evident in his feeling for the importance of Martin Luther's attack on the mediating function of the Church and his discovery of the *significatio passiva*. But it is not this living connection Luther sought which came to dominate Western consciousness. Corbin admits with sadness that the religions of the Book tend always to succumb to idolatry, dogma, and literalism.[25]

---

24. Corbin, *Creative Imagination*, 185.
25. Corbin, *Le paradoxe du monothèisme*, 251.

THE ANGELIC FUNCTION OF BEINGS

For Corbin the bridge is *ta'wil*, the transformation of the sensory world into symbols, into open-ended mysteries that shatter, engage, and transform the entire being of the creature. Its metaphysical grounding is provided by the experience of creation as theophany, as the realization of Divine Compassion. This is not creation of the universe of matter or energy as science now conceives it: a single, unimaginably vast explosion creating in an instant an expanding universe of self-sufficient, physical substance and a primordial flux of energies, extending outward in quantitative space, evolving through time in a ceaseless evolution. This Creator is not a maker of something from nothing; not an artisan shaping any stuff into an object; not a physicist, whose distant, abstract Mind is structured by a Theory of Everything. There are no fundamental particles, no basic forces playing out through time. Those relations all are based upon Power, Distance, and the Otherness of Creation. The god of modern science created something from nothing, established the laws of Nature, and has kept His distance ever since.

It is hard to overstate the contrast between the feeling for the world which must accompany these conceptions and that implicit in the doctrine of Ibn 'Arabi:

> The *leitmotiv* is not the bursting into being of an autarchic Omnipotence, but a fundamental sadness: "I was a hidden Treasure, I yearned to be known. That is why I produced creatures, in order to be known in them." ...[T]he origin, the beginning is determined by love, which implies a movement of ardent desire...on the part of him who is in love. This ardent desire is appeased by the divine Sigh.
>
> ... [C]reation springs not from nothingness, from something other than Himself...but from His fundamental being....
>
> Thus Creation is Epiphany...it is an act of the divine, primordial Imagination. Correlatively, if there were not within us that same power of Imagination, which is not imagination in the profane sense of "fantasy," but the Active Imagination ...or *Imaginatrix*, none of what we show ourselves would be manifest....

> … To the initial act of the Creator imagining the world
> corresponds the creature imagining the worlds, his God,
> his symbols.[26]

The archetypal creative act is not based on Power but on Love.
The imagination in us is not manipulative, not coercive, it does not even
engage in "laying bare." We are not creators of what we imagine, if by
creation we mean the act of a Master. To create is to Love, to let
flower. Not *ens* or *esse*, but *esto!*—the imperative inauguration of
being which grounds the meaning of *significatio passiva*. This is the
meaning of *himma*: real being is created not by thought, but by
passion. Creation as Imagination is founded upon Desire, Love, and
Sympathy. Symbolic perception, mystic perception, gives birth to
forms, to things, to personifications, out of the depths of the mysteries
of the Heart. And these beings, lifted thus away from their entrapment in the opacity of the world perceived as merely physical, have
their true being revealed in the light of the *mundus imaginalis*.

The Image thus created and perceived is no phantasm, no flut-
tering wisp of spirit. It is more real than any "thing" can ever be.[27]
Every theophany "announces something other, which is more than
itself; it is more than appearance, it is apparition."[28] To modern
consciousness, "apparition" is synonymous with the unreal. Not so
here. *Ta'wil* is possible "because there is symbol and transparency."

> This form itself presupposes an exegesis which carries it
> back to its source, or rather apprehends simultaneously the
> many planes on which it is manifested. Without the Active
> Imagination the infinite exaltations provoked in a being by
> the succession of theophanies which that being bestows on
> himself would be impossible.[29]

The world of sensory perception becomes transparent. It can be
seen through. But this is because what lies on the other side, what

---

26. Corbin, *Creative Imagination*, 184-88.
27. Corbin, *Spiritual Body and Celestial Earth*, x.
28. Corbin, *Creative Imagination*, 194.
29. *Ibid.*

draws the world out of itself, and which has the power to turn it inside out, is more real, more true, more powerful than any of those realities, both autonomous and opaque, which make up the world of objects. The only true autonomy is granted by the One, which lies in the direction of heaven. The realm of the beyond, the succession of heavens, is not populated by things: the inhabitants of these heavens are transparencies in perpetual Return, perpetually Opening, "an ocean without a shore." The world perceived in this way invites a Fall into and through the world, which is itself a Return. This Return is not a negation of the world, not a rejection or denial of a sinful state. It is an awakening to and celebration of the immensity of the true Journey.

We in the West have fallen prey to the catastrophic results of an exclusive emphasis on the exoteric meaning of the *tawhid*, the witnessing of the Unique, which is the assertion of the existence of an *Ens supremum* that transcends all of Creation. This is the unintended idolatry of abstract monotheism. In necessary counterpoint to this outer meaning is the esoteric *tawhid*: this reveals that the Unique that is witnessed is in fact the unity of Love, Lover, and Beloved. In the doctrine of yet another figure of that crucial 12th century who is of great importance for Corbin's vision, Ruzbehan Baqli Shirazi, God cannot be witnessed by an Other, since then there would have to be a creature extrinsic to God to witness Him from outside.[30] There can be no Other than God, and creatures are truly not Other, but rather God's own "sense organs" by which He knows Himself. For Ruzbehan, since "God can only be looked at by Himself," a "world which wishes itself other (either by agnosticism or by piety [an idolatry masquerading as piety]) is not a world that God looks at. Literally, it is a *world that God does not look at*."[31] Such a world must have come into existence in the first place in order that "Nietzsche's tragic

---

30. See Corbin, *History of Islamic Philosophy*, 284-86. Ruzbehan Baqli Shirazi was born in Pasa near Shiraz in 1128 and died in Shiraz in 1209. This great mystic of "extreme emotionalism" taught a doctrine of Divine love and theophanic beauty, "rejecting any asceticism which opposes divine to human love, for he sees both as two forms of a love which is one and the same."

31. Corbin, "The Jasmine of the *Fedeli d'Amore*: A Discourse on Ruzbehan Baqli of Shiraz," 209.

exclamation...*God is dead* can resound and spread in it."[32]

Thus the Creation itself as the realization of the Divine Compassion, the Breath of the Merciful, is itself the link between the human soul and the Divine. And because it is a living connection, it must be active, continually alive, subject to perpetual *ta'wil*. This Creation is a recurrent Creation, not accomplished once and for all, such that we can at some time hope to know the ends of it. "*Creation* as the 'rule of being' is the pre-eternal and continuous movement by which being is manifested *at every instant* in a new cloak."[33] There can be no Theory of Everything in the cosmos as understood by Ibn 'Arabi, because Creation is never closed and completed. Beings are not independent existents that can be known and manipulated as if they are only what they are, in the manner that we conceive of things. Utilitarianism, or our contemporary equivalent, engineering, is far too restrictive to be universalized into a cosmology, because there can be no autonomous objects for use. Such objects are by definition dead, opaque, literal.

This ceaseless creation is invisible to us,

> because when something passes away, something like it is existentiated at the same moment.... At every *breath* of the "Sigh of Compassion"...being ceases and then is; we cease to be, then come into being. In reality there is no "then," for there is no interval.... For the "Effusion of Being" that is the "Sigh of Compassion" flows through the things of the world like the waters of a river and is unceasingly renewed.[34]

And so the identity of objects and persons is not granted by their continuity in an illusory linear time, but rather comes from the eternal archetype or form, the principle of individuation of that being.

"At every instant:" each being is created anew perpetually—and so ceases to be and becomes at every instant. This ceasing to be is

---

32. Corbin, "The Jasmine of the *Fedeli d'Amore*: A Discourse on Ruzbehan Baqli of Shiraz," 209.

33. Corbin, *Creative Imagination*, 200.

34. *Ibid.*, 201.

fana,' annihilation, the disappearance of the one substance that is "pluralized in its epiphanies." The other side of this, the perpetuation of each being, is accomplished through its existence in the One Divine Being, which must however flower into multiple theophanic forms through out all the planes of beings, all the worlds, terrestrial and supraterrestrial. This manifestation and annihilation occurs eternally, perpetually, instantaneously, and in all the hierarchy of worlds from the terrestrial upwards. The interpenetration of this world and the other means that "this is the other world, or rather, this already is the other world."[35] This is the key to the "secret of Resurrection:" there is a *"continuous ascension* of beings, beginning with the untying of the knot of the dogmatic faiths, when dogmatic science gives way to the science of vision."[36]

The metaphor of the "knot of belief" is found in Ibn 'Arabi, and some knowledge of his meaning can shed light on Corbin's use of it here. Chittick writes,

> The Arabic word...which is typically translated as "belief" derives from the root...which means to knit, knot or tie; to join together, to convene, to make a contract.... [T]he eighth verbal form from the root...[as] a technical term signifying belief...suggests a knot tied in the heart that determines a person's view of reality. The Shaykh employs the word to refer to all the knottings that shape understanding—the whole range of cognitions, ideas, theories, doctrines, dogmas, prejudices, perceptions, feelings, and inclinations that allow people to make sense of the world.... Beliefs lie at the root of every human thought and action.[37]

In the hierarchy of spiritual stations potentially attainable by humans, the pinnacle is "the Station of No Station." From this viewpoint of perfect knowledge, it is clear that to every knot there corresponds a

---

35. Corbin, *Creative Imagination*, 203.
36. *Ibid.*, 205.
37. Chittick, *Imaginal Worlds*, 138.

truth, yet no knot is complete:

> Having actualized the Station of No Station, perfect human
> beings recognize that all beliefs are true and all lead to
> God.... They understand the legitimacy of every belief and
> the wisdom behind every knot tied in the fabric of Reality.... By
> accepting each knot for what it is, they learn what it has to
> teach, and by not allowing themselves to be limited and
> defined by it, they allow for the untying of every knot.
> Only by standing in all stations of human possibility and
> not being defined by any of them can they achieve the
> Station of No Station.[38]

This exalted station lies far beyond any simplistic relativism. At yet
the intuition of this possibility lies close to Corbin's heart: "He...who is
the disciple of Khidr possesses sufficient inner strength to seek freely
the teaching of all the masters."[39]

The beginning of the ascension is that spiritual birth which gives
one access to the *mundus imaginalis* and so "an increasing capacity
for acceptance of forms forever new." The eschatology of Resurrection must be understood not only as referring to the worlds after death,
but to spiritual birth in this world also. And it applies not only to humanity: "every being is in a state of perpetual ascension, since its
creation is in a perpetual recurrence from instant to instant."

This cosmology presents a radical challenge to the understanding of the meanings of Transcendence and Immanence, of
Creation and Imagination, which have molded Western thought.
It is not only that there can be no autonomous objects knowable
in their concrete and literal opacity, but the world itself becomes
transformed, transparent, eternally permeable to the Breath of the
Compassionate. This world is indeed terrestrial, but not irremediably trapped at the level of the nihilism of "mere matter," of a
world without Presence:

---

38. Chittick, *Imaginal Worlds*, 154.
39. Corbin, *Creative Imagination*, 67.

> If we consider the creature in relation to the Creator, we
> shall say that the Divine Being *descends* toward concrete
> individualizations and is epiphanized in them; inversely, if we
> consider these individualizations in their epiphanic function,
> we shall say that they *rise*, they ascend toward Him.
> And their ascending never ceases because the divine
> descent into the various forms never ceases.... That is why
> *the other world already exists in this world*; it exists in every
> moment, in relation to every being.[40]

Corbin recounts a conversation with D. T. Suzuki in Ascona in 1954:

> We asked him what homologies in structure he found
> between Mahayana Buddhism and the cosmology of
> Swedenborg in respect of the symbolism and correspon-
> dences of worlds: I can still see Suzuki suddenly brandishing
> a spoon and saying with a smile "This spoon *now* exists in
> Paradise.... We are *now* in Heaven."[41]

Apophatic Theology and the Antidote to Nihilism

The hermeneutic ability of the creative Imagination to transmute
all things into symbols destroys the distinction between psychology and cosmology and unites them in a psychocosmology in which
Creator and creature participate not as opposing terms with an
unbridgeable gulf separating them, but as complementary poles of a
divine drama. These poles are conceived very differently by the
dogmatic theologies. These restrict Revelation to a single literal meaning that must be accepted equally by all. In this are the seeds of
totalitarianism. And this is because if there is One Law for all then all
are equal under that law, and as far as the law is concerned, their
individual differences are of no account. This is just that same
metaphysical leveling which makes objects out of the icons of
creation. Persons become no more than units in a social machine.

---

40. Corbin, *Creative Imagination*, 207.

41. *Ibid.*, n. 41, 354-55. On Suzuki and Swedenborg, see Suzuki, *Swedenborg: Buddha of the North.*

Without the action and the passion of the principle of individuation, the uniqueness of each thing disappears as its divine connection is broken. Things fall apart, no thing can be oriented towards its celestial pole, no thing can be more or less itself, more or less real, and there remains only one level of being with one set of laws for all. Religion becomes psychology becomes biology, becomes chemistry becomes physics, and there is nothing innate in the soul anymore—we are at the mercy of the all-powerful environment: genes, parents, culture. Corbin puts this neatly, commenting tongue-in-cheek, "Haven't we gone almost as far as to say that chromosomes are a 'fascist invention!'"[42]

For Corbin of course, the roots of all this lie in the loss of the *mundus imaginalis* with the entire cosmology, anthropology, and angelology that it entails. A metaphysics and therefore a psychology not centered on Imagination and the cognitive function of sympathy must sooner or later degenerate into idolatry and literalism. In such a world there can be no psychology of Presence and no means of effecting the intensifications of being required for true vision.

But Corbin distinguishes yet another thread in the complex web of metaphysical mistakes and existential decisions which have cut us off from the divine Presence. The mistake in question is one of confusing Being with "a being," "a confusion between *Theotes* (Divinity) and the *theoi* (gods)."[43] This mistake is itself rooted in the distinction long made in the Abrahamic traditions between positive and negative theology. The former, the *via eminentia*, or *tashbih* in Arabic, confers upon the divinity the characteristics of creatures, raised as it were to a higher power. God is the Compassionate, the Merciful, the Forgiver, the Loving, and so on. In the Islamic tradition these Names of God stress His nearness and similarity to his creatures. We have just seen how attributes such as sympathy can lead all things back to God. But if not balanced by its opposite, this can amount to a kind of hyperinflation of the creatural world and makes of the Absolute nothing more than a Most Perfect Creature. The Absolute Divinity

---

42. Corbin, *Le paradoxe du monothèisme*, 247 and 258, n. 32.
43. Corbin, Prefatory Letter to *The New Polytheism* by David L. Miller, 2.

becomes a being, a *Summum Ens*. This is the essence of just that idolatry which dogma tries so hard to avoid. This is totalitarianism, an absolutization of the finite attributes. It threatens to erect an opaque and immoveable God, fixed forever in its various perfections; placed there, what is more, by the acts of the creatures, and reflecting them. And worse: this idolatry gives rise inevitably to nihilism. For the finite attributes themselves cannot in the end survive the inflation. They disappear into the abyss of the Absolute Infinite. Nietzsche saw this with shattering clarity and declared the Death of God. Thus idolatry and nihilism are inseparable; and this may be the central claim of the Religions of Abraham.

The antidote to this nihilism of idolatry lies on the *via negativa* of negative or apophatic theology. In Islam, this is *tanzih*, "declaring incomparability." No attributes can be predicated of the Divinity—the Absolute is *no thing*. The *Qur'an* says: "There is nothing like Him" (42:11). But this is the *no-thing* of Being itself, the beyond-being which yet is, as we have seen, that which gives being to each thing: the very principle of individuation. The unity of the divinity, of the *Theotes*, is what entails the unity and the individuality of every thing. But also, this Absolute of negative theology is the source and origin of all Creation, the Beyond beings from which they all descend, the Nothing from which all things are derived. The Supreme Divinity, the *deus abscondita*, can never be any kind of thing and is only encompassed by indirection by a negative theology. It is Being, not "a being." "It is impossible to express this mystery of Being which brings each existent into being, that is, this mystery of the One which brings each being into being as an existent."[44]

We must at all costs avoid

> two symmetrical nihilisms: that of an affirmative theology (kataphatic) erecting its absolute dogma, beyond which there would be nothing to search; that of a negative theology (apophatic) which would only aspire to the indetermination of

44. *Ibid.*

the Absolute, and which would lose from view that it is the
nihil a quo omnia procedunt (the Hidden Treasure...). On one
side and the other one has a theology without theophany.[45]

The rigid closure of fundamentalist nihilism is balanced by the
"mortal danger" of a negative theology that sees in the *Nihil* only
the Abyss, rather than "another name of God."[46] The danger and
the paradox lie in the fact that during the journey from unconsciousness through consciousness towards suprasconsciousness the
soul is confronted by two darknesses:

> there is one Darkness which is only Darkness; it can intercept
> light, conceal it and hold it captive. When the light escapes
> from it (according to the Manichean conception or the Ishraq
> of), this Darkness is left to itself, falls back upon itself; it
> does not become light. But there is another darkness, called
> by our mystics the Night of light, luminous Blackness, black
> Light.
>
> [O]*rientation* requires here a threefold arrangement of
> planes: the day of *consciousness* is on a plane intermediate
> between the luminous Night of superconsciousness and the
> dark Night of unconsciousness. The divine Darkness, the Cloud
> of unknowing, the "darkness at the approaches to the Pole,"
> the "Night of symbols" through which the soul makes its
> way, is definitely not the Darkness in which the particles of
> light are held captive."[47]

And so the approach to the Pole is fraught with perils only
too well known in the West, for Nietzsche himself "perished in
the moment of triumph" and fell victim to a "failed initiation,"
"prey to extravagant thoughts and delirium." When the newborn,
higher, spiritual *Ego* begins to open and faces the station of the

---

45. Corbin, *Le paradoxe du monothèisme*, 237-38.

46. St. Gregory of Nyssa, John Scotus Erigena, and Jacob Boehme in the West
all agreed on this supra-essential Non-Being of God. See Nasr, *Religion and the
Order of Nature*, and Michael Sells, *Mystical Languages of Unsaying*, on the apophatic
tradition.

47. Corbin, *Man of Light*, 6-7.

luminous darkness, then the danger is greatest. "The Sufi would need an experienced shaykh to help him avoid the abyss and to lead him to the degree that is in truth the divine center of his being...."[48] But Nietzsche's cry of anguish "is precisely what, for a Sufi, is experienced as the Supreme Test, the *Test of the Veil*,"[49] as a Divine Withdrawal:

> Here we can see how imaginatively and spiritually disarmed we are in comparison with those Spirituals whose certainties we have evoked.... What we experience as an obsession with nothingness or as acquiescence in a nonbeing over which we have no power, was to them a manifestation of divine anger, the anger of the mystic Beloved. But even that was a real Presence, the presence of that image that never forsook our Sufis."[50]

And yet that very witnessing of the Unique which is ever Present, ever Withdrawn, which is Love, Lover, and Beloved unified through compassion and longing which draw all things onward towards Union and Unity, is in each case unique, wholly present to each according to his capacity. Corbin cites again and again the *hadith* central to the spirituality of Sufism: "He who knows himself knows his Lord." It is this knowledge that is the foundation for and the true esoteric meaning of monotheism, beyond all idolatry, beyond even the black Light:

> Through [the] redemptive path of pure love, the consciousness of the *fidele* [love's faithful] becomes that of the mystic who knows that he is the eye with which God contemplates himself; that he himself, in his being, is the witness by which God witnesses himself, the revelation by which the Hidden Treasure reveals itself to itself.[51]

This then is the Angel of the Face, the only God that we can ever know. Not the *deus abscondita* beyond all Being, but the God who knows himself in and through us.

---

48. *Ibid.*, 127.
49. Corbin, "The Jasmine of the *Fedeli d'Amore*," 209.
50. Corbin, *Creative Imagination*, 282.
51. Corbin, "The Jasmine of the *Fedeli d'Amore*," 208.

> Israel was able to serve only "its" God, and could proclaim the
> unity of only "its" God.... Each of us, as well, has to recognize
> "his" God, the one to which he [is able to] respond....
> The Angel is the Face that our God takes for us, and
> each of us finds his God only when he recognizes that
> Face.[52]

The necessity for the pluralization of the Unique Divinity into an
unlimited number of theophanic forms, Corbin calls the "paradox of
monotheism."[53] Even at the furthest extremes of mystical experience, we
are as nothing when compared with the Absolute and our vision of the
Divinity is necessarily partial.

> "Each being," says Ibn 'Arabi: "has as his God only his
> particular Lord, he cannot possibly have the Whole."
> Here we have a kind of *kathenotheism*[54] verified in
> the context of a mystic experience; the Divine Being is
> not fragmented, but wholly present in *each* instance, individual-
> ized in *each* theophany....[55]

It is this ungraspable Unity of the One God that provides the possibility for
the unification, the individuation, of each of the infinite plurality of things. It
is the principle of Individuation itself. Exoteric monotheism immobilizes
God and the cosmos in a static and deadly structure when it confuses God as
Being, the principle of Individuation, with God as an *ens supremum*, as a
supreme being. "It is the 'death of Being' to confuse the unity of Being (*Esse*)
with a pseudo-unity of beings (*ens*) which is essentially multiple."[56]

This Absolute of which nothing can be predicated can never be an
idol—it is the Hidden Treasure that became known in and through
Creation. And the supreme form of its manifestation in being is in the

---

52. Corbin, Prefatory Letter, 4.
53. See Corbin, "Le paradoxe du monothèisme" and "Le necessité de
l'angelologie," both in *Le paradoxe du monothèisme*.
54. From the Greek, "one by one." In Vedic polytheism this expresses the idea
that each god is for a time, considered as single and supreme.
55. Corbin, *Creative Imagination*, 121.
56. Corbin, Prefatory Letter, 2.

mode of Presence of the Absolute Person, each time unique, the God, the Angel, whose divine birth is the signal of the birth of the soul in each seeker.

> The Angel is the Face that our god takes for us, and each of us finds his God only when he recognizes that Face.[57]

> The Absolutely indeterminant only becomes the *Deus revelatus*... by relation to the creature in so far as this *Deus revelatus* is the creator of it. It is necessary therefore that the Absolute come out of its absoluity, to posit a creature of which it is personally the God....[58]

In order to prevent God and creation both from closing off, solidifying into idols, in order to keep the sympathy alive and ensure the perpetual angelic function of beings, *tashbih* must be balanced by *tanzih*. Nearness and distance both are essential attributes of God: together they make up *tawhid*, the declaration of Unity. We can now understand the full import of the Hidden things and just what it is of God that lies within. *Tanzih* corresponds to *batin*, and *tashbih* corresponds to *zahir*. That is: the Outward and Manifest is the Nearness of God; the Inward and Hidden is the Oneness, the incomparability, the no-thing-ness of the Divinity. The manifest tends to descend into idolatry; the hidden opens onto the Infinite. God's Nearness is external. It is His Distance that lies within. It is through the no-thing-ness of the divinity that the essential infinitude of a person, of a presence, is determined. And so, by turning the world inside out, by giving birth in the world to that interiority which is characteristic of the things of the soul, by winning each skirmish in the Battle for the *Anima Mundi*, we return the hidden dimension to the manifest and uncover the depths that lie just under the surface of the world.

Corbin sees in Jacob Boehme the principal Western exponent of the apophatic path taken also pre-eminently by the Shi'ites. He quotes Alexander Koyré:

---

57. Corbin, Prefatory Letter, 4.
58. Corbin, *Le paradoxe du monothèisme*, 236.

> What Boehme believes in advance of all doctrine, what
> he searches for, what all his doctrine is destined to justify,
> is that God is a personal Being, more than this, that he is
> one person, a living person, self-conscious, an active person,
> a perfect person.[59]

"Note well," Corbin comments, "the words 'that he searches for.'
The personal God is not given primitively. He is encountered at the
end of a Quest (as of that for the Holy Grail)"[60] The end point of this
search is not an idol, not a thing at all, and therefore not an end but a
beginning. The openness of the Personal God means that persons, even
finite, limited ones, through their likeness to the Divinity are not things
at all. And the God that the mystic seeks is a real person, infinite,
living, symbolic—all of this is guaranteed by the "nothing from which
all things arise," a *nihil* whose primary atttribute is not the Abyss but
unending determinations of the Plenitude of Beings. It is the Emptiness, the Unknown, and Unknowable into which one falls upward in
an unending series of theophanies.

---

59. Corbin, *Le paradoxe du monothèisme*, 237.
60. *Ibid.*

CHAPTER EIGHT

A Life in Sympathy with Being

Music and Mirrors

Daryush Shayegan relates the following anecdote:

Corbin was extremely sensitive to the topography of Iran, he saw it as the terrestrial and sensible form of the *mundus imaginalis*. I remember a trip we took together to Isphahan. We were settled in a little lunchroom of the Hotel Shah-Abbas, which reproduced, after a fashion, the small empty niches of the music room of the Palace of Ali Ghapou.[1] In the walls and the partitions there were cut out of the emptiness innumerable small silhouettes of vases, flasks, laces of cuttings of all the forms conceived by an overflowing imagination. It gave to the space a sensation of levitation, the feeling that everything was in suspension. Everything seemed to be an apparition, vanishing as in a dream. I saw Corbin rise, his eyes lit by an interior gaze, then he took me by the arm, and led me to one of these empty niches, said to me in a voice soft and sensual, "This is the phenomenon of the mirror, put your hand into this space and you will touch no form there; the form is not there: it is elsewhere, elsewhere..."[2]

---

1. See page 186 in this book and the photographs in Blair and Bloom, *The Art and Architecture of Islam: 1250-1800*, 191.

2. Daryush Shayegan, *Henry Corbin: La topographie spirituelle de l'Islam iranien*, 23-24.

The ability to be carried away, through the forms of this world, to the infinite expanses of the other worlds is mystical, imaginative, symbolic perception. Not a flight from Reality, but a Journey towards it.

The capacity to perceive forms in the spaces of these heavens requires neither the passive perception which we think is necessary to experience external objects, nor the rationality of the philosophers, but a "con-formism," achieved through sympathy, with the forms of Desire.

> One does not penetrate into the Angelic World by housebreaking, one does not move around mentally in the world of Hurqalya by the assistance of a formal logic or of a dialectic which leads from one concept to the next by deduction.[3]

Corbin's fully charged "gnosiology," wholly unlike any rational "theory of knowledge," is based upon Love and its transfiguration by Beauty as the supreme theophany.[4] The ecstasy which is inherent in the Angel, in the Hidden Imam of Shi'ism, can "shatter the rock of doubt," and "paralyse the 'agnostic reflex'" by breaking "through the mutual isolation of consciousness and its object, of thought and being; here phenomenology becomes ontology."[5] The infinite succession of Heavens and the unending openings they accomplish communicate with one another by means of correspondences of "forms," of isomorphisms, between one level and the next, in a kind of *Gestalt* cosmology.[6] It is the perception of these that makes possible the Journey beyond. The correspondences are not in the head, but of the heart.

Two primary metaphorical treatments of these forms and their correspondences that derive from Sufi and Shi'ite gnosis are complimentary in their illumination of the isomorphisms of the heart and the heavens. On the one hand, there is the phenomenon of the

3. Corbin, *Spiritual Body and Celestial Earth*, xix.
4. Corbin, *Creative Imagination*, 98.
5. Corbin, *Swedenborg and Esoteric Islam*, 31-32.
6. Corbin, *En islam iranienne*, v. 1, 141, n. 107.

Mirror and the Image, based upon a metaphysics of Light. On the other, there is Music. But more than this, there is a mystical, cosmological *synaesthesia* in play, such that categories that the analytical mind must keep separate, here interpenetrate. For Mulla Sadra, the exercise of active Imagination gives substance to the subtle body in which all the five external senses are fused to "constitute a single *synaesthesis.* "[7] Recall the phenomenology of reading in Hugh of St. Victor, in which the ontologically remedial hermeneutic of *studium*, or sympathy, engages all the senses and is at once physical, intellectual, and spiritual. In Abram's view, a synaesthetic experience lies at the heart of the "animistic consciousness" which is the essence of pre-reflective perception.[8] In that case, the alchemical purification of the soul by the gnostic which results in the re-animation of the world is indeed a return to a lost Paradise which is always at hand. Just as the *Heliotrope* reaches towards its angel, so do the rocks of the earth and the animals of the wilderness. The world of the soul is here in this one if we only have the eyes to see it. Da'ud Qaysari, a Sufi of the 13th century C.E., and an influential commentator on Ibn 'Arabi writes "animals *see* things which, among human beings, can be seen only by the visionary mystics."[9]

Islam indeed sees itself as the Primordial Revelation. And listen again to the comments of Norman Brown:

> The Islamic imagination, Massignon has written, should be seen as the product of a desperate regression, back to the primitive, the eternal pagan substrate of all religions—that proteifirm cubehouse, the *Ka'ba*—as well as to a primitive pre-Mosaic monotheism of Abraham. The Dome is built on the Rock.[10]

But this return, Corbin would say, is not a regression, but a reacquisition at another level of something we have lost through our exile. The perception of homologies between the primordial Mazdean Revelation

---

7. Corbin, *Swedenborg and Esoteric Islam*, 16.
8. Abram, *The Spell of the Sensuous*, 130.
9. Corbin, *Spiritual Body and Celestial Earth*, 146.
10. Brown, "The Apocalypse of Islam," 92.

and those that followed is based upon a *progressio harmonica.*[11] There
is no need to regress: the forms are always there for those with the
subtle ears with which to hear and the eyes of fire with which to see.
We can always find a way to achieve that primordial state of the
dokhema, before appearance and belief were sundered in the archetypal moment of doubt, that primordial agnostic moment. This is the
return to the mythic—not regression, but *progressio.*

Light and sound, space and time, word and being, all resonate
together in worlds replete with archetype-images. Events in time are
exemplars of eternal Events in the time of the Soul, and these can
only be evaluated by a measure that varies with their intensity.

> And this intensity measures a time in which the past remains
> present to the future, in which the future is already
> present to the past, just as the notes of a musical phrase,
> though played successively, nevertheless all persist together
> in the present and thus form a phrase.[12]

And it is in music that we can most readily express this synaesthetic
space-time in which the Word itself is the music that speaks the forms
of beings in the spaces of the heart.

> This homologation of forms in time with forms in space
> offers a particularly subtle case of *isomorphism*. It is this,
> in reality, which leads us to conceive of *many modes of
> spatiality*, among which the visual mode, corresponding to
> sensible perception, is not perhaps even the privileged case.
> Speech, the Divine Word...is the sonorous incantation which
> evokes beings and which remains the profound and secret
> nature of each being. Stabilized in this being, this nature
> does not reveal itself, however, to the empirical point of view,
> but to another visual sense, to an *interior vision* perceiving
> other spaces. But precisely these spaces, and this psycho-
> spiritual spatiality, which has other properties than sensible
> space, require in their turn a homologation of sonorous space

---

11. Corbin, *Spiritual Body and Celestial Earth*, xvii.
12. Corbin, *Creative Imagination*, 35-36.

to supersensible spaces where the vibrations of the Word propagate as "arpeggios charged by distant lights...."[13]

The "theophanic method of discourse" recommended by Ibn 'Arabi is perhaps "nothing other than a form or an appeal of the *progressio harmonica.*" "Something in the nature of harmonic perception is needed in order to perceive a world of many dimensions."[14] The reverberations of the Word correspond both to the Images reflected and multiplied in a room of mirrors and to the repetitions of a melody in ascending octaves. Each repetition of a form thus echoed preserves and alters that form—the form of a person, a situation, an event—but each time at a different level of being.[15] And it is the Active Imagination that is the mirror *par excellence* and so is the locus of the sonorous spaces in which the being of things reverberates.

For these reverberations to occur there must be active the power to "absolve" which is the true, esoteric function of the Absolute: "the *absolute* is not that primary and primordial aspect which one has the habit of signifying by this word. It is a past participle which supposes a *nomen agentis....*"[16] To perceive these reverberations, to see things as they really are in the realm of the Imaginal,

> [i]n order to grasp the Image in its *absolute* reality, that is to say, *absolved,* detached, from the sensory mirror in which it is reflected, it is undoubtedly necessary to have...an *"eye of the world beyond..."* that is, an organ of vision which is itself part of the absolute activity of the soul, and which corresponds to our *Imaginatio vera.*[17]

These beings that are so known do not dissipate into vague, universal, or abstract forms. They are not the ghosts of things but the things themselves: more real, intense, beautiful, alive, more themselves than they could be in this world.

---

13. Corbin, *En islam iranienne,* v. 1, 140-41.
14. Corbin, *Spiritual Body and Celestial Earth,* xxviii.
15. Corbin, *En islam iranienne,* vol. 1, 144.
16. Corbin, *Le paradoxe du monothèisme,* 231.
17. Corbin, *Spiritual Body and Celestial Earth,* 81.

Corbin speaks also in this context of the iconography, the theosophy of art, as it were, which accompanies this vision of the world. It is not only towards music and mirrors that we can turn for sensual means in which to accomplish the intensification of beings, but also to the visual arts and to architecture.[18] What is required of such art is not that it be representational, but symbolic. Thus there is not only no need for the perspectival space of the Renaissance, but a positive rejection of it. Perspectival realism corresponds to historical linearity and imposes the same self-sufficient independence upon things in abstract sensory space as historical consciousness does upon the events of linear time.[19]

In the spaces of iconographic, symbolic art,

> All the elements are represented in their real dimensions ("in the present"), in each case perpendicularly to the axis of the viewer's vision. The viewer is not meant to immobilize himself at a particular point, enjoying the privilege of "presentness" and to raise his eyes from this fixed point; he must *raise himself* toward each of the elements represented. Contemplation of the image becomes a mental itinerary, an inner accomplishment; the image fulfills the function of a *mandala*. Because each of the elements is presented not *in* its proper dimension, but *being* that same dimension, to contemplate them is to enter into a multidimensional world, to effect the passage of the *ta'wil* through the symbols. And the whole forms a unity of qualitative time, in which past and future are simultaneously in the *present*.[20]

The function of such an art is not representation, however beautiful, but transformation and transfiguration of the soul and of the world "by that Light of Glory which the soul projects onto it."[21] The purpose of this sacred symbolic art is to enact the psycho-cosmic transformation that it symbolizes.

---

18. There is of course also a hermeneutics of literary forms, particularly poetry. See, for instance, references to Hafiz in Corbin's *Creative Imagination* and in Corbin's writings on Ruzebehan Baqli of Shiraz. For a complementary analysis along the same lines, see Nasr, *Islamic Art and Spirituality*.

19. Corbin, *Creative Imagination*, 90-91 and n. 34.

20. *Ibid.*, 91, n. 34.

21. Corbin, *Spiritual Body and Celestial Earth*, 30.

In architecture as well, the functional meaning of the forms
is this concentration and intensification provided by the form of
the *mandala*, or more properly in architecture, the *templum*, the
temenos. Speaking of the Friday Mosque at Isphahan,[22] Corbin writes,

> At the geometrical center of the enclosure we find a
> basin whose fresh water is perpetually renewed. This is
> a *water-mirror*, reflecting at the same time the dome of
> heaven, which is the real dome of the *templum*, and the
> many-colored ceramic tiles which cover the surfaces. It
> is by means of this mirror that the *templum* brings about
> the meeting of heaven and earth. The mirror of the water
> here polarizes the symbol of the centre. Now this phenomenon
> of the mirror at the centre of the structure of the *Templum*
> is also central to the metaphysics professed by a whole
> lineage of Iranian philosophers, among whom the most
> famous lived at one time or another in Isafahan. Thus
> there must certainly have been a link between the different
> forms of the same Iranian conception of the world, perhaps a
> link so essential that it will explain how the painters and
> miniaturists of Islamic Iran felt in no way that their art was
> subject to the traditional anti-iconic interdict. They had
> produced neither sculptures in space nor easel-paintings.[23]

Here in this sacred place, mirror, space, and contemplation come
together at the center of the world. The image of the mosque is
reversed and reflected in the mirror of the water.

> Let us now transpose this idea of a virtual image to the
> plane of a mystical reflection. To transpose the image of
> virtuality into actuality is to accomplish the very operation
> which, for the metaphysicians of the school of Sohravardi,
> signifies penetration into the *mundus imaginalis*...."[24]

---

22. See Henri Steirlin, *Ispahan: image du paradis* and Blair and Bloom, *The Art and Architecture of Islam: 1250-1800.*
23. Corbin, "Emblematic Cities," 16.
24. *Ibid.*

The phenomenon of the mirror enables us to understand the internal dimension of an object or a building situated in the space of this world, because it leads us to grasp its spiritual dimension, the metaphysical image which precedes and shapes all empirical perception.[25]

Rebuilding the Temple

The perception of this mosque as something other than a subject for study by the architect or architectural historian, whatever its artistic merit might be, requires the *Imago Templi*, the interior "mirror reflecting the *Imago Animae* [where] contemplator, contemplation and temple are one."[26] To understand this Temple requires a phenomenology of the *temenos*, a "temenology" of the imaginal world. It is in this sacred precinct that Heaven and earth communicate, and it is this *locus* that we lack.[27]

Modern historical consciousness is twice removed from the original, cosmic temple. In pre-Christian antiquity the image of the world as temple was well known. In Plato, Plutarch, Cleanthus, Manilius, and others, the cosmos itself is the divine spectacle contemplated with awe and reverence.[28] But, Corbin says, there is a profound difference between this vision of the world and that of

25. Corbin, "Emblematic Cities," 21.

26. Corbin, *Temple and Contemplation*, 387.

27. *Ibid.*, 267. The architect Christopher Alexander has attempted to revive a science of sacred space. His work is of interest in light of the conception of form and space that Corbin is analyzing. Of immediate relevance is *A Foreshadowing of 21st Century Art: The Color and Geometry of Very Early Turkish Carpets*, Alexander's study of Turkish "Sufi" carpets and their implications for our understanding of sacred geometry. Alexander has described the goal of his work with humor and an intense seriousness as "the attempt to make God appear in the middle of a field" (See the video recording, "An Architecture for the Soul," University of California Media Center and The Center for Environmental Structure). Anyone with a taste for Corbin would do well to become acquainted with Alexander's work. See also Alexander's initial book in the series called, *The Timeless Way of Building*, and Stephen Grabow's essay on Alexander and his work, *Christopher Alexander: The Search for a New Paradigm in Architecture*, which includes extensive interviews.

28. Corbin, *Temple and Contemplation*, 270-71.

Suhrawardi, Avicenna, and the other gnostics for whom the world itself is the crypt of the Temple.

> This visible world is no longer itself the temple; it is the *crypt* of the Temple, or cosmic crypt. The initiation conferred by the Angel consists in showing the initiate how to leave this crypt and reach the Temple to which the Angel belongs, and to which the initiate, by virtue of his origin, also belongs. Inside the crypt, he is merely an exile.[29]

> The sages of antiquity prayed in a temple that was intact; the prayer of 's sage rises from the depths of the temple crypt, because he has been exiled from the Temple. We are situated between two catastrophes: one is the premise of salvation, the other is perhaps irremediable. The first is the descent into exile.... The second is in some sense the sending of the exile himself into exile: this occurs at the moment when the world ceases to be experienced as the Temple crypt. This is not simply the destruction of the Temple, but the destruction of the Temple crypt: the crypt in which the exiles awaited their return to the Temple.[30]

The first catastrophe, the descent into exile, is the descent into time. "The history of humanity begins with exile, which in turn begins with the destruction of the Temple."[31] Here Corbin is referring not to the origins of humanity, since the "sages of antiquity" were human, but to the origins of history itself. The destruction of the Temple of Solomon in Jerusalem by Nebuchanezzar marks the profanation of the sacred that is the entry into historical time. Salvation is possible only by virtue of the *Imago Templi*, by means of which the exiles are oriented towards their goal, and by means of which their existence in the crypt is made known. But to understand the *Imago templi* one must "reach the meeting place of the two seas."

---

29. Corbin, *Temple and Contemplation*, 271.
30. *Ibid.*, 275.
31. *Ibid.*, 278.

Who among the exiled can reach this place that is no place? Only those who can escape the confines of history. Corbin relates an esoteric Jewish interpretation of the story of Moses:

> [O]ne of the symbolic properties of Water is to typify the sense of time and of engulfment in time. Pharaoh's aim is to make all male children who sink into time succumb to the indifferent uniformity of all that is encased in time, and to prevent them from rising to the heights of the worlds revealed by the divine Word. They are to drown in the waters of secular, one-dimensional history. The little "ark" in which, according to esoteric tradition, his "celestial parents" saved Moses, was in fact the divine Word, and Moses was preserved from the flux of historical time.[32]

And only so could he meet Khidr.

The second catastrophe is the destruction of the crypt itself. This is a tale we have heard before: The crypt has been emptied of the presences that inhabited it, of the hierarchies of the *Animae caelestes*.

> Without the world of the Soul there is no *Imago*. Thus man had lost his own soul as the heavens had lost theirs.... The ordeal of exile no longer exists; instead there is a deliberate refusal to feel exiled.... The world is "disoriented": there is no longer an "Orient." One thinks one is out in the open, that there is neither an above or a below."[33]

Without the Orient, there is only History, that "out in the open" which leaves a place only for "...a totalitarian sense of the existent..."[34] uniform, void, and without Presence, or even the nostalgia for it. This describes the frenzied world of modern secular humanity for whom no amount of activity, no amount of expansion can compensate this loss of soul.

> The destruction of the Temple is destruction of the field of vision: contemplation collapses for lack of space, for lack of a

---

32. Corbin, *Temple and Contemplation*, 279.
33. *Ibid.*, 276-77.
34. Corbin, Prefatory Letter, 2.

horizon beyond this world....

... For many of our contemporaries...[t]he Temple is destroyed. There is no longer any link between Heaven and earth.

The norm of our world can assume all manner of names: sociology, dialectical or non-dialectical materialism, positivism, historicism, psychoanalysis and so on.... The knot which paralyses our awareness is well-tied. The difficulty is that most men live outside themselves, even though they may never have gone outside themselves, for the good reason that they have never been inside themselves. Of course there is no lack of therapies to make them go inside themselves; but if these are successful, it is often even more difficult to make them come outside of themselves. Deprivation in the external world is followed by sterile stagnation, endlessly hammering out the contours of a false subjectivity. I would say that the virtue of the *Imago Templi* lies in making us be *within ourselves outside ourselves*. For we must not confuse introspection, introversion, with contemplation: there is no contemplation without the Temple. The virtue of the *Imago Templi* lies in delivering the man-temple both from the dangers of an invasive sociology and from the dangers of a sujectivity which is its own thrall. It unties the knot because it re-establishes communication between Heaven and earth, opening up for all men the spaces beyond.[35]

---

35. Corbin, *Temple and Contemplation*, 388-89.

Conclusion: A Voyage into the World

He who believes a lot,
Experiences a lot.
—Peasant woman from the Gospel of Mark[1]

Henry Corbin's immense work is the result of the meditations of a man living a life in sympathy with beings. We perhaps need the example of such a life in a world where, in the words of Kathleen Raine, "the idea of energy has replaced the presence of beauty."[2] That his meditations are theosophical and grounded in what were for him the central truths of Abrahamic monotheism will make them difficult for some to accept. But for Corbin the failure of the West lies in the rejection of the sacred, and the dominant religious tradition for this culture is Christianity, a prophetic religion founded upon Revelation and a sacred book. If we are to understand ourselves and the source of our current catastrophes and perhaps prevent, or at least mitigate catastrophes still to come, it will not be through a wholesale rejection of this tradition. Nor, does Corbin argue, will it be through a blind acceptance of it.

Henry Corbin never converted to Islam. He considered himself an Occidental and a Christian and so in some sense outside of the Islamic spirituality which he presents. And yet clearly he had made a

---

1. Quoted in Hans Peter Duerr's *Dreamtime: Concerning the Boundary Between Wilderness and Civilization.*
2. Quoted in Robert Sardello's "Taking the Side of Things: Notes on Psychological Activism," 128.

place for it in himself. Nasr says:

> When speaking of Shi'ism, he usually spoke of 'us' and con-
> sidered himself to be identified with Shi'ism in spirit as well as
> mind.... Corbin displayed an attachment to Shi'ism which was
> not only that of the usual Western scholar engaged in the
> subject of his research. Rather, it was participation in a spiri-
> tual world in which it can be said that Corbin possessed faith.[3]

And yet his overarching goal was ecumenical: to reveal by means of
comparative philosophy and comparative spiritual research the common
bonds which unite the Peoples of the Book into a single destiny and which
must be understood so that there can be a dialogue between persons:

> since a dialogue takes place between "persons," it is neces-
> sary, in order that there be dialogue, that the persons dialoguing
> have between them something in common. A dialogue takes
> place between "thou" and "I." It is necessary that "thou" and
> "I" be invested with the same responsibility for a personal
> destiny.[4]

There can be no dialogue if one member of the pair has lost all
hope, or even the memory of the hope, of ever being promoted to
the rank of Person.

The alternative to the catastrophe of the Death of God is the
theophanic cosmology of the gnostics in the Abrahamic tradition. Corbin
devoted his life to articulating this vision of the essential harmony at the
root of all of the religions of the Book, the Vision of what he was to call in
his late work the *Harmonia Abrahamica*. It is based on a Christology
radically different from the one that became dogma. It requires a return
to the Christology of the Ebionites, who had no doctrine of the Trinity or of
the substantial union of the divine and human in Jesus. For these Jewish-
Christians, Jesus was a manifestation of the celestial Son of Man, the
Christos Angelos, who was consecrated as Christ at his baptism.

---

3. Nasr, *Henry Corbin: The Life and Works of the Occidental Exile in Quest of
the Orient of Light*, 280.
4. Corbin, *Le paradoxe du monothèisme*, 214-15.

Jesus then takes his place in the lineage of the True Prophets.
Corbin writes,

> for Ebionite Christianity...sacred history, the hierology
> of humanity, is constituted by the successive
> manifestations...of the celestial *Anthropos*, of the eternal
> *Adam-Christos* who is the prophet of Truth, the True
> Prophet. We count seven of these manifestations, eight if
> we include the terrestrial person of Adam himself. They are
> Adam, Noah, Enoch, Abraham, Isaac, Jacob, Moses,
> Jesus.... The fundamental basis of this prophetology is
> therefore the idea of the True Prophet who is the celestial
> *Anthropos*, the *Christus aeternus*, hastening from
> christophany to christophany "toward the place of his
> repose." Now, this is the same structure that Islamic
> prophetology presents, with this difference, that the suc-
> cession of christophanies is no longer completed with the
> prophet Jesus of Nazareth, but with the prophet of Islam,
> the "Seal of the Prophets" whose coming Jesus himself an-
> nounced, and who is the "recapitulation" of all the
> prophets.[5]

Thus Mohammad is identified with the figure of the Paraclete in the
Gospel of John. Among the Shi'ites, the Twelfth Imam, the Hidden
Imam, is sometimes identified with this final manifestation of the True
Prophet, the central figure of the Eternal Gospel.

Corbin understood his primary tasks as a philosopher to be to
aid in the salvation of soul, both *anima humana* and *anima mundi*,
from two complementary catastrophes: imprisonment in the absolute
truths of dogma and the fall into the abyss of nihilism. He wished to
serve as midwife for a rebirth of possibilities abandoned by the
dominant ideologies of the West. It is surely not only the content
of Surawardi's vision which makes him such a central figure in
Corbin's development, but also the fact that his mission too was a
revival, an attempt to make a future for the "Oriental wisdom of
the ancients."

---

5. Corbin, "Harmonia Abrahamica," preface to *Évangile de Barnabé*, 11.

Corbin's passionate stand against the prevailing spirit of his own times derives from the same sense of the centrality of the hidden things of the soul that gave him such a feeling for the esoteric strains in Shi'ite Islam. The Shi'ites have always been a minority within Islam as a whole, and Corbin was most drawn to those among them who regard themselves as defenders of the secret things of God against a dogmatic majority. He quotes a contemporary Shi'ite: "Never forget that there have been only a handful of faithful around our Imams, and that it will be thus until the end of time."[6] Perhaps he also shared the their "tragic sense of history:"

> An eminent Iranian shayk, from whom I have learned much, went so far as to say to me, some time before he died, when we were speaking about the confident pessimism of Shi'ite traditions: "Never forget! The day will come when one will no longer be able even to utter the name of God in this world."[7]

The theme of exile is central to Corbin's thinking. A colleague comments, "He lived in a world in which, he used to say with irony, most of his contemporaries had been dead for a thousand years."[8] And yet it is clear that his is neither a pessimistic vision, nor a world-denying asceticism. Corbin offers a view of the Abrahamic religions that is based on a complex, varied, and yet consistent group of cosmologies common to the esoteric branches of all of them and centered on the cosmic priority of the individual Person. These Platonist cosmologies are hierarchical, without being narrowly patriarchal in the pejorative sense, and they are oriented towards divinity without demonizing this world. It is not easy for everyone to understand that this is possible. The contemporary politically correct view of monotheism is that it is radically male-biased, other-worldly, and anthropocentric. That it has been so in its dogmatic forms is undeniable. Whether it must be so is thrown into serious question by Corbin's work.[9]

---

6. Corbin, *En islam iranienne*, Vol. 1, 86.

7. Corbin, *Temple and Contemplation*, 388.

8. Robert Bosnak, *Tracks in the Wilderness of Dreaming*, 48.

9. See Murata's *The Tao of Islam: A Sourcebook of Gender Relationships in Islamic Thought*.

CONCLUSION

Even more difficult to entertain in our time is the stance towards historical and scientific truth that Corbin adopts. There have been innumerable attempts since the beginning of the scientific revolution to reconcile scientific truth with revealed truth. All have failed to do justice to one side or the other. This may be because of the split between spirit and matter that Corbin attacks with such depth and rigor. Dogmatists on either side claim all of reality for themselves so that any solution results in a single dominant vision. But a unified Theory of Everything, whether based upon spirit or matter or upon some union between them, will be of necessity monistic, abstract, and totalitarian. Corbin would be uninterested in any such undertaking.

Instead we should listen when Corbin says that one can admit and celebrate a plurality of spiritual universes, and

> without taking up one's abode in them, keep an abode for them in oneself... In addition, it is necessary to understand the mode of perception proper to each of them, the *modus intelligendi* that is each time the direct expression of a mode of being, of a *modus essendi... The more perceptions and representations of the universe each monad integrates, the more it unfolds its own perfection and differs from every other.*[10]

If we can accept the absolute priority of the soul in this sense, it becomes possible to believe that there can be a diversity of competing forms of life, without feeling the overwhelming need to unite them into a single vision. There can be no final theory, because there are no finished things. The cosmos is in process, but not, or perhaps not only, in the evolutionary sense. Only the fixed and finished can be known with finality. The divine creativity that is the source of all things is beyond the reach of human knowledge. In the end to be fully human is to attain to the state of the mystic, of the philosopher, and for Corbin, "To be a philosopher is to take to the road, never settling down in some place of satisfaction with a theory of the world..."[11]

---

10. Corbin, *Avicenna*, 9. My italics.
11. Corbin, *The Voyage and the Messenger*, 140.

We should learn to grasp all our truths less tightly, to avoid the heavy handed, hard-hearted certainty of the dogmatist. We must learn the lesson Jacob Bronowski teaches: there is a difference between knowledge and certainty, between *dokema* and dogma. Our modern world is said to be scientific. There is no doubt that science supplies the paradigm for what counts as knowledge for many, perhaps most, people. It is supposed to be a characteristic of scientific thought that it remains always open, always hypothetical. Science in the West may well have developed partly as a response to the dogmatic closure of official Christianity in an attempt to recover something of the angelic function of beings and to re-establish the means for the individual to attain knowledge.[12] Bronowski is the most powerful spokesman I know of for this view of the scientific process, for what he calls the Principle of Tolerance. In the powerful and forever unforgettable moments of his television series, *The Ascent of Man*, filmed at Auschwitz, he says

> It is said that science will dehumanize people and turn them into numbers. That is false, tragically false. Look for yourself. This is the concentration camp at Auschwitz. This is where people were turned into numbers. Into this pond were flushed the ashes of some four million people. And that was not done by gas. It was done by arrogance. It was done by dogma. It was done by ignorance. When people believe they have absolute knowledge, with no test in reality, this is how they behave. This is what men do when they aspire to the knowledge of gods.
> ... We have to cure ourselves of the itch for absolute knowledge and power.[13]

Of course he is right. Yet his error is not to see that the reality in which he hopes to test hypotheses is restricted beforehand by a too narrow scientism. And though there is something special about science

---

12. This argument is set forth by Nasr in *Knowledge and the Sacred* (39), who credits Etienne Gilson with the same intuition.
13. Jacob Bronowski, *The Ascent of Man*, 374.

as Bronowski understands it, there is nothing special about scientists—they fall all too easily into the traps of dogmatism like the rest of us. All our actions in this world must be taken cautiously, with humility, and in the face of uncertainty.

Perhaps Corbin's greatest gift to us is the transmission of a tradition in which the principle of individuation is allied with the concept of imagination. We are ultimately responsible for ourselves and for making ourselves capable of our God. And so too, because of the chivalrous bond between the individual and the Angel, we are responsible for the determination of that God in the world. But more than this the spiritual birth accomplished by the soul, for the Angel, far outstrips both the bounds of the *ego* and the bounds of the literal world as well. Every battle for the Angel is a battle for the soul of the world, for the transfiguring light that brings into being a transformed and transforming world. This is why alchemy is the sister of prophecy; the transformation of the individual cannot be accomplished without the transformation of the world. It is not that we must escape this world to find salvation in another, for the world too is in Exile and must be returned to Paradise. This Return is accomplished as we begin to see that "the other world already exists in this world." It only remains to actualize it. To do so we must have access to a cosmology that has the spaces and the times into which this world can unfold.

Yet that reanimated world, alive to our senses and in sympathy with that which is best in us, is fragile. Its fragility is a measure perhaps of its worth, not of its irreality. That others do not see, or that our experiences are fleeting, are not reasons for doubt or despair. As Heraclitus said, "Nature loves to hide."

In the end we must come to see with wider eyes, with more acute and subtler senses than we have been taught to do. For those open to this possibility, the obstacles are great enough. But what can one say to the skeptic, to the rationalist critic, buried, it may be, inside most of us? By what criteria can we judge this psycho-cosmology that runs so counter to the trends of the contemporary world? David Abram gives the best answer that I know of:

> If they do not aim at a static or "literal" reality, how can
> we discern whether one telling of events is any better or
> more worthy than another? The answer is this: a story
> must be judged according to whether it *makes sense*. And
> "making sense" must here be understood in its most direct
> meaning: to make sense is *to enliven the senses....* To make
> sense is to release the body from the constraints im-
> posed by outworn ways of speaking, and hence to renew
> and rejuvenate one's felt awareness of the world. It is to
> make the senses wake up to where they are.[14]

This "making sense" can be understood as the function of
that *synaesthesia* which can perceive the *progressio harmonicum*,
of that *aisthesis* which Hillman invokes in his own homage to
Henry Corbin, *The Thought of the Heart and the Soul of the
World.*[15] It is expressed and realized in a gasp, a breathing in of
the world in a primary aesthetic response. The making of our soul
can be judged through aesthetic responses. Hillman quotes
Plotinus: "We possess beauty when we are true to our own being;
ugliness is in going over to another order."[16] Then when the senses
do awaken to where we are, we find that where we are is neither
defined by, nor limited to, the world of material causality, the world
where history is a terror and where the despair of nihilism spreads
like a shroud over us all.

Corbin has said that there is an element of decision involved
in spiritual awakening. The decision to orient oneself toward the
search for the invisible Guide does not guarantee the finding, but
it is the required submission for embarking upon the Way. And to
those who refuse to so decide? To those who by nature, or delib-
erately, reject the symbolic life?

> The Gospel parable of the Feast (Matt. 22:2-10, Lk. 14:16-24)
> means precisely what it says.... It would be ridiculous to

---

14. Abram, *The Spell of the Sensuous*, 265.
15. Hillman, *The Thought of the Heart and the Soul of the World*, 47 ff.
16. *Ibid.*, 59.

engage in polemics against the men or the women who refuse to come to the Feast; their refusal inspires only sadness and compassion.[17]

No one would claim that access to the world Corbin opens up can be achieved without effort and perhaps not without guidance. Even to approach it requires commitment and the "courage of Love." But we can perhaps measure our halting progress in our attempts to be true to ourselves and to those we love and to make sense of our lives and of our work. If we can begin to enact that prophetic-poietic passion which is the root of *aiesthesis* and the source of the imagination, then all our quests can be seen not as solitary journeys inward but as voyages outward into the world.

---

17. Corbin, *The Man of Light*, 145, n. 3.

The Porcelain Room on the third storey of the palace of the Ali Ghapou.

186

Works Cited

Works by Henry Corbin

1. Books and Collected Essays.

Works that are available in English are listed only in their translated versions. A complete bibliography of works published during Henry Corbin's lifetime can be found in *Henry Corbin*, ed. Christian Jambet, and referenced below.

Avicenna and the Visionary Recital. Trans. Willard Trask. Bollingen Series LXVI (Princeton: Princeton UP, 1960).

The Concept of Comparative Philosophy. Trans. Peter Russell (Ipswich: Golgonooza, 1981).

Creative Imagination in the Sufism of Ibn 'Arabi. Trans. Ralph Manheim. Bollingen Series XCI (Princeton: Princeton UP, 1969).

Cyclical Time and Ismaili Gnosis. Trans. Ralph Manheim and J. Morris (London: Kegan Paul, 1983).

"Cyclical Time in Mazdaism and Ismailism" (Eranos, 1951)
"Divine Epiphany and Spiritual Birth in Ismailian Gnosis" (Eranos, 1954)
"From the Gnosis of Antiquity to Ismaili Gnosis" (1956)

Face de Dieu, Face de l'homme: Hermeneutique et soufisme (Paris: Flammarion, 1983).

"Mundus Imaginalis ou l'imaginaire et l'imaginal" (1964)
"Hermeneutique spirituelle compareé" (Eranos, 1964)
"De l'épopeé heroique à l'épopeé mystique" (Eranos, 1966)
"Face de Dieu et face de l'homme" (Eranos, 1967)
"L'idee du Paraclet en philosophie iranienne" (1970)

Henry Corbin. Ed. Christian Jambet. *Cahier de l'Herne*, no. 39. Consacré à Henry Corbin (Paris: Editions de l'Herne, 1981).

"De Heidegger à Sohravardi, entretiens avec Phillipe Nemo"
"Post-Scriptum à un entretiens philosophique"
"Transcendental et Existential"

A History of Islamic Philosophy. Trans. L. Sherrard and P. Sherrard (London: Kegan Paul, 1993).

L'Homme et son ange: initiation et chevalerie spirituelle (Paris: Fayard, 1983).

"Le récit d'initiation et l'hermeticisme en iran" (Eranos, 1949)
"L'initiation ismaèlienne ou l'esoterisme et le verbe" (Eranos, 1970)
"Juvenilité et chevalerie en islam iranien" (Eranos, 1976)

En islam iranienne: aspects spirituels et philosophiques. 4 Vol. (Paris: Gallimard, 1971-73).

Vol. I: *Le shi'isme duodècemain,* 1971
Vol. II: *Sohrawardi et les platoniciens de perse,* 1973
Vol. III: *Les Fidèles d'amour—Shi'isme et soufisme,* 1973
Vol. IV: *L'Ecole d'Ispahan—L'Ecole Shaykhie—Le Douzieme Imam,* 1973

The Man of Light in Iranian Sufism. Trans. Nancy Pearson (New Lebanon: Omega, 1994).

Philosophie iranienne et philosophie compareé (Tehran: Acad. Imp. Iran. de Phil., 1977).

La philosophie iranienne islamique aux XVII et XVIII siecles (Paris: Buchet-Chastel, 1981).

Le paradoxe du monothèisme. Ed. de l'Herne (Paris: Editions de L' Herne, 1981).

"Le paradoxe du monothèisme" (Eranos, 1976)
"Nécessité de l'angélologie" (1977)
"De la théologie apophatique comme antidote du nihilisme" (1977)

Spiritual Body and Celestial Earth: From Mazdean Iran to Shi'ite Iran. Trans. Nancy Pearson. Bollingen Series XCI: 2 (Princeton: Princeton UP, 1977).

Swedenborg and Esoteric Islam. Trans. L. Fox (West Chester: Swedenborg Foundation, 1995).

"*Mundus Imaginalis* or the imaginary and the imaginal (1964) [also in *Face de Dieu, face de l'homme: Hermeneutique et soufisme,* cited *supra*]
"Comparative Spiritual Hermeneutics" (Eranos, 1964) [also in *Face de Dieu, Face de l'homme: Hermeneutique et soufisme*]

*Temple and Contemplation.*Trans. by P. Sherrard and L. Sherrard (London: KPI, 1986).

The Realism and Symbolism of Colours in Shiite Cosmology (Eranos, 1972)
The Science of the Balance and the Correspondences between Worlds in Islamic Gnosis (Eranos, 1973)
Sabean Temple and Ismailism (Eranos, 1950)
The Configuration of the Temple of the Ka'bah as the Secret of the Spiritual Life (Eranos, 1965)
The *Imago Templi* in Confrontation with Secular Norms (Eranos, 1974)

The Voyage and the Messenger: Iran and Philosophy. Trans. Joseph Rowe (Berkeley: North Atlantic, 1998) [translation of *L'Iran et la philosophie,* Fayard, 1990].

Iranian Studies and Comparative Religion (1948)
Iranian Studies and Philosophy (1951)
Problem and Method in Religious History (1968)
A Theory of Visionary Knowledge (1977)
The Theme of the Voyage and the Messenger (1973)
A Shi'ite Liturgy of the Grail (1974)
Prophetic Philosophy and the Metaphysics of Being (1966)
Sufism and Sophia (1956)
The Musical Sense of Persian Mysticism (1967)

2. Articles, Extracts & Essays

"Emblematic Cities: A Response to the Images of Henri Steirlin." *Temenos Journal* 10 (1990): 11-24. Trans. Kathleen Raine. Orig. in Henri Steirlin's *Ispahan: Image du Paradis.* (Geneva: Editions SIGMA, 1976).

"Epistle on the State of Childhood, by Sohravardi, translated with Introduction, Presentation and Notes by Henry Corbin." Trans. Liadain Sharrard. *Temenos Journal* 4 (1984): 53-76.

"Eyes of Flesh and Eyes of Fire: Science and Gnosis." *Material for Thought* 8 (1980): 5-10.

"Harmonia Abrahamica," preface to *Évangile de Barnabé: Recherches sur la composition et l'origine*, par Luigi Cirillo, *Texte et Traduction* par Luigi Cirillo and Michel Frémaux. (Paris: Editions Beauchesne, 1977).

"The Jasmine of the *Fedeli d'Amore*: A Discourse on Ruzbehan Baqli of Shiraz." *Sphinx* 3 (1990): 189-223.

Prefatory Letter to *The New Polytheism* by David L. Miller. (Dallas: Spring, 1981).

"The Question of Comparative Philosophy: Convergences in Iranian and European Thought." Trans. Jane A. Pratt. *Spring* (1980): 1-20.

"Theophanies and Mirrors: Idols or Icons?" Trans. Jane A. Pratt and A. K. Donohue. *Spring* (1983): 1-2.

Works by Other Authors

Abram, David. *The Spell of the Sensuous: Perception and Language in a More-Than-Human World* (New York: Pantheon, 1996).

Adams, Charles J. "The Hermeneutics of Henry Corbin." *Approaches to Islam in Religious Studies*. Ed. Richard C. Martin (Tucson: University of Arizona Press, 1985), 129-50.

Alexander, Christopher. *A Foreshadowing of 21st Century Art: The Color and Geometry of Very Early Turkish Carpets* (New York: Oxford UP, 1993).

Alexander, Christopher. *A Timeless Way of Building* (New York: Oxford UP, 1979).

Ali, Ahmed. *Al-Qur'an* (Princeton: Princeton UP, 1984).

Armstrong, Karen. *Islam: A Short History* (New York: Modern Library, 2000).

WORKS CITED

Avens, Roberts. "Corbin's Interpretation of Imamology and Sufism." *Hamdard Islamicus* XI (2), Summer (1988): 67-79.

Avens, Roberts. "Henry Corbin and Suhrawardi's Angelology." *Hamdard Islamicus* XI (1), Spring (1988): 3-20.

Avens, Roberts. *Imagination as Reality: Western Nirvana in Jung, Hillman, Barfield & Cassirer* (Dallas: Spring, 1980).

Avens, Roberts. *The New Gnosis* (Dallas: Spring, 1984).

Avens, Roberts. "The Subtle Realm: Corbin, Sufism and Swedenborg." *Immanuel Swedenborg: A Continuing Vision.* Ed. Robin Larson (New York: Swedenborg Foundation, 1988), 382-91.

Avens, Roberts. "Theosophy of Mulla Sadra." *Hamdard Islamicus* IX (3), Autumn (1986): 3-30.

Avens, Roberts. "Things and Angels, Death and Immortality in Heidegger and in Islamic Gnosis." *Hamdard Islamicus* VII (2), Summer (1984): 3-32.

Bamford, Christopher. "Esoterism Today: The Example of Henry Corbin." *The Voyage and the Messenger: Iran and Philosophy.* Trans. Joseph Rowe (Berkeley: North Atlantic, 1998) [Translation of *L'Iran et La Philosophie*, Fayard, 1990].

Barfield, Owen. *Saving the Appearances: A Study in Idolatry.* 2nd ed. (Middletown: Wesleyan UP, 1988).

Baring, Anne, and Jules Cashford. *The Myth of the Goddess: Evolution of an Idea* (New York: Viking, 1991).

Barks, Coleman. *The Essential Rumi* (New York: HarperCollins, 1995).

Blair, Sheila and Jonathan Bloom. *The Art and Architecture of Islam: 1250-1800* (New Haven: Yale UP, 1994).

Bloom, Harold. *Omens of Millennium: The Gnosis of Angels, Dreams and Resurrection* (New York: Riverhead, 1996).

Bly, Robert, ed. *Leaping Poetry: An Idea with Poems and Translations* (Boston: Beacon, 1975).

Bly, Robert. ed. *News of the Universe: Poems of Twofold Consciousness.* (San Francisco: Sierra Club, 1980).

Bly, Robert, James Hillman, and Michael Meade. *The Rag and Bone Shop of the Heart* (New York: HarperCollins, 1992).

Bosnak, Robert. *Tracks in the Wilderness of Dreaming* (New York: Delacorte, 1996).

Bronowski, Jacob. *The Ascent of Man* (New York: Little, Brown, 1974).

Brooke, Roger. *Jung and Phenomenology* (London: Routledge, 1991).

Brown, Norman O. "The Apocalypse of Islam." *Apocalypse &/or Metamorphosis* (Berkeley: Univ. of California Press, 1991), 69-94.

Brown, Norman O. "The Prophetic Tradition." *Apocalypse &/or Metamorphosis.* (Berkeley: Univ. of California Press, 1991), 46-68.

Campbell, Joseph. *The Masks of the Gods: Oriental Mythology* (New York: Viking, 1969).

Cheetham, Tom. (forthcoming). "Before I Was a Planet: Poverty, Poetry and the Theory of Things." *Eranos Yearbook.* 71 (2001).

Cheetham, Tom. "Black Light: Henry Corbin, C. G. Jung and the Secret of the Secret. A Contribution to the Differentiation of Darkness." *Spring—Jungian Fundamentalism (and others).* 67 (2001).

Cheetham, Tom. "Consuming Passions: The Star, The Feast and the Science of the Balance." *Temenos Academy Review.* Spring 2002.

Cheetham, Tom. "Dogmas, Idols and the Edge of Chaos." *Human Ecology Review* 7 (1): 68-71.

Cheetham, Tom. "Harmonia Abrahamica: The Lost Language and the Battle for the Soul of the World." *Temenos Academy Review.*

Cheetham, Tom. "Within This Darkness: Incarnation, Theophany and the Primordial Revelation." *Esoterica: the Journal for Esoteric Studies* IV (2002): 61-95.

WORKS CITED

Chittick, William. *Imaginal Worlds: Ibn al-'Arabi and the Problem of Religious Diversity* (Albany: SUNY Press, 1994).

Chittick, William. *The Self-Disclosure of God: Principles of Ibn 'Arabi's Cosmology* (Albany: SUNY Press, 1998).

Chittick, William. *The Sufi Path of Knowledge: Ibn 'Arabi's Metaphysics of the Imagination* (Albany: SUNY Press, 1989).

Cohn, Norman. *Cosmos, Chaos and the World to Come: The Ancient Roots of Apocalyptic Faith* (New Haven: Yale UP, 1993).

Cranz, F. Edward. "1100 AD: A Crisis for Us?" *De Litteris: Occassional Papers in the Humanities.* Ed. M. Despalatovic (New London: Connecticut College Library, 1978), 84-108.

"The Reorientation of Western Thought c. 1100 A.D.: The Break with the Ancient Tradition and Its Consequences for Renaissance and Reformation," delivered at the Duke University Center for Medieval and Renaissance Studies, March 24, 1982.

Duerr, Hans Peter. *Dreamtime: Concerning the Boundary between Wilderness and Civilization.* Trans. Felicitas Goodman (London: Blackwell, 1985).

Eliade, Mircea. *A History of Religious Ideas, Vol. 1: From the Stone Age to the Eleusinian Mysteries* (Chicago: Univ. of Chicago Press, 1978).

Eliade, Mircea. *A History of Religious Ideas, Vol. 2: From Gautama Buddha to the Triumph of Christianity* (Chicago: Univ. of Chicago Press, 1982).

Eliade, Mircea. *A History of Religious Ideas, Vol. 3: From Muhammad to the Age of Reforms* (Chicago: Univ. of Chicago Press, 1985).

Eliade, Mircea. *The Myth of the Eternal Return, or Cosmos and History* (Princeton: Princeton UP, 1954).

Ettinghausen, Richard and Oleg Grabar. *The Art and Architecture of Islam: 650-1250* (New Haven: Yale UP, 1994).

Faivre, Antoine. *Access to Western Esotericism* (Albany: SUNY Press, 1994).

Grabow, Stephen. *Christopher Alexander: The Search for a New Paradigm in Architecture* (Boston: Oriel, 1983).

Heidegger, Martin. *Being and Time.* Trans. J. Macquarrie and E. Robinson (San Francisco: Harper, 1962).

Hillman, James. *Anima: An Anatomy of a Personified Notion* (Dallas: Spring, 1985).

Hillman, James. *Archetypal Pshychology: A Brief Account* (Dallas: Spring, 1983).

Hillman, James. *Inter Views* (1983; rpt. Dallas: Spring).

Hillman, James. "On the Necessity of Abnormal Psychology." *Facing the Gods* (Dallas: Spring, 1980), 1-38.

Hillman, James. *Re-Visioning Psychology* (New York: Harper & Row, 1975).

Hillman, James. *The Soul's Code: In Search of Character and Calling* (New York: Random, 1996).

Hillman, James. *The Thought of the Heart and the Soul of the World* (Dallas: Spring 1992).

Hodgson, Marshall S. *The Venture of Islam: Conscience and History in a World Civilization.* 3 Vols. (Chicago: Univ. of Chicago Press, 1994).

Idel, Moshe. *Kabbalah: New Perspectives* (New Haven: Yale UP, 1988).

Illich, Ivan. *H_2O and the Waters of Forgetfulness: Reflections on the Historicity of Stuff* (Dallas: Dallas Institute of Art and Humanities, 1984).

Illich, Ivan. *In the Vineyard of the Text: A Commentary to Hugh's Didascalicon* (Chicago: Univ. of Chicago Press, 1993).

Irving, Clive. *Crossroads of Civilization: 3000 Years of Persian History* (London: Weidenfeld and Nicholson, 1979).

WORKS CITED

Jambet, Christian. *Henry Corbin.* Ed. Christian Jambet. *Cahier de l'Herne.* No. 39 (1984).

Khan, Inayat and Coleman Barks. *The Hand of Poetry: Five Mystic Poets of Persia* (New Lebanon: Omega, 1993).

Landolt, Hermann. "Henry Corbin, 1903-1978: Between Philosophy and Orientalism." *Journal of the American Oriental Society.* 119 (3) (1999): 484-90.

Mackey, Sandra. *The Iranians: Persia, Islam and the Soul of a Nation* (Harmondsworth: Dutton, 1996).

Masani, Rustum. *Zoroastrianism: The Religion of the Good Life* (New York: Collier, 1962).

Merchant, Carolyn. *The Death of Nature: Women, Ecology and the Scientific Revolution* (New York: Harper, 1980).

Merchant, Carolyn. *Ecological Revolutions: Nature, Gender and Science in New England* (Chapel Hill: Univ. of North Carolina Press, 1989).

Miller, David L. *The New Polytheism* (Dallas: Spring, 1981).

Minsky, Marvin. "Will Robots Inherit the Earth?" *Scientific American,* October 1994.

Moore, Thomas. *The Care of the Soul: A Guide for Cultivating Depth and Sacredness in Everyday Life* (New York; HarperCollins, 1992).

Morrow, Glen and John Dillon. *Proclus' Commentary on Plato's Parmenides* (Princeton: Princeton UP, 1987).

Murata, S. *The Tao of Islam: A Sourcebook of Gender Relationships in Islamic Thought* (Albany: SUNY Press, 1992).

Murata, S. and W. Chittick. *The Vision of Islam* (New York: Paragon 1994).

Nasr, Seyyed Hossein. "Henry Corbin: The Life and Works of the Occidental Exile in Quest of the Orient of Light," Ch. 17. *Traditional Islam in the Modern World* (London: Kegan Paul, 1987).

Nasr, Seyyed Hossein. *Ideals and Realities of Islam* (London: Allen & Unwin, 1966).

Nasr, Seyyed Hossein. *An Introduction to Islamic Cosmological Doctrines*. Rev. ed. (Albany: SUNY Press, 1993).

Nasr, Seyyed Hossein. *Islamic Art and Spirituality* (Albany: SUNY Press, 1987).

Nasr, Seyyed Hossein. *Knowledge and the Sacred.* (Albany: SUNY Press, 1989).

Nasr, Seyyed Hossein. "Oral Transmission and the Book in Islamic Education: The Spoken and the Written Word." *The Book in the Islamic World: The Written Word and Communication in the Middle East,* Ed. George N. Atiyeh (Albany: SUNY Press, 1995), 57-70.

Nasr, Seyyed Hossein. "Shi'ism and Sufism: Their Relationship in Essence and in History." *Sufi Essays* (Albany: SUNY Press, 1991), 104-20.

Nasr, Seyyed Hossein. *Religion and the Order of Nature* (New York: Oxford UP, 1996).

Nasr, Seyyed Hossein, *et al. Expectation of the Millennium: Shi'ism in History* (Albany: SUNY Press, 1989).

Nasr, Seyyed Hossein, *et al. Shi'ism: Doctrines, Thought and Spirituality* (Albany: SUNY Press, 1988).

Oelschlager, Max. *The Idea of Wilderness: From Prehistory to the Age of Ecology* (New Haven: Yale UP, 1991).

Radding, Charles. *A World Made by Men: Cognition and Society, 400-1200* (Chapel Hill: Univ. of North Carolina Press, 1985).

Raine, Kathleen. *Golgonooza: City of Imagination. Last Studies in William Blake* (Hudson: Lindisfarne, 1991).

Rhodes, Robert. *The Making of the Atomic Bomb* (New York: Simon and Schuster, 1986).

WORKS CITED

Rothenberg, J. and Pierre Joris, eds. *Poems for the Millennium, Volume 1: From Fin-de-Siecle to Negritude* (Berkeley: Univ. of California Press, 1995).

Rothenberg, J. and Pierre Joris. *Poems for the Millennium, Volume 2: From Postwar to Millennium.* Berkeley: Univ. of California Press, 1998).

Sardello, Robert. "Taking the Side of Things: Notes on Psychological Activism." *Spring* (1984): 127-35.

Schimmel, Annemarie. *Mystical Dimensions of Islam* (Chapel Hill: Univ. of North Carolina Press, 1975).

Scholem, Gershom. *Origins of the Kabbahlah* (Princeton: Princeton UP, 1962).

Schuon, Frithjof. *The Essential Writings of Frithjof Schuon.* Ed. S. H. Nasr (Shaftesbury, England: Element, 1986).

Sells, Benjamin, ed. *Working with Images: The Theoretical Foundations of Archetypal Psychology* (Woodstock: Spring, 2000).

Sells, Michael. *Approaching the Qu'ran: The Early Revelations* (Ashland: White Cloud, 1999).

Sells, Michael. *Early Islamic Mysticism* (Mahwah: Paulist, 1996).

Sells, Michael. *Mystical Languages of Unsaying* (Chicago: Univ. of Chicago Press, 1994).

Shayegan, Daryush. *Henry Corbin: La topographie spirituelle de l'Islam Iranien* (Paris: Ed. de la Difference, 1990).

Sherrard, Philip. *The Eclipse of Man and Nature* (Hudson: Lindisfarne, 1987).

Sherrard, Philip. *Human Image—World Image* (Ipswich: Golgonooza, 1992).

Smart, Ninian. *The Religious Experience of Mankind* (New York: Scribner's, 1969).

Steiner, George. *Martin Heidegger* (Chicago: Univ. of Chicago Press, 1989).

Steirlin, Henri. *Ispahan: Image du Paradis* (Geneva: Editions SIGMA, 1976).

Suhrawardi, Yahyá ibn Habash. *The Philosophy of Illumination: a new critical edition of the text of Hikmat al-ishr⁻aq, with English translation, notes, commentary, and introduction by John Walbridge and Hossein Ziai* (Provo: Brigham Young UP, 1999).

Suzuki, D. T. *Swedenborg: Buddha of the North.* Trans. and introduction Andrew Bernstein. Afterword David Loy (West Chester: Swedenborg Foundation, 1996).

Verenne, Jean. "Pre-Islamic Iran" in *Mythologies*, Vol. 2 ed. by Yves Bonnefoy (Chicago: Univ. of Chicago Press, 1991), 870-90.

Versluis, Arthur. *Theosophia: Hidden Dimensions of Christianity* (Hudson, New York: Lindisfarne, 1994).

Wasserstrom, Steven M. *Religion After Religion: Gershom Scholem, Mircea Eliade, and Henry Corbin at Eranos* (Princeton: Princeton UP, 1999).

Williams, Michael Allen. *Rethinking "Gnosticism:" An Argument For Dismantling a Dubious Category* (Princeton: Princeton UP, 1996).

Index

A

Abraham 113, 167, 179

Abrahamic Tradition 113

Abram, David 12, 12 n25, 13, 13 n27, 60, 60 n 15, 118, 119, 119 n15, 120, 137 n47, 167, 167 n8, 184, 184 n14

Abu'l-Hasan Kharraqani 99, 99 n37

Achaemenids 27

Active Imagination 69 n31, 70, 71, 79, 97

Adam 127-130, 179

Adams, Charles J. 31 n25, 121 n19

Agathodaimon 41

Ahmed Ali 23 n13

Ahriman 20-24, 95, 135

Alamut 106, 107 n57

Alchemy vii, 31, 122, 139, 147

Alexander, Christopher 90 n14, 172 n27

Alexander of Macedon 25

Ali 37, 38, 102

Ali Ghapou 165, 186

Allah 32, 33, 34

Amesha Spentas 20

Anima Mundi 59, 60, 61, 163

Animae caelestes 174

Archetypal psychology vi, vi n2, 80 n58

Ardeshir 27, 27 n18

Aristotelians 77, 86

Aristotle 41, 42, 68, 86, 86 n4, 87, 87 n6, 120 n17

Armstrong, Karen 31 n24

Arsacids 25

Assyrians 24 n15

Avens, Roberts 2 n3, 4 n8, 28, 29 n22, 51 n16, 127 n35, 146 n14

Averroes 68, 68 n30, 86, 87, 92, 110

Avesta 19, 24, 25, 77

INDEX

INDEX

N

Nasir Tusi 115

Nasr, Seyyed Hossein ix n1, 13 n28, 18 n3, 29 n22, 31 n24, 35, 36 n28, 39, 39 n32, 40 n33, 50 n10, 51, 51 n17, 53 n23, 75 n48, 81 n58, 100, 100 n39, 101 n42, 102 n43, 109, 109 n64, 116, 116 n7, 119 n16, 125, 125 n30, 142, 160 n46, 170 n18, 178, 182 n12

Nasr, S. H. et al 31 n24

Nebuchanezzar 173

Nemo 2 n3

Neoplatonism ix

New Sciences 44 n1

Newton, Isaac 26, 44 n1, 66

Nicolas of Cusa 141

Nietzsche, Friedrich 83, 154, 160, 161

Noah 113, 179

Nwyia 11

O

Oelschlager, Max 149 n23

Oetinger, Friedrich Christoph 101 n41

Ohrmazd 20, 21, 23, 24, 25

Ong, Walter J. 118

Oppenheimer, Robert 149 n22

Oresme, Nicholas 133 n43

Ortega y Gassett 133 n43

Orwell, George 111

P

Palace of Ali Ghapou 165

Paracelsus 26, 71, 98

Paraclete 89, 116, 138, 179

Parmenides 141, 142

Parry, Milman 118

Pentecost 89

Plato 42, 66, 67, 77, 141, 172

Platonist cosmologies 180